Nadia Boulanger and the Stravinskys

Eastman Studies in Music

Ralph P. Locke, Senior Editor
Eastman School of Music

Additional Titles of Interest

The Courage of Composers and the Tyranny of Taste: Reflections on New Music
Bálint András Varga

A Dance of Polar Opposites:
The Continuing Transformation of Our Musical Language
George Rochberg
Edited by Jeremy Gill

Dane Rudhyar: His Music, Thought, and Art
Deniz Ertan

In Search of New Scales: Prince Edmond de Polignac, Octatonic Explorer
Sylvia Kahan

Leon Kirchner: Composer, Performer, and Teacher
Robert Riggs

Ralph Kirkpatrick: Letters of the American Harpsichordist and Scholar
Edited by Meredith Kirkpatrick

Samuel Barber Remembered: A Centenary Tribute
Peter Dickinson

Stravinsky's "Great Passacaglia":
Recurring Elements in the Concerto for Piano and Wind Instruments
Donald G. Traut

The Substance of Things Heard: Writings about Music
Paul Griffiths

Variations on the Canon: Essays on Music from Bach to Boulez
in Honor of Charles Rosen on His Eightieth Birthday
Edited by Robert Curry, David Gable, and Robert L. Marshall

A complete list of titles in the Eastman Studies in Music series may be found
on the University of Rochester Press website, www.urpress.com

Nadia Boulanger and the Stravinskys

A Selected Correspondence

Edited by
Kimberly A. Francis

UNIVERSITY OF ROCHESTER PRESS

The University of Rochester Press gratefully acknowledges generous support from the Manfred Bukofzer Endowment of the American Musicological Society, funded in part by the National Endowment for the Humanities and the Andrew W. Mellon Foundation.

First published 2018

University of Rochester Press
668 Mt. Hope Avenue, Rochester, NY 14620, USA
www.urpress.com
and Boydell & Brewer Limited
PO Box 9, Woodbridge, Suffolk IP12 3DF, UK
www.boydellandbrewer.com

ISBN-13: 978-1-58046-596-0
ISSN: 1071-9989

Library of Congress Cataloging-in-Publication Data

Names: Boulanger, Nadia, author. | Stravinsky, Igor, 1882–1971, author. | Francis, Kimberly A., 1979– editor.
Title: Nadia Boulanger and the Stravinskys : a selected correspondence / edited by Kimberly A. Francis.
Other titles: Eastman studies in music ; v. 143.
Description: Rochester : University of Rochester Press, 2018. | Series: Eastman studies in music ; volume 143 | Includes bibliographical references and index.
Identifiers: LCCN 2017048920 | ISBN 9781580465960 (hardcover : alk. paper)
Subjects: LCSH: Boulanger, Nadia—Correspondence. | Stravinsky, Igor, 1882–1971—Correspondence. | Conductors (Music)—Correspondence.
Classification: LCC ML423.B52 A4 2018 | DDC 780.92/2—dc23 LC record available at https://lccn.loc.gov/2017048920

This publication is printed on acid-free paper.
Printed and bound in Great Britain by TJ International Ltd, Padstow, Cornwall

Dedicated to Pamela and Thomas Francis

Contents

Photographs follow p. 14.

Acknowledgments

An entire team of research assistants, colleagues, and archivists brought this project to life, and it is my pleasure to express here, in some small way, my gratitude to all involved.

To Sonia Kane, Ralph Locke, and Julia Cook, I thank you for supporting this project and helping to make it a reality. My thanks, too, to the anonymous reviewers who helped refine this project through their thoughtful, constructive feedback.

Essential financial support for this text was provided by the Social Sciences and Humanities Research Council of Canada, Office of Research and the College of Arts at the University of Guelph, American Association of University Women, American Musicological Society, Graduate School of the University of North Carolina at Chapel Hill, and private donations from Don Campbell. Earlier versions of this work were read at conferences and colloquia in Canada, the United States, and England. My thanks to all involved for their provocative insights.

The letters cited in this edition, both in translation and in footnotes, draw on archives throughout Europe and North America. Materials from the Boulanger archives are reprinted with the permission of the Centre international Nadia et Lili Boulanger; materials from the Paul Sacher Stiftung and the Stravinsky Family papers of the Bibliothèque nationale de France are reprinted with the permission of John Stravinsky; and materials from the Théodore Strawinsky archives are reprinted with the permission of the Fondation Théodore Strawinsky. Special thanks are due especially to the staff and scholars associated with the three major collections wherein the majority of the correspondence is housed: Catherine Massip and Élisabeth Giuliani of the Département de la musique of the Bibliothèque nationale de France; Heidy Zimmermann, Carlos Chanfón, and Isolde Degen of the Paul Sacher Stiftung; and Sylvie Visinand of the Fondation Théodore Strawinsky in Geneva, Switzerland.

This entire project began when I was a graduate student at UNC–Chapel Hill and had the great fortune to work as a research assistant to Annegret Fauser. I learned from her the nuances of archival research and the discipline necessary for success. It was her encouragement and exacting standards that pushed me past my initial fear of working with Stravinsky's handwriting and drove me to engage with this material in myriad ways. I consider myself immensely lucky that she continues to act as a mentor and friend, serving as an example of erudition and compassion. I must also thank Alexandra Laederich and Jeanice Brooks, who have supported this project from its inception and have shared so generously of their deep knowledge of French culture, Boulanger's world, and the nature of exacting scholarship. Alexandra, especially, read through the entire French portion of this text and provided invaluable insights concerning Boulanger's prose.

The translations and transcriptions found here involved a veritable army of research assistants. To Jamie Jackson, Matthew Toth, Victor Fernandez, Krisandra Ivings, Erin Maher, Jennifer Walker, and especially Melissa Laporte, I extend my thanks. To Rosheeka Parahoo, who built and populated this book's companion website, I thank you for your hard work, your fresh perspective, your infectious energy, and your commitment to excellence. May this be your first academic project of many. Dawn Cornelio served as an indefatigable collaborator when it came to untangling Boulanger's prose. Your virtuosity with translation continues to inspire me. And to Connor Maitland, who served as this manuscript's extraordinary copy editor, I cannot thank you enough. Finally, while this edition exists because of this marvelous team, the final text is mine alone, particularly any mistakes or infelicities.

To my colleagues, especially Sally Hickson, Margot Irvine, Sofie Lachapelle, Paola Meyer, Sandra Parmagiani, and Christina Smylitopolous, I thank you for the inspiring and supportive environment in which I have the pleasure of working every day. I also thank my friends, especially Stephanie and Michael Berec, Kristen Meyers-Turner, Christine O'Connor, and Matthew Carl Todd for their support, encouragement, and guidance. A special debt is owed to Emily Abrams Ansari, Kevin Bartig, Annegret Fauser, William Gibbons, Alicia Levin, Avila Lotoski, Friedemann Sallis, and Karen and Doug Shadle, who so kindly read drafts of this text and whose comments helped shape the final result.

I thank my parents for everything they have given me and for their support over the years. I lovingly dedicate this book to them and their example. And to Brian, Emily, Ellison, and Quinton, thank you for your love and patience. In one of Boulanger's favorite anecdotes about Stravinsky, she would tell of his refusal to bow to critics: he didn't need their applause, he would say, because he had his *boussole* (compass) in his pocket. My dear children, my brilliant and wonderful husband, I don't need a compass: I have you. I thank you for your patience and love through thick and through thin.

Note on Companion Website

All transcriptions of this book's corresponding French originals can be consulted on the book's companion website, https://digex.lib.uoguelph.ca/exhibits/show/boulangerandstravinskys. Indeed, I designed the website to serve as a reference tool in itself. All letters may be sorted by author, date, and indexed items. For example, it is possible to isolate all letters written by Boulanger that reference the *Symphonie de psaumes*, if one so desires. One may also choose between viewing French and English texts side by side, or viewing French or English letters in isolation. All editorial comments and footnotes appear in the print version only.

Abbreviations

F-LYc	Conservatoire national supérieur musique et danse de Lyon, Lyon, France
CINLB	Centre international Nadia et Lili Boulanger
F-Pn	Bibliothèque nationale de France—National Library of France
CH-Fts	Foundation Théodore Strawinsky, Genève, Switzerland
N.L.a.	Lettres autographes, nouveau fonds—Autograph letters, new collection
US-NYp	New York Public Library
Rés. Vm. Dos.	Réserve Vm. Dossier—Miscellaneous reserved (unpublished/autograph) materials in the Bibliothèque nationale de France
CH-Bps	Stravinsky collection, Paul Sacher Stiftung

To condense score citations, the following abbreviations have been employed:

ph.	Photostat (used to describe all manner of reproduced scores, particularly as "photostat" is the word used by Boulanger and Stravinsky regardless of the actual means of reproduction).
a.	autograph
2p	two piano
2pr	two-piano reduction
p/v	piano/vocal reduction

Introduction

It all began with music lessons for Stravinsky's son in October of 1929. By that fall, Nadia Boulanger, thirty-two-year-old professor at the École normale de musique in Paris and at the Conservatoire américain at Fontainebleau, had garnered a reputation as an extraordinarily gifted music educator. The daughter of a Parisian composer, the distinguished Ernest Boulanger, and an exiled Russian princess and former Conservatoire vocal student, Raïssa [née Mychestky], Boulanger had made her place in Paris as a composer, performer, and pedagogue.[1] Her musical prowess had been tested and proven already by her prodigious graduation with four first prizes from the Conservatoire de Paris at the age of sixteen. By 1929, despite abandoning her own moderately scandalous career as a composer in favor of performing and teaching, Boulanger had ascended to a compelling position in modernist circles as a charismatic, passionate teacher of musical composition, harmony, history, accompaniment, and performance. Above all, she championed new music.

Contemporaneously, by the late 1920s, Igor Stravinsky held both an imperious and a controversial place within the modernist musical community. Son of a Russian opera singer, Fyodor, and a Ukrainian-born mother, Anna [née Kholodovskaya], Stravinsky returned from Switzerland to Paris following the First World War to find that his new neoclassical aesthetic divided the city that had earlier celebrated him for works such as *The Firebird* and *Petrushka*. Though his professional world and social acquaintances appear to have had little connection to Boulanger's at this time, Boulanger had already developed a deep devotion to Stravinsky's music, and was actively promoting it. Sparse evidence

---

1. Raïssa (Rosalie) Mychestky came to Paris in 1876, claiming to be an exiled Russian princess. Rumors exist that Raïssa may in fact have been Jewish and from Poland. Jérôme Spycket argues that Raïssa was the daughter of Princess Yekaterina Ivanovna Myshchetskaya, who was German in background and had converted from Lutheranism. Spycket suggests that Raïssa was in fact illegitimate, and the title came to her mother as a means of covering up an affair with a member of the imperial family. Spycket, *À la recherche*, 65. Raïssa Boulanger never spoke Russian at home. Nadia Boulanger did not know the language and had to ask students to translate for her. Boulanger's later claims that she understood the Slavic soul were never autobiographical in nature.

and anecdotal references describe Stravinsky's visits to Boulanger's studio in the 1920s, a teaching space that must have reminded him of the *jours fixes* that he had attended at the home of his own beloved teacher, Nikolay Rimsky-Korsakov (1844–1908).[2] During visits with Boulanger's students, Stravinsky spoke about his works and provided feedback on the compositions of Boulanger's pupils. These occasional exchanges, as well as Boulanger's extraordinary reputation as a pedagogue, led Stravinsky to approach Boulanger about facilitating the education of his son, Sviatoslav Soulima. Boulanger accepted the eighteen-year-old as a student, and in so doing drew the Stravinskys into her world just as she entered theirs, eventually corresponding with Catherine, Anna, Denise, Théodore, Soulima, Françoise, Milène, "Kitty," and of course Igor Stravinsky (table I.1).

The Paul Sacher Stiftung, the Fondation Théodore Strawinsky, and the New York Public Library all hold Boulanger's letters to members of the Stravinsky family. The Stravinskys' letters to Boulanger can be consulted at the Bibliothèque nationale de France. Stravinsky's letters reveal his professional ambition and bear witness to his thirst for praise, his struggle with detractors, and his businesslike approach to composition. He operates in these letters as both friend and foe, by turns officious and doting. His words underscore his deep love of family and friends as well as his ready manipulation of those who could help him cement his legacy.

Boulanger's letters offer a candid glimpse of the praise she lavished on Stravinsky and her professional strategies employed for his benefit. Particularly rich are her comments on the *Symphony of Psalms*, the *Dumbarton Oaks Concerto*, the Symphony in C, and *The Rake's Progress*. Invaluable are her accounts of the early reception of *The Rake* and her general reportage on the reestablishment of European cultural traditions after the Second World War, especially the place of post-tonal composition and its effect on young composers. Her words allow for an intimate experience of both her response to the way in which Stravinsky distanced himself from her after 1952 and her concern over his health and well-being as reported to her by Stravinsky's children. Overall, this epistolary exchange paints a firsthand account of the transatlantic nature of musical life during the modernist era for both Boulanger and Stravinsky. It speaks of the complex relationship between creation and reception, between composition and transmission, and between friendship and careerism.

Boulanger's Stravinskys

Adding an additional layer of nuance and interest to this epistolary account are the letters exchanged between Boulanger and Stravinsky's immediate family.

---

2. Brooks, *Musical Work*, 27–28, 174.

Table I.1. Stravinsky Family Correspondence with Boulanger, Bibliothèque
nationale de France

Name	Relation to Igor Stravinsky	Shelfmark (*F-Pn*)	Dates
Stravinsky, Anna	*Mother*	N.L.a. 108 (85–87)	1930–35
Stravinsky, Catherine	*First wife*	N.L.a. 108 (88–96)	1929–37
Stravinsky, Catherine ("Kitty")	*Granddaughter*	N.L.a. 108 (97–101)	1967–70
Stravinsky, Denise	*Daughter-in-law*	N.L.a. 108 (102–7)	1939–76
Stravinsky, Françoise	*Daughter-in-law*	N.L.a. 108 (108–14)	1946–72
Stravinsky, Igor		N.L.a 108 (115–310)	1929–69
Stravinsky, Milène	*Daughter*	N.L.a. 108 (312–18)	1969–75
Stravinsky, Soulima	*Son*	N.L.a. 108 (319–87)	1929–77
Strawinsky, Théodore	*Son*	N.L.a. 109 (1–62)	1931–80

The Stravinsky family, excluding Igor, sent 140 letters to the French pedagogue between 1929 and 1979. At either end of this edition, Igor Stravinsky's
words retreat into the background, and those of his immediate family frame
and fill the narrative. This edition would be incomplete without a discussion
of the correspondents beyond Igor Stravinsky who so enrich this collection
(table I.1).

Yekaterina (Catherine) Gavrilovna Stravinsky (née Nossenko) (1880–1939) and Anna Kirillovna Stravinsky (née Kholodovskaya) (1854–1939)

The letters of Anna Stravinsky, Igor's mother, and Catherine Stravinsky, his first
wife, appear in this collection twice and five times, respectively. I have chosen in this collection to refer to his first wife as Catherine, as this is how she
self-identified in letters to Boulanger, and it is what her children called her.
I link Anna and Catherine within this introduction neither to diminish their
importance as individual authors nor to suggest a sort of uniformity of voice
within their texts—quite the contrary. Instead, I join them to draw attention to
their role as matriarchs, to emphasize the power this title granted them within
the Stravinsky domestic framework, and to underline the impact they had on
the lives of those within the household. Given the tremendously patriarchal
portrayal and framing of Stravinsky's career and his family's structure in the

current literature, I wish to emphasize here the women's voices in this family and the dynamic nature of their personalities. I argue that it was the Stravinsky women who facilitated and nurtured the lines of communication between Igor Stravinksy and Nadia Boulanger in the early 1930s. Without them, Boulanger's connection to Stravinsky would likely have faltered.

Anna Stravinsky, the composer's strong, intimidating mother, was the youngest of four daughters. Though her decision was frowned upon, she chose to marry Fyodor Stravinsky at the age of nineteen.[3] Beyond this brief biographical reference to his mother's background, stories of Igor's parents center primarily on his father. In 1876, Fyodor Stravinsky premiered the role of Mephistopheles in Gounod's *Faust* at the Mariyinsky Theatre to great acclaim. That same year, Anna and Fyodor moved to St. Petersburg with their first son, Roman, then only a year old. By October 1881, the family was living in an apartment at 8 Kryukov Canal, and on June 17 [o.s. June 5], 1882, their third son, Igor, was born.

Anna remained in Russia during the revolution and emigrated west to live with Igor (by all accounts her least-favorite son) and his family in June 1922.[4] She died in 1939, the same year as Catherine and just six months after Stravinsky's daughter Lyudmila. Anna's letters to Boulanger are polite and respectful, extending warm wishes to Boulanger's mother. Indeed, Anna's mention twice in her letters of the relationship between mother and daughter leads me to suspect it was a bond she respected and valued. It is quite likely that Boulanger's mother's claims to a Russian royal background may have heightened the affinity between Anna Stravinsky and the Boulangers, though none of the Boulangers' letters to the Stravinskys contains Russian text.[5] Indeed, Nadia did not speak the language.

Catherine Stravinsky is the other matriarchal figure with whom Boulanger maintained a conversation.[6] Catherine has often been painted as dutiful,

---

3. For one such depiction of Anna and Fyodor Stravinsky, see Walsh, *Creative Spring*, 4–15. Richard Taruskin also provides details about Stravinsky's upbringing as related to his father and particularly to his father's work as an opera singer. He provides very little background information about Anna Stravinsky. Taruskin, *Stravinsky and the Russian Traditions*, 77–92.

4. Robert Craft states this in his foreword to the Stravinsky correspondence, before presenting some of Catherine Stravinsky's letters. See Craft, *Stravinsky: Selected Correspondence*, 3. Walsh repeats this idea, *Creative Spring*, 4–15.

5. The Stravinsky archives at the Paul Sacher Stiftung contain only one letter written by Raïssa Boulanger to the Stravinsky family. Much of the letter is illegible, and it was most likely written at the end of Raïssa's struggle with Parkinson's disease. The entire text is in French, except for a brief valediction in Russian.

6. Life in Catherine and Igor Stravinsky's home is considered in Théodore Strawinsky's *Catherine and Igor Stravinsky*. The book is dedicated to Boulanger

though resentful of her husband's extramarital affairs. She is rarely allowed moments of agency or assertiveness in the current literature, with perhaps the exception of Stephen Walsh's presentation of her as an "intelligent, profound, and exceptionally warm-hearted woman."[7] The letters included here reinforce Catherine's agency, showing her to have been a caring mother and certainly not a shrinking violet. Every bit the fiery counterpart to her husband, Catherine Stravinsky appears in these letters as an authoritarian—someone who expected her vision for her children's care enforced and who did not hesitate to impose her expectations on Boulanger. I have chosen to include the last letter sent from Catherine to Boulanger (undated, but likely from late 1936 or early 1937). It is touching that the last extant exchange between the two involved Catherine thanking Boulanger for the flowers the latter had arranged to have waiting when Catherine returned from the Sancellemoz sanatorium for what all hoped—in vain—would be a lasting recovery from her battle with tuberculosis.

Théodore Strawinsky (1907–89)

Of all Stravinsky's children, Théodore Strawinsky arguably bore the most striking resemblance to his father and yet was often at odds with him. Théodore never employed the "v" in the family last name. Even his posthumous foundation remains the Fondation Théodore Strawinsky. For this reason, and as a means of emphasizing the arm's-length connection Théodore appears to have had with the American Stravinskys, I have retained the different spelling of Théodore's last name in this edition. No evidence exists in his letters as to why he maintained the older spelling, though I suspect it related in part to his artistic identity and in part to cherished family memories from before 1939 and the mixture of cultural influences—particularly Russian, French, and Swiss—that both fractured and forged his upbringing.

Théodore's correspondence reveals him as a passionate, devoted, and deeply religious man. Trained as a painter at l'Académie André Lhote à Paris, he achieved international acclaim by the age of twenty-four, and worked as a professional artist for the remainder of his life. Of Théodore's numerous

---

and she played a pivotal role in facilitating its publication. Walsh also discusses Catherine at length in his own biography, particularly *A Creative Spring*, 90–91.

7. Walsh, *Creative Spring*, 90–91. The most recent account of Catherine Stravinsky's relationship with Igor Stravinsky can be found in Robert Craft, *Stravinsky: Discoveries and Memories*. Indeed, Craft's text is provocative in many ways, particularly his portrayal of the Stravinsky family as "dysfunctional." *Discoveries and Memories* serves as an intriguing counterpoint to the correspondence presented in this volume.

accolades, the most treasured was likely his appointment as Commander of the Order of St. Gregory the Great by Pope Paul VI in 1977.

Théodore was the only one of Stravinsky's children never to emigrate to the United States. Following his marriage to Denise Guerzoni in 1936, his adult life was spent in Le Mans, France, and after 1946, in Geneva, Switzerland.[8] In 1941 he was singled out as a potential communist and detained at Camp Récébédou near Toulouse by the French government for several months—a terrifying reality his father tried desperately to mitigate while in the United States, as the correspondence demonstrates. After the war, Théodore and Denise assumed care for their niece Catherine (Kitty), the daughter of Théodore's sister, Lyudmila (Mika), and Yuri Mandelstam. Mandelstam's story adds further tragedy to this branch of the Stravinsky family tree. Arrested in Paris during the Second World War, despite having converted from Judaism to the Orthodox faith in 1935, he died in a concentration camp in Jarworzhno, Poland, on October 15, 1943, leaving Kitty an orphan.[9] Théodore and Denise officially adopted Kitty in 1952, when she was fifteen years old.

Théodore's first surviving letter to Boulanger dates from March 22, 1935; it was sent to offer condolences after he learned of her mother's death. Few clues remain to explain how or why Boulanger grew close to Théodore, and this element of the Boulanger–Stravinsky network remains a mystery. Yet after 1936, and particularly following the Second World War, they corresponded quite regularly and visited each other often, especially after Théodore's conversion to Catholicism in 1947. Boulanger became a sort of adopted mother/aunt figure to Théodore, and their shared faith is often referenced in the correspondence. The later, deeply emotional letters reveal Théodore's complicated relationship with his father, whom he dearly loved; his deep-seated resentment and dislike of his stepmother Vera; and his distrust of Robert Craft, his father's amanuensis after 1946. Théodore's correspondence with Boulanger, it would appear, served as an outlet for his frustrations and a source of comfort. Théodore Strawinsky's letters aid in understanding the final years of Igor Stravinsky's life, and though they must be read through the lens of a son who never forgave his father's remarriage, they nonetheless reveal the complicated nature of the Stravinsky family's inner workings and the role Boulanger played as a sort of adopted family member.[10]

---

8. For details about the marriage, see Walsh, *Second Exile*, 50–52. Walsh quotes Vera Sudeikina's letter on the wedding from July 10, 1936. This letter is now housed at the Paul Sacher Stiftung.
9. Walsh, *Second Exile*, 161; and Weeda, *Yuriy Mandel'shtam*, xxi.
10. Tamara Levitz similarly cautions others about reading Théodore Strawinsky's letters as objective texts. See Levitz, *Modernist Mysteries*, 295 (especially n. 12).

Denise Strawinsky (née Guerzoni) (1914–2004)

Denise Strawinsky was the daughter of Swiss artist Stephanie Guerzoni (1887–1970). Guerzoni was the only female student of painter Ferdinand Hodler (1853–1918, with whom she studied from 1915–18. Denise appears to have been a loving wife and devoted daughter-in-law When, in 1938, the Stravinsky family found itself convalescing at the sanatorium in Sancellemoz after the death of Lyudmila, Denise was there to serve as nurse. Elsewhere, Denise actively participated in family matters. Her letters to Boulanger, three of which I have included in this edition, often show her acting as intermediary between Boulanger and Igor or Théodore. In moments of crisis, it was Denise, rather than her husband, who took up the pen to correspond with Boulanger. This collection reveals Denise as diplomat—carefully lying to protect Boulanger from news of Igor Stravinsky's brazen travels executed against doctor's orders in 1939—and as witness to the Stravinsky family dynamic, supporting, with her husband, the post-1971 counternarratives that celebrated Catherine Stravinsky. Denise Strawinsky's letters represent another strong, assertive female voice in the Stravinsky family environs—a voice that helped smooth over dissent or facilitate action so as to protect a certain brand of the Stravinsky family legacy.[11]

Sviatoslav (Soulima) Stravinsky (1910–94)

The younger son and third child of Igor and Catherine Stravinsky, Soulima was born in Lausanne, Switzerland.[12] Boulanger taught Soulima—or Sviétik, as she referred to him in her diaries during the 1930s—composition and analysis every Tuesday morning at 11:30 a.m.[13] Piano performance was likely also discussed, especially given that Boulanger and Soulima Stravinsky concertized together in the late 1930s as well as in 1946, performing two-piano reductions of Igor Stravinsky's works they themselves created.[14]

Soulima met his wife, Françoise Bon (Blondlat), in Paris where she was studying law during the war.[15] Their son Jean was born shortly after the war ended. From across the Atlantic, Boulanger sent numerous care packages to

---

11. Indeed, seventeen years following Igor's death, Denise Strawinsky published her own account of the domestic life of Catherine and Igor. See Denise and Théodore Strawinsky, *Au cœur du foyer*.
12. Walsh, *Creative Spring*, 146.
13. Francis, "A Dialogue Begins," 22–44. The typical spelling of this Russian nickname is Svétik, but Boulanger very clearly added the "i" to her spelling of the name.
14. For further details of their performance practice, see Brooks, *Musical Work*, 112–13.
15. Walsh, *Second Exile*, 179.

the young family, whose vulnerability in early postwar Paris concerned her greatly. After returning to the French capital herself, Boulanger grew close to the trio, and the accounts she sent to Igor Stravinsky warmly depict the time she spent in Soulima and Françoise's apartment. After the war, Igor Stravinsky convinced his 35-year-old son and daughter-in-law to relocate to the United States. Boulanger remained a faithful reference writer for Soulima as he applied to American teaching positions after emigrating.

The correspondence suggests that Soulima, like so many others of her alumni, remained a student in Boulanger's mind for her entire life, and she often references him in her letters first and foremost in terms of his musical development. As for Soulima, this collection presents the youthful, spirited nature of his letters before World War II and the reverent, sober voice of those that followed it. In the early years, Soulima approached Boulanger as more of a governess and confidante, while in the later years, his candor is replaced by humble respect. After 1950, when Soulima was appointed to a professorship in piano performance at the University of Illinois, his letters depict him at once excited about establishing a reputation for himself outside of his father's shadow and deeply concerned about his father's legacy. Unlike his brother, Soulima does not discuss the family drama that surrounded Stravinsky's physical care post-1968 in letters to Boulanger. The sobriety of Soulima Stravinsky's own brief messages at this point serve as a foil to his brother's angry and disillusioned prose.

Expressive Markings: The Question of Love

A central theme found in the letters concerns the question of love shared between Boulanger and Igor Stravinsky. Boulanger's letters, especially those after the Second World War, often reference her love for the composer. Few of her letters post-1945 fail to mention that she "loves ... both [Igor and Vera] madly" (January 27, 1946) and "loves [Stravinsky] so" (November 25, 1946). Stravinsky, similarly, ends letters with expressions of affection for Boulanger. His first letters after Boulanger leaves the United States end with "love and kisses" (November 23, 1946) and "[from Stravinsky,] who loves you" (September 5, 1948). But it was not a passionate, romantic love.

We now know Boulanger had at least three affairs during her lifetime with married men (Raoul Pugno, Camille Mauclair, and Prince Pierre of Monaco), and there is no lack of evidence for these relationships. Alexandra Laederich and Rémy Stricker engage compellingly and thoughtfully with the complicated and convoluted nature of Boulanger's romantic relationships, as recorded in her diaries at length.[16] There is no such evidence of an affair with Stravinsky.

---

16. Stricker, "La Critique de Nadia Boulanger," in *Témoignages et études*, 131–18.

If nothing else, Boulanger's devotion to Stravinsky, to his children, and to his first wife, Catherine, stood as a formidable obstacle to her own pursuit of the composer—not to mention that a public alliance with a foreigner, and such a high-profile musician, would have jeopardized if not altogether undone the professional identity she had built for herself.[17]

Instead, Boulanger's was a platonic love built around Stravinsky as an artist, as the composer of the music in which she so deeply believed. In many respects, Boulanger lived an isolated life. Talent, age, and circumstance distanced her from the majority of her peers, and the death of loved ones separated her from family. Her gender marked her as the exception in almost all the professional circles she frequented. Stravinsky, however, realized her vision. His music satisfied all of Boulanger's criteria for great masterworks. When handed the opportunity to learn of Stravinsky's kindness and humanity, Boulanger connected his warmth and friendship to his compositions. Indeed, she found him to be art incarnate, and he assumed for her both a human and a superhuman quality. Boulanger blended her love for Stravinsky and her love of Stravinsky's music in her lectures and her writing, treasuring this unique and intimate connection. Regardless of how sincerely that love was reciprocated, her intimate knowledge of the composer remained something Boulanger treasured.

In fact one wonders, at times, if the Stravinskys in general and Igor in particular ever completely returned Boulanger's devotion. Yet, to deem Boulanger naïvely enraptured and Stravinsky only selfishly exploitative contradicts the evidence, to a degree. When at his most professional, Stravinsky can seem almost dismissive and cold in his letters to Boulanger, but the reader should not confuse expediency with apathy. Stravinsky expresses his affection in specific contexts—there is a time and a place. And yet there are moments, particularly after 1952, when Stravinsky is clearly guilty of callous and calculating behavior. I argue that these letters reveal an uneven and ultimately platonic love centered around and fed by Stravinsky's art and ego, a love that blossomed in the context of a friendship that in and of itself relieved Boulanger's sense of isolation.

Editorial Apparatus

Publishing both the French and English versions of these letters would amount to an excessively large text. Instead, the French transcriptions have been included as part of this book's companion website, where one can choose to view the fully indexed and searchable French and English letters, consulting them in isolation or with both languages side by side.

---

17. Francis, *Teaching Stravinsky*, 116–19.

The letters presented here were chosen because of their narrative power and ability to walk the reader both through forty years of the tumultuous twentieth century and through the reactions of their authors to said events. If letter content became predictable (for example, Boulanger's annual well-wishes on the anniversary of the death of Stravinsky's first wife on March 2), I chose not to publish them. Likewise, Christmas and birthday greetings, unless accompanied by additional information, have not been included here. Whenever possible, I have endeavored to present the writers in dialogue with one another rather than produce sequences of unanswered letters.

Unfortunately, most material sent by Boulanger to extended family members no longer exists in the archives, though it would have been delightful to read her response to Catherine's letter of April 1931 or her letter to Anna Stravinsky after the premiere of the *Symphony of Psalms* in Brussels in December 1930. The lack of extant letters sent to Soulima Stravinsky also disappoints. Those letters in Boulanger's hand retained in Soulima's papers at the New York Public Library fail to be of consequence, and so have been omitted. Along these same lines, it would appear Boulanger did not bond with Stravinsky's daughter Milène to the same extent she did with his sons, and so the only surviving letter from Stravinsky's younger daughter that I have included here appears on October 27, 1969, as a response to Boulanger's presentation of her condolences concerning the situation that surrounded Stravinsky's final convalescence in New York. One would have hoped for more from Milène's voice, and it remains curious to me that Boulanger failed to connect with her as strongly as with the other women of the family. I have also chosen not to include any letters written by Françoise Stravinsky, not because of a lack of extant documents but because of a lack of germane material. Finally, I have omitted the letters written by Stravinsky's granddaughter Kitty (Catherine) to Boulanger. Though gracious enough, and indicative of the lengths to which Boulanger went to remember the birthdays of her friends' children and grandchildren, the letters from Kitty to Boulanger are rather perfunctory.

Nothing that remains was chosen to sensationalize, but neither were letters excluded to protect the correspondents in question. This rich collection often presents Boulanger at her most vulnerable and candid, and Stravinsky at his more playful and paternal. I remain sensitive to the private nature of Boulanger's and Stravinsky's prose, and yet, the significant moments of these letters often lie at the interstices of the guarded and the candid.

In the editorial apparatus itself, it has been my intention to stay out of the way as much as possible. Important figures, events, and works have been identified in a footnote at first mention, but otherwise I have endeavored to let the voices represented by these letters speak for themselves—as much as any historical document can indeed do so. All references to Stravinsky's works remain in the language in which they were discussed, most commonly French—e.g., *L'oiseau de feu,* not *The Firebird;* the *Symphonie de psaumes,* not the *Symphony of Psalms.*

In the interest of comprehensiveness and fidelity to the narrative to which this correspondence attests, I have chosen to include materials published elsewhere, including the forty letters previously released in Robert Craft's *Stravinsky: A Selected Correspondence.* Indeed, my edited collection seeks to ameliorate the image of Boulanger constructed by Craft's editorial work, an image Craft in several publications tied to subservience and the macabre.[18] I and others have criticized elsewhere the errors in Craft's edition, including translation issues and his conflating of letters.[19] Consider, for example, that Craft confuses the letters from May 19, 1941, and July 29, 1941, intermingling the paragraphs of the two. Elsewhere there are translation issues that—though not fatal— nevertheless detract from the accuracy of the text. And finally, Craft did not at all understand the scope of the correspondence, claiming that Boulanger and Stravinsky's early dealings "were not documented in epistolary form" and that Boulanger's "chapter in the eventual Stravinsky biography will have to be constructed from the letters and memoirs of others."[20] Surely, my own edition sheds further light on this matter.

Each letter included here is preceded by the author's name and the name of the intended recipient. The shared last name of six of the correspondents in this collection makes the use of the Stravinsky surname potentially confusing. For this reason, I have chosen to use the surname alone only when referencing Igor. All other Stravinskys appear either with both first and last name or by first name only. I have also chosen to retain the different and ever-evolving transliterations of the Strawinsky/Stravinsky surname in the body of the letters published here. The question of when and why Strawinsky became Stravinsky—and Boulanger's seeming difficulty in adopting this change—becomes yet another subtlety worth tracking in the correspondence.

Every letter appears in its entirety. Nothing has been omitted; ellipsis points are as their authors wrote them. All postscripts have been included here at the bottom of each letter, regardless of where they were written in the original. Geographical names appear in English, for the most part, though French street names and diacritics have been used for addresses in Paris, e.g., St.

---

18. Craft, *Stravinsky: Selected Correspondence,* xvii. In my own conclusions, I agree with and am indebted to Matthew Toth's work on the Stravinsky–Craft relationship. See Toth, "Editorial Craft: Reconsidering Igor Stravinsky's Letters to Nadia Boulanger," Gossip Conference/ Colloque Le Potin, University of Guelph, ON, May 2012.

19. Jeanice Brooks, "The *fonds* Boulanger at the Bibliothèque Nationale," *Notes* 51 (1995): 1235.

20. Craft, ed. *Selected Correspondence,* xvii.

Honoré, rue Ballu, and 9ème for the *arrondissement* where Boulanger lived. Whenever possible, letters have been dated by the time they were written, not postmarked, if both pieces of information existed. I have assumed some dates incorrect based on the content of the letters, and have inserted what I take to be the correct date in square brackets.

I have tried, whenever possible, to render Boulanger's various punctuation habits intelligible. She would often employ dashes as all manner of punctuation (periods, commas, question marks). My main goal was readability, and so any editorial changes I made to punctuation have been done with the intention of clarifying, not altering, Boulanger's meaning. All underlining, whether single or multiple, is here transcribed as italics. I have reproduced strikethroughs where appropriate. In the case of telegrams or letters typed on an American typewriter that are therefore missing all diacritics, said markings remain also absent in the transcriptions. Similarly, all telegrams remain in capital letters, as they were in the originals.

It bears mentioning that there are numerous errors within Boulanger's original prose. These vary from the simple omission of a word or a hyphen when using the imperative, to capitalizing the first letter in the names of French months, to what appears to have been a struggle with the subjunctive mood and some Anglicisms and *maladresses*. Boulanger never received formal schooling outside of the study of music, and would later lament that this resulted in deficiencies with the written language.[21] And whether due to haste, fatigue, or a sincere struggle to express herself, the letters to Stravinsky contain some errors. Wherever possible, I have attempted to fill these gaps and smooth out the prose. Footnotes indicating editorial choices exist within the English version of the text, but the transcriptions of the French originals, consultable on the companion website, read faithful to the originals, mistakes and all, rather than overburdening the text with [*sic*] markings. Moreover, the significance of these errors extends beyond the question of editorial methodologies. Boulanger's willingness to send incomplete, unpolished letters to Stravinsky speaks to her comfort and candor with the composer. Though the pair never stopped the formal and polite French custom of *vouvoyer*, the errors allowed into the epistolary record are in and of themselves an indication of a certain familiarity on Boulanger's part with the Stravinskys, assuming she herself was aware of the imperfection of her texts.

---

21. Interview with Émile Naoumoff, January 10, 2011.

Chapter Outline

The letters proceed chronologically, beginning with a Christmas card from the Stravinsky family to the Boulangers in 1929 and ending with Boulanger's well-wishes to Théodore and Denise Strawinsky on the anniversary of Igor's death in 1972. The texts between are divided along historical or artistic fault lines. The first two chapters consider the early establishment of Boulanger's dialogue with the Stravinskys through her position as Soulima Stravinsky's music teacher. They progress through the loss of her own mother on March 19, 1935, her involvement with the *Dumbarton Oaks Concerto,* and her role in mourning Stravinsky's lost loved ones—Lyudmila, Catherine, and Anna.

The third chapter concerns the relocation of both Boulanger and Stravinsky to the United States during the Second World War and their subsequent dialogue, including Boulanger's painfully emotional letter of March 17, 1941, which contains a near-transcription of the mental breakdown guilt was causing her to have. The letters from the World War II era are especially moving, with a Europe at war as their backdrop. They also touch upon artistic events such as the publication of Stravinsky's *Poétique musicale,* the post-compositional editing of his Symphony in C, the reorchestration of the "Danse Sacrale" movement of his *Rite of Spring,* and the somewhat fraught premiere of the *Sonata for Two Pianos.* The chapter ends with the letters sent by Boulanger as she prepares to return to Paris and separate from Igor and Vera Stravinsky. They prove especially poignant—and prescient. Boulanger would never again visit with the Stravinskys on American soil. Soulima Stravinsky's letters from France at this time paint an image of newly liberated Paris and Igor Stravinsky's tenuous place within it.

Chapter 4 details Boulanger's return home in 1946 and her interpretation of early reconstruction conditions. She follows Stravinsky's career from afar while also feeding the composer information about his children and new grandchild, Jean. Boulanger makes palpable her frustration and sadness over separating from the Stravinskys of Hollywood, a frustration that serves as a touching foil to the sheer delight she expresses at reuniting with Stravinsky in Venice in September 1951 at the premiere of his opera, *The Rake's Progress.*

In chapter 5, the tone of the dialogue shifts again as Stravinsky begins to redefine himself as a post-tonal composer. His letters, commonly dictated at this point, become colder in tone, and his once-jovial prose becomes infrequent. The chapter ends with correspondence relaying that Stravinsky has had a stroke in Berlin and that Théodore Strawinsky fears for his father's long-term care.

The final chapter presents the closing decades of Stravinsky's life, the concerns of his children over his health and well-being, and Boulanger's adaptation to increasingly fettered access to the composer. The once commanding and assertive tone of Boulanger's prose takes on a couched, veiled nature after the mid-1950s. From 1969 onward, Boulanger's letters become bifurcated— one stream of missives, sent to Igor, remains supportive if not somewhat stuffy and clichéd; the other stream, sent to Théodore, relays her frustration and increasing despair over the composer's care. While Stravinsky's voice falls from the record, Boulanger's final words mirror her very first letters from the early 1930s as she finds herself supporting Stravinsky's children, celebrating the composer she admired, and defending a music she dearly loved.

Unknown location, n.d., Boulanger and Stravinsky, contact sheet for unidentified photo shoot (SIS FO 50 001). Reproduced with permission of the Igor Stravinsky Collection, Paul Sacher Stiftung, Basel, Switzerland.

Sancellemoz (Haute-Savoie, France) 1939, Milène and Igor Stravinsky with
Denise and Théodore Strawinsky (1213 d). © Fondation Théodore Strawinsky.
Reproduced with permission.

Magnanac (Haute-Garonne, France) 1941, Théodore et Denise Strawisnky (1284).
© Fondation Théodore Strawinsky. Reproduced with permission.

Villars (Vaud, Suisse) 1957, in back, the Prince of Monaco, in the foreground,
Boulanger and Théodore Strawinsky, the day of Boulanger's seventieth birthday
(1650). © Fondation Théodore Strawinsky. Reproduced with permission.

Hollywood, California, 1945, Boulanger and Stravinsky sitting on "her couch."
Inscriptions written by Boulanger and Stravinsky are for Winifred Johnstone,
administrator for the Lili Boulanger Memorial Fund. Author's collection.

Chapter One

October 1929–August 1938

The first piece of correspondence kept by either Boulanger or Stravinsky appears in Boulanger's archives and is a single calling card, dated December 19, 1929, sent to her by Stravinsky to wish her season's greetings.[1] This small gesture suggests that Stravinsky and Boulanger had been in contact, however superficially, in the years preceding Soulima Stravinsky's studies with Boulanger. One wonders if Raïssa Boulanger, who had previously corresponded with Pyotr Ilyich Tchaikovsky, may have in some way aided or encouraged the connection between her daughter and Stravinsky.[2] The first steady trickle of documents begins nine months after this greeting card, with Stravinsky's request that Boulanger oversee his son's musical education. During the course of his first year of study, Soulima became romantically involved with one of Boulanger's American students, Diantha Walker (May 9, 1930). Soulima's affection for Walker grew increasingly intense, and a year later Boulanger found herself trying to smooth matters over with his mother (April 8, 1931). Though sympathetic to the couple, Boulanger yielded to the wishes of Catherine Stravinsky, who clearly articulates her vision for her son and for married life in general in this first chapter.

Upon growing closer with the family, Boulanger found herself invited to attend the world premiere of Stravinsky's mature neoclassical work, the *Symphony of Psalms*. The concert took place in Brussels, Belgium, under the baton of Ernst Ansermet on December 13, 1930.[3] Following this concert and

1. Letter, Stravinsky family to the Boulangers, January 19, 1929, N.L.a. 108 (115), F-Pn.
2. Ernest and Raïssa Boulanger met Tchaikovsky during his visit to Paris in June 1886. His diaries describe a concert wherein Raïssa Boulanger sang for him. Lakond, transl., *The Diaries of Tchaikovsky*, 47. By December of that year, Raïssa Boulanger had written Tchaikovsky to request some music from him. Spycket, *A la recherche*, 61; Rosenstiel, *Nadia Boulanger*, 15–16.
3. Boulanger retained an autographed photostat copy of the original score dating from the premiere. See "Symphonie de psaumes," Boulanger, F-Pn, Gr Vma. 476.

through her role as teacher to Soulima, Boulanger gained increased access to the music of Igor Stravinsky. She attended rehearsals for the symphony in Paris as well as the work's Parisian premiere on February 24. She also began teaching courses on the symphony at the École normale de musique, promoting the *Symphony of Psalms* as a true modernist masterpiece.[4]

Likely dating from a few months after the composition's premiere is the first piece of correspondence of Boulanger's present in Stravinsky's archives. Rather than a prose letter, the document is instead a list of inconsistencies Boulanger documented between Stravinsky's recording of the symphony and his piano/vocal score, prepared by Soulima. The somewhat clumsy letters that follow detail the original, cautious exchange between Boulanger and Stravinsky as she oversaw the editorial revision of the piano/vocal score. Boulanger's letters reveal her to be a fastidious though easily distracted partner, and she carefully protects her actions by framing them within the context of her work as a teacher.[5] Stravinsky's responses appear cordial though at times cursory, and an underlying air of impatience (or perhaps even apathy) permeates his responses to Boulanger's ever-exacting inquiries.

In the years that followed, Boulanger and the Stravinsky family corresponded concerning myriad matters, both professional and personal. They exchanged birthday greetings and sympathies following the final convalescence and death of Boulanger's mother on March 19, 1935. They reveal Boulanger's fledgling efforts to secure performances for Stravinsky through her involvement with the Société musicale indépendante (June 19, 1932) and the Princesse de Polignac (February 25, 1933).[6] Boulanger also writes here of obtaining appointments for Stravinsky, first at the École des hautes études in Fontainebleau and then at the École normale de musique. Boulanger assumed full responsibility for paying Stravinsky's salary (ca. December 1935)[7] and in her letters, Boulanger insists that the work of her students will inspire Stravinsky's own projects. In 1936, Stravinsky, we learn, attended the first combined memorial mass Boulanger held for her mother and sister, arranging for flowers to be laid on their tomb (March 19, 1936). That same year, Stravinsky provided Boulanger with a copy of his newly published autobiography, *Chroniques de ma vie* (January 1935).[8]

---

4. See Francis, "A Dialogue Begins," 22–44.
5. For more on Boulanger's editorial involvement with the *Symphonie de psaumes*, see Francis, *Teaching Stravinsky*, 37–65; and Francis, "A Dialogue Begins," 22–44.
6. There is disappointingly little in Boulanger and Stravinsky's correspondence concerning the Princesse de Polignac. See also n. 28 of this chapter.
7. Francis, *Teaching Stravinsky*, 83–87.
8. Igor Stravinsky, *Chroniques de ma vie*.

Between 1937 and 1939, Boulanger completed three tours of the United States. These tours marked the apex of her transatlantic influence and were an opportunity for her to be fêted by her alumni who had gone on to become professors and even senior administrators at some of the country's most prestigious institutions for musical training. While on tour, Boulanger connected with wealthy women philanthropists, including Mildred Woods Bliss and Mrs. John Alden Carpenter.[9] Boulanger used these connections to champion Stravinsky's works and attempt to win him new commissions. The *Dumbarton Oaks Concerto*, commissioned by the Blisses for their thirtieth wedding anniversary, was the result of Boulanger's negotiations.[10] She also conducted the premiere on May 8, 1938. The letters reveal how frantic the entire process was. Indeed, some letters must have crossed paths, and this makes for difficulty establishing a specific chronology. The chapter ends on this intense note.

Music Lessons

Stravinsky to Boulanger

I. Strawinsky
Pleyel
Paris

Mme [*sic*] Nadia Boulanger
Garganville [*sic*]
[August] 26, 1929

Dear friend,
    I called your home to learn where to find you and was told it was necessary to write to you at Garganville [*sic*], which is what I'm doing.[11]

---

9. For more on women patrons of the United States, see Locke and Barr, *Cultivating Music in America*.
10. For more on Boulanger and the *Dumbarton Oaks Concerto*, see Brooks, "Collecting Past and Present," in *A Home of the Humanities*, 75–91; and Brooks, *Musical Work*, 224–50.
11. Gargenville is the city just to the northeast of Paris where the Boulanger family's summer cottage, "Les Maisonettes," was located. Boulanger's mother bought the cottage in 1908, and it was where Lili died in 1918. When the cottage was occupied by Nazis during the Second World War, the news devastated Boulanger. She never returned. Rosenstiel, *Nadia Boulanger*, 55–56; and Spycket, *Nadia Boulanger*, 18.

I absolutely need to see you to consult about a matter that is very important to me and concerns the musical education of my younger son, who is a
nineteen-year-old pianist.

Is it possible to see one another? I am staying in Paris for another ten
days and I have come here almost especially to settle his musical education
in Paris and would be much obliged if you were to arrange an appointment
for me either here or at Pleyel's, or (in case it is impossible for you here) at
Garganville,* where, in that case, I will come see you next week.[12]

This weekend (which is to say Saturday, Sunday, and Monday until Tuesday
afternoon) I will be in the country, which is why I would be very grateful if you
could send me a short note by *return post* so that I will have it before heading to
the countryside.

Thank you in advance, dear friend, and believe me to be your dearly devoted,
Igor Stravinsky

*Simply let me know
**How does one find you there?

❧   ❧   ❧

Soulima Stravinsky to Boulanger

Paris
252 rue du F[aubourg] St-Honoré
May 9, 1930

Dear Mademoiselle,

I tried just now to call but was unable to reach you.

My father will be at home, in his Pleyel apartment, between 7 and 8 o'clock
this evening. I believe this is a good time for you, as you have told me. I spoke
with Diantha yesterday evening and I am now much more at ease.[13] But, I very
much hope that you will be able to give my father a sense of this young girl,

---

12. At this time, Stravinsky was staying in an attic apartment offered him by
    Gustave Lyon, then director of the Pleyel firm. The apartment was on rue de
    Rochechouart in the 9th arrondissement, not far from Boulanger's own Paris
    apartment at 36 rue Ballu, also in the 9th. Walsh, *Creative Spring*, 323.
13. Diantha Walker, a Boulanger pupil from the United States, attended
    Fontainebleau in the summer of 1931. She corresponded with Boulanger
    from 1931 until 1944. Despite what appears to have been a heated love affair
    between herself and Soulima Stravinsky, Diantha eventually married William
    Boardman in 1937. F-Pn, N.L.a. 57 (1–10).

because I have complete confidence in God and faithfully believe that what is clearly impossible right now will be done in its own time with His help.

Thank you again for everything you are doing for me.

Your ever-devoted student,
Sviétik

❧ ❧ ❧

Catherine Stravinsky to Boulanger

Nice
April 8, 1931

Dear Mademoiselle,

Please allow me to write to you this letter on an issue concerning Sviétik that worries me greatly. He spoke to me quite frankly about it and I told him all our thoughts on the subject. I would like to share a few words with you regarding it as well.

My husband and I are not very sympathetic toward the idea of a marriage to someone from outside our race and religion, a marriage which above all else seems very much premature to us, seeing as Sviétik is still practically a child.

Nor can we forget that he is preparing himself for a career as a pianist, which particularly complicates his case. Indeed, this field requires a a great deal of travel and a lifestyle that, in our opinion, at least at the beginning of artistic life, does not lend itself well to starting a family (children are always to be expected). Moreover, one must remember that he still depends on us entirely, that he is only a student of music and that he is not yet an established artist, earning his own living.

For two years now, Sviétik has lived most of his life away from his family, and under these conditions it has been difficult for us to exert an influence over him. It seems to us, dear friend, that you are the best placed to help us with our difficulties. Permit us to believe you do not think harshly of us for troubling you with our concerns.

As for the sentimental side of this affair, and without wanting to rush anything, we beg you to support our point of view around Sviétik so that he sees, among all those who matter to him, a uniform opinion on the questions that are tormenting him. I say this to you freely, because it seems to us Sviétik is inclined to believe that you welcome favorably the idea of this union so desired by him. As for us, we do not want Sviétik tied up by promises that perhaps shouldn't be fulfilled. I have suggested (and this so as to not sadden him entirely) that he wait at least a year to return to the overall question of marriage.

I think that you share our views, which is why we have addressed this in all frankness and in an appeal to your good friendship and would like to count firmly on your support and it is in this hope that I extend to you, dear Mademoiselle, my best wishes,

Catherine Stravinsky

[P.S.] Please do forgive this slightly confusing letter, but having been extremely busy these last few days I did not have time to put everything in order in this hurriedly written letter because I would like for you to read it before Sviétik's arrival.

❧   ❧   ❧

Catherine Stravinsky to Boulanger

Nice

May 7, 1931

Dear Friend,

Thank you so much for your very sincere letter reassuring us.

We are very grateful to you for having honestly shared your feelings and your point of view with us. Unfortunately, it differs significantly from our own, but as you have given us your promise that, in appearance, you will support us, we are firmly counting on you. Besides, the attitude to take right now concerning young people is to interfere in no way in their relationships. The young woman will return to America soon; one need neither try to make her return, nor oppose it, but as for the future, leave it all up to the will of God, because it is not up to us to unite or separate them. It is only important that Nini does not extend any formal promises, that is all.

I hope that everything is now clear between us.

I have not yet thanked you for having thought of us (Nini's performance). Your telegram was a great joy for us all.[14]

Sviétik wrote to me that he will defer his exams until next year. So much the better! We approve of it entirely. It was an effort well beyond his abilities as he now understands.

I will finish this letter by thanking you very sincerely for all the interest you have shown our son and for your kind friendship toward us.

Believe that I am, dear Friend, your cordially devoted,
C. Stravinsky

---

14. I have identified no such telegram.

Symphonie de psaumes

Boulanger to Stravinsky

[No Date, ca. 1931]

I

1) Dedication—omitted—voluntarily?
> —Psalm numbers, can they be indicated?

2) *Domine* in capital letters beginning at the fourth measure after R17
> —Should we reserve putting *Dominum* in capital letters until the end—or for the third movement, for the end of the second, or is it to be in *capital letters* throughout?

3) At R9, the part in ♪:

> At R12:

> Is this correct?

4) Fugue

> Sixth measure of R4, orchestra: *sub. meno f*
> piano: *sub. dolcissimo*
> —The second version seems more accurate

Remarks on the recording[15]

I

At R4, left hand *staccatissimo*
7 after R12 the altos sing B-natural on the record—the correction seems to indicate C-natural on the first beat.

---

15. Boulanger's copy of the recording can still be consulted at the Bibliothèque nationale de France. Igor Stravinsky, *Symphonie de psaumes*. Alexis Vlassoff choir, Walter Straram orchestra, Stravinsky (conductor). Columbia, LFX 179–81. Vinyl.

II Fugue
Before R12, *retenu*
1 after R13 *retenu*
The movement is slower than 60 = ♪ in the fugue.

III
6 after R2, the sopranos and altos drop out on the third beat—this creates a silence which I find excellent before the tenors' *Laudate*, don't you think?

R20 is a little closer to 66 = ♩ noticeably slower than 48 to the ♩
At R22, the tempo is nearly OK here, maybe it's slightly slower than 48= ♩, but only slightly.
3 after R28 there is a C-natural in the recording, but I believe I heard a C-sharp at the performance. *You corrected this as a C-sharp*—Is it better like this?

II Fugue
3 after R8, l*u*to or l*a*to?
4 after R17, *Do' mi–no* (the comma's in the right place, yes?)

III
Aren't you afraid that by writing:
Al-le-*lui*-a
there will be an emphasis on the "i" rather than the "u?" Shouldn't you isolate the "i?"

♩   ♩
Al-le-lu . . . i – a
R1, maybe indicate *poco meno p* and reserve the *p* for four after R1.
3 after R2, *fir-ma-men-to* or *tés*?
3 after R2 you've indicated in the piano *me-nto*, but left in the orchestral part: *men-to*?

5 after 22 in the trumpet (actual notes):

But at 5 after R26:

Are the two different versions accurate? I think so, but . . .

&   &   &

Boulanger to Stravinsky

Les Maisonettes
Hanneucourt
by Gargenville (S&O) PTH 28

Mr. Igor Stawinsky
August 13, 1931

Dear Friend,

It is not because of negligence, but out of respect for your work that I have not responded—given the circumstances, I thought that the only reasonable solution would be to send you the proofs: they arrived today at the same time as your letter.

Unfortunately, I'm leaving for Fontainebleau. They will be corrected. No, I will send you as early as today the exemplar Païchadze returned to me. Would you please answer my questions *as soon as you can*, on this exemplar, and I will transfer them to the proofs.[16]

(I hope that you still have my little list.)

I am sorry at the thought of annoying you with all this, but though there are several cases where I'm not afraid to take "responsibility," there are also two or three spots where you alone can decide.

Need I tell you what a place you hold here in all our minds and hearts? Unbeknownst to you, you are constantly present through your work. You have managed to inspire such affection that is, I believe, only equaled by the admiration we have for you. And so . . .

Our very faithful thoughts surround you.

To you, Dear, Great Friend, all we have that is the most sincere and profound,
Nadia Boulanger

₞   ₞   ₞

---

16. There are two extant copies of Boulanger's editorial work: *Symphonie de psaumes, réduction chant/piano* (Paris: Édition Russe de Musique, ca. 1930) F-Pn, Rés. Vma. 317; and F-LYc, UFNB M 531 STR.

Gavryil Païchadze to Boulanger

Paris
22 rue d'Anjou (8ème)

G. Païchadze
Director
Des Editions S & N Koussevitzky:
Editions Russes de Musique
Edition A. Gutheil
September 5, 1931

Dear Mademoiselle,

I sent you the new proofs of Stravinsky's *Symphonie de psaumes* (piano/vocal) yesterday by registered mail along with the exemplar of the first edition that you corrected.[17]

I would ask you to look at these proofs at your first available opportunity and to return them to me as soon as will be possible for you.[18] This urgency is caused by the fact that the first edition of the score has been sold out to the last copy for quite some time, and we have been forced to refuse requests for this work, which is most unpleasant for both the composer and the editor. The new printing is therefore very urgent, especially because we must give several performances of the *Symphonie* during the first months of this upcoming season.

In the hopes that you will understand this S.O.S. call and thanking you in advance, please accept my most respectful sentiments, Madame.

Sincerely,
G. Païchadze

❧   ❧   ❧

17. Only two pages of these proofs remain in Boulanger's archives. The rest were sent to Éditions Russes: F-Pn, Rés. Vma. Ms. 245, "pages bleues."

18. In the original document found in the Paul Sacher Stiftung, this paragraph has been bracketed off in an unidentified hand.

Boulanger to Stravinsky

Les Maisonettes
Hanneucourt
by Gargenville (S&O) PTH 28

Igor Strawinsky
La Virronière
Voreppe
Isère
September 7, 1931

Dear Friend,

I've made the corrections—everything is at rue d'Anjou—but unfortunately, a few questions remain.[19] I'm sorry to bother you, but what can be done? Respond on these sheets, make use of this envelope, and forgive me for not having spared you this annoyance.

You know with what deep sentiments of admiration, affection, and confidence I call myself your,
NB

[P.S.] My respects to your dear Mother.

    ❧   ❧   ❧

Boulanger to Stravinsky

Les Maisonettes
Hanneucourt
By Gargenville (S&O) PTH 28

Igor Strawinsky
Isère
La Virronière
Voreppe
September 8, 1931

Dear Friend,

I see that certain points have already been set by you. I'm only sending you the pages containing questions. Could you respond to the following all at once:
1) Indication of Psalm numbers?

---

19. The street address for Édition Russe.

2) Wouldn't it be good to indicate that you want men's voices and children's (or women's) voices?

The rest is as follows:

1) Compare the trumpet on p. 33 with that on p. 35.

2) the A-natural added in pencil but not by yourself on p. 22, second measure of R7.

3) And the chord on the last page—I believe very much that the C-sharp is correct, in spite of the recordings, because when the issue arose in the orchestral part, you played a C-natural with a shocked expression—and added the C-sharp immediately after.

Excuse me for having been slightly late—Please be sure, it was not my fault.

With deep devotion,
NB

🔊 🔊 🔊

Stravinsky to Boulanger

Isère
La Virronière
Voreppe

Les Maisonettes
Hanneucourt
by Gargenville (S&O) PTH 28
September 12, 1931[20]

Very dear friend,

Thank you with all my heart for the trouble you have taken with this, and please kindly forgive the haste of my responses.

Attached are the blue pages with my answers written beside them in the margins.

As for the first two questions of your letter—(1) indication of the Psalm numbers and (2) the use of men's and children's voices, and in their absence, women's voices in the composition—it is *completely essential* to include this in the piano/vocal reduction. For the rest, if I remember, I've already spoken to Païchadze about the matter. But my memory fails me to such a point [I have

---

20. Boulanger signed a document stating she had received from Stravinsky the material mentioned in this letter, September 12, 1931, CH-Bps.

even forgotten what my *Symphonie de psaumes* is called] that I can't seem to remember anything anymore! *It's becoming terrible.*[21]

Please believe in my loyal friendship and my infinite thanks,
Your
Igor Strawinsky

❧   ❧   ❧

Boulanger to Stravinsky

Les Maisonettes
Hanneucourt
By Gargenville (S&O) PTH 28

Isère
Mr. I. Strawinsky
La Vironnière
Voreppe
September 17, 1931

Dear Friend,

I've received your letter—everything is finished and sent off. It is unfortunate about the C-sharp because of the C-natural in the following measure, but . . . at the heart of the matter I am sure you are correct, naturally.

No need to thank me, we would all be deeply honored and happy if we could help you with anything at all. These are certainly not tasks for you.

In all haste, and with sincere affection,
Nadia Boulanger

[P.S.] I recommended to Païchadze that he have someone review the orchestral score and ensure the corrections are incorporated. I hope that there is someone who can do that with care.

❧   ❧   ❧

---

21. The bracketed portion of this sentence appears in the carbon copy located at the Paul Sacher Stiftung but not in the version sent to Boulanger.

Boulanger to Stravinsky

36 rue Ballu

I. Strawinsky
167 Brd. Carnet [*sic*]
Nice

My dear *Friend,*

Thank you with all my heart—your thoughts touched me greatly.

I can never tell you what these months with the symphony have been and the daily discoveries that come from reading and rereading this extraordinary score.

If I knew how, I wish I could express the importance of this work, in all aspects. But actually, that would be pretentious—it speaks so well for itself!

In this letter, please find our wishes, affection, and fervent admiration,
Nadia Boulanger

1932–1937

Boulanger to Igor Stravinsky

36 rue Ballu 9th
Téléph: Trinité 90–17

June 17, 1932

My dear Friend,

How gladly I would have liked to greet you tomorrow, to join with those who love you and to show you my inexpressible affection.

You are such a great light for us. You give me joy that is renewed each day—and you wish to honor me with a friendship [and] a trust that is most precious to me.

Difficulties of the sort that you can imagine prevent us—my students and I—from sending you the souvenir we reserved for you. I would like to hope that we will succeed in the end, because losing this chance to do something for you is very hard on us.

Happy birthday, dear friend—and *thank you,* if only I could tell you what affection, what admiration I have for you,

Yours,
Nadia Boulanger

❧   ❧   ❧

Stravinsky to Boulanger

Voreppe (Isère)

June 5–8, 1932

How can I thank you, dear Nadia, for your sketches that are so full of a friend-ship, which is particularly precious to me since I know only too well the price-less virtues of your heart and ears![22]

But, I beg of you, do not be extravagant in finding me things that I love pas-sionately but which are, because of the dark times in which we live, unafford-able for us other musicians. Leave those to the rich, if there are any left.

Most fondly,
Your 50-year-old friend*
Igor Strawinsky

*OK, I know it's "Quinquagenarian," but the number sounds better.[23]

❧ ❧ ❧

Boulanger to Stravinsky

36 rue Ballu 9th
Téléph: Trinité 90–17

June 19, 1932

Dear friend,

Excuse this business letter.

We would like to stage either a festival of your work or a half program at the Société musicale indépendante: including in either case the first performance of the *Duo concertant* in Paris, and maybe *L'Histoire du soldat* or other works of your choice (we cannot, for financial reasons, have many instruments.) A final program will have to be settled—but first we would like to know what fee you would accept. We don't wish to question you on this matter and will do every-thing possible to accommodate you, it goes without saying. But our account is pitiful. I must raise the funds myself and, before going into details, I need to know that one thing.

May I ask you to respond to me *as soon as possible.*

---

22. These "esquisses" are now held in the Bibliothèque nationale, Rés. Vma. Ms. 984.

23. This passage loses some of its wit in translation, but it is a play on words in the original French between the word for "fifty-year-old" (*quinquagénaire*) and the word "*cinquantenaire*," which translates as "a person in his or her fifties."

The concert wil take place at the École normale, in the autumn if it is possible.

Believe in my deep affection,

Dear Friend,
Nadia Boulanger

❧ ❧ ❧

Soulima Stravinsky to Boulanger

Voreppe

May 3, 1932

Dear Mademoiselle,

We were very touched by your kind thoughts for Easter and we thank you with all our hearts.

Thank you as well for your kind letter, which I am very embarrassed not to have answered until today.

Is Madame Boulanger doing a bit better, is she suffering a bit less?[24] I cannot express how much I am affected by her long, painful suffering. I send my sympathy to you and to her.

I will probably see you again soon, which delights me greatly. I intend to come to Paris for a couple of days at the end of May. Perhaps you will see my father beforehand, because he leaves for Paris this week to record *L'Histoire du soldat* and the *Octuor*.[25]

I believe he wants to see you about me. I have every intention of seeing Philipp to get some technical advice and some guidelines from him for my work. It needs to be done without offending Madame Chailley at all and therein, it seems to me, lies the difficulty.[26]

---

24. Based on anecdotal evidence, it is believed Boulanger's mother suffered from Parkinson's disease.

25. Stravinsky recorded *L'histoire du soldat* and the *Octuor* in Paris May 6–7 at the Studio Albert in Paris. The work has since been released as Igor Stravinsky, *Stravinsky: Composer & Conductor*, vol 1, Andante CD3-1-3 (rerelease), 1960 of 1932 (original) vinyl,. Performers include: Raphaël Delbos (trombone), Eugène Foveau (trumpet), Marcel Darrieux (violin), Gustave Dhérin and Marius Piard (bassoon), Jean-Paul Morel (percussion), Louis Moyse (flute), and Emile Godeau (clarinet).

26. Soulima's original piano teacher, Céliny-Chailley-Richez, was a Raoul Pugno prodigy. It would appear Soulima also chose to work with Isidor Philipp from time to time. See Brooks, *Musical Work*, 112.

I am sure you will give me good advice about this and, in waiting to see you again soon, when I can tell you all that I have done this winter, I send to you, my very dear Mademoiselle, my most devoted affection and to Madame Boulanger my utmost respect.

Your
Sviatoslav Strawinsky

❧ ❧ ❧

Anna Stravinsky to Boulanger

Voreppe

June 23, 1932

Dear Mademoiselle,
    Your kind and affectionate note, which I received on the day of my son's birthday, touched me greatly. Thank you wholeheartedly for having thought of me, and I ask you to express my gratitude to your Mother for thinking of me. Knowing her suffering of late, I wish for her recovery.

Dear Mademoiselle, trust in my very sincere sentiments,
A[nna] Strawinsky

❧ ❧ ❧

Soulima Stravinsky to Boulanger

Voreppe (Isère)

January 16, 1933

My very dear Mademoiselle,
    It is certainly much too late to wish you a Happy New Year. All the same, I wish you all the happiness and health possible for the fifty weeks to come, as well as to Madame Boulanger, while apologizing for my tardiness. It is because I recently had concerts in Switzerland from which I have just returned for the holidays. We were profoundly touched by your good thoughts and we thank you wholeheartedly.
    I must come to Paris for the 25th, and on the 26th (it's a Wednesday) rue Ballu? I have a lesson with M. Philipp at 5 o'clock. I hope to see you again a little after 6 o'clock. If not, I will telephone you, because I would *so much* like to see you again.

In this hope, please always remember, my dear Mademoiselle, my most grateful
and respectful affection,
Sviétik

᷾   ᷾   ᷾

Boulanger to Stravinsky

36 rue Ballu 9th
Téléph: Trinité 90–17

Monsieur I. Strawinsky
Voreppe
Isère
February 25, 1933

Dear Friend,

Forgive me for coming to bother you about a matter that truthfully is none
of my business. But I am currently working on the *Oedipus Rex* project—I now
have the greatest hopes of being successful.[27] Your absence at the March 21
concert greatly distressed our mutual friend, just when she is taking such pleasure in convincing herself of her active admiration for your work.[28]

All things considered, this is what I found. Would you accept, without *anyone* learning [of it] (*no* exceptions, you have my word), compensation of five,
maybe six thousand francs to come conduct *Renard?* I want to finalize this and
without fear of *the least indiscretion*—send an urgent telegraph because the OSP
must decide by Tuesday at the latest.[29] It would be unthinkable to do it without
you and it would be so beautiful to hear *Renard* with you.

Forgive me and know I am your deeply devoted,
NB

᷾   ᷾   ᷾

---

27. Boulanger owned one copy of *Oedipus Rex* in her library. It is a photostat
    of the handwritten fair copy with numerous of Stravinsky's annotations. I
    remain uncertain about what Boulanger means here by "*Oedipus Rex* project."
    "Oedipus Rex," F-Pn, Vma. 4006.
28. The "mutual" friend referenced here by Boulanger was Winaretta Singer, the
    Princesse de Polignac, one of Stravinsky's most important patrons at the time.
    For more on Boulanger, Stravinsky, and the Princesse de Polignac, see Kahan,
    Music's Modern Muse, 294–325; and Brooks, "Nadia Boulanger and the Salon,"
    415–68.
29. By OSP, Boulanger means Orchestre symphonique de Paris.

Stravinsky to Boulanger

Grenoble [Suisse]
36 rue Ballue
Paris 9

February 27, 1933[30]

HAVE CONCERT 19 MARCH OSP PSAUMS, SACRE, ROSSIGNOL AND 21 MARCH CONCERT WITH DUSHKIN LAUSANNE. STOP ~~HAVE YET~~[31] ~~TO CLEARLY EXPLAIN IT OUR FRIEND~~

FONDLY STRAWINSKY

↪   ↪   ↪

Anna Stravinsky to Boulanger

March 22, [19]35

My dear Mademoiselle,
  I am deeply upset to learn of the great misfortune that has befallen you. I did not know your Mother, but I know the deep filial love you felt for her and with all my heart I share in your grief.[32]

Very sincerely,
Anna Strawinsky

↪   ↪   ↪

---

30. This is a draft of a telegram in Vera Sudeikina's handwriting found in the Paul Sacher Stiftung. The telegram does not exist in Boulanger's archives. As a rule for this edition, telegrams by nature contain errors, and so I have not flagged them.
31. Most likely the writer of the telegram confused "pourtant" with "encore." I have chosen the latter translation.
32. Boulanger's mother died on March 19, 1935, just four days after the seventeenth anniversary of Lili's death. The event was a staggering blow to Boulanger. Spycket, *Nadia Boulanger*, 86; Rosenstiel, *Nadia Boulanger*, 257–8; and Francis, *Teaching Stravinsky*, 82–83.

Théodore Strawinsky to Boulanger

Paris

March 22, 1935

Know, dear Mademoiselle, that all my heart is with you in the great misfortune that has so cruelly befallen you.

Your most sincerely devoted,
Théodore Strawinsky

⌘ ⌘ ⌘

Boulanger to Igor Stravinsky

36 Rue Ballu 9th
Téléph Trinité 90–17

Mr. I. Strawinsky
To read on the way

Dear Friend,

To give you complete freedom, I have specified to the School at Fontainebleau that you will only see students and offer a course for them if the *number* of students is sufficient. Rest assured the matter remains open—but understand clearly that you can count on seeing them [the students] in June and July. It is *essential* for the completion of projects. The projects are related to your work and you—projects that, I believe, will interest you. And you are under no obligation, given the way things have developed.

Your help is of such moral support, and I am in such need of it.

May God be with you on this journey during which so many thoughts accompany you.

Your
Nadia B.[33]

---

33. Boulanger convinced the faculty at the École normale to keep Stravinsky on following the success of his work with her students at Fontainebleau. Auguste Mangeot and Alfred Cortot, the École normale's directors, wrote to Stravinsky on September 17, 1935, to confirm the appointment and to clarify that Boulanger had taken it upon herself to cover Stravinsky's payments: "Mademoiselle Nadia Boulanger nous a informés qu'elle avait pris les dispositions pour vous assurer et pour vous remettre elle-même la rétribution dont vous avez convenu avec elle." Letter, Mangeot and Cortot to Stravinsky, CH-Bps.

❧ ❧ ❧

Boulanger to Igor Stravinsky

January 1936

They tell me, Dear Friend, that you have sent me the second volume of *Chroniques* [*de ma vie*].[34] *I do not want to wait* for the return post *to tell you what your thoughtfulness means to me.* In the very *painful* hours that *I must endure,* your affection, your *trust is a great support,* and in the memory of Mother, and my dear Lili, I thank you with all my heart,

Your
NB

❧ ❧ ❧

Stravinsky to Boulanger

Paris

March 19, 1936
My very dear friend,

I am still under the influence of yesterday evening's serene memorial.[35] I really would have liked to see you, but the number of people going to greet you made it difficult for me.

I am thinking of you, believe me, and please accept these flowers intended for the grave of your dearly departed.[36]

Your
Igor Stravinsky

❧ ❧ ❧

---

34. I have yet to find a copy of this text in Boulanger's archives.
35. Reference to the memorial mass Boulanger held for her mother and sister that year. It would have been the first held for both family members.
36. Both Lili and Raïssa Boulanger were buried in the family crypt in Montmartre along with Boulanger's father and paternal grandmother.

Boulanger to Igor Stravinsky

36 rue Ballu, 9th

March 27, 1936

Dear Friend,

Here is the sheet music for *Perséphone*.[37] I cannot tell you my sorrow in part-
ing with it—not a day went by that I did not owe it for profound and radiant
joys. I was hoping to make a two-piano reduction—this will [have to wait] for
your return. Allow me also to enclose a cheque—if the circumstances and my
stupid illness were not complicating everything, you would have had it sooner.[38] But what you've given is so meaningful that many years will pass before we
will have exhausted its richness.

How can I thank you—need I tell you. You know, don't you, what you mean
to all of us, and above all, I add to a limitless admiration my whole-hearted
affection, dear Friend,

Your
Nadia Boulanger

∛ ∛ ∛

Catherine Stravinsky to Boulanger

Paris

April 15, 1936

My dear friend,

Thank you for your affectionate note that I received for Easter. Mother and
I thank you with all our hearts.

We were able to exchange telegrams with our travelers Easter Sunday and I also
received three letters.[39] Now we need to wait for their arrival in Rio, from where

---

37. Boulanger's copy of the *Perséphone* score referenced here remains missing.
    Still within her collection are a series of piano/vocal proofs that she edited
    in a manner similar to her involvement with the *Symphonie de psaumes* and a
    copy of the orchestral score bearing annotations used for the 1949 revision.
    See Stravinsky, "Perséphone (proofs)," F-Pn, Rés. Vma. 316; and "Perséphone,"
    photostat of orchestral score, Gr. Vma. 474. For more on Stravinsky's melo-
    drama, see Levitz, *Modernist Mysteries*.

38. Boulanger agreed to pay Stravinsky's salary for co-teaching her classes at the
    École normale de musique.

39. The reference here is to a tour of South America made by Soulima and Igor
    Stravinsky. Walsh, *Second Exile*, 44–51. Tamara Levitz also discusses this tour.
    See Levitz, "Igor the Angeleno," 153.

they will write to me. So far the sea is very calm and their trip has been enjoyable and very restful. I am sure this long crossing will be good for the two of them. I hope these two months will go by very quickly for them and maybe for me as well, and that God will grant me progress in my recuperation, so that I will be refreshed for the arrival of my husband and for Théodore's wedding.[40] I don't know if Nini will come back with his father or he will stay for his own concerts.

I hope, dear friend, that the calm of your country house has been a great rest for you, which you certainly need.

Thinking affectionately of you,

Your
C. Strawinsky

[P.S.] (I return to Sancellemoz on Friday)

❧   ❧   ❧

Soulima Stravinsky and Théodore Strawinsky to Boulanger

Mlle. Nadia Boulanger
36 rue Ballu
Paris

You spoil me too much, dear Mademoiselle. Théodore just brought me those delicious candies.

Fondly,
Sviétik

My most devoted wishes,
Théodore Stra[winsky]

❧   ❧   ❧

---

40. Théodore Strawinsky and Denise Guerzoni were married on June 29, 1936, in Paris. Though allowed to attend the wedding, Catherine soon had to return to Sancellemoz for further treatment of her tuberculosis. At this time, Mika (Lyudmila), who had married Yury Mandelstam eight months before, announced she was pregnant, despite being warned against it because of her own tubercular state. Walsh, *Second Exile*, 52.

Soulima Stravinsky to Boulanger

Paris

September 25, 1936

Very dear Mademoiselle,

Your note touched me so! My wholehearted thanks for it. Mother has returned to Paris for good this time and this is such a delight for all of us.

I hope to see you soon and send along my most respectful and devoted wishes,

Your
Sviétik

❧   ❧   ❧

Catherine Stravinsky to Boulanger

[1936–37]

My very dear Friend,

How can I thank you for these beautiful flowers brought to me at the exact moment of my arrival. I am so touched and send my love.

Thinking of you,
C. Strawinsky

❧   ❧   ❧

Boulanger to Stravinsky

36 rue Ballu 9th

Mr. I. Strawinsky
25 Faubourg St. Honoré
Paris
[December 7, 1937]

The concert has just concluded—I do not know what to tell you, dear, special friend—but you know, don't you?[41] Your genius has changed our path, our thought, our awareness, and never will we be able to thank you enough! But you know what awkwardness keeps me from saying!

---

41. Most likely a reference to the Parisian premiere of *Jeu de cartes*, possibly even the one recorded for French radio in December 1937.

Fondly, and with very great affection, I am

Your
Nadia

Family Tragedy and the *Dumbarton Oaks Concerto*

Boulanger to Mildred Woods Bliss

[MILDRED ROBERT BLISS],[42] WASHINGTON

WITHOUT NEWS STRAWINSKY DESIRES KNOW SHOULD HE BEGIN COMPOSITION (STOP) FOR YOR SUGGESTED 2500 ACCEPTS COMPOSE MUSIC BRANDENBURG CONCERTOS DIMENSIONS

~~GREETINGS~~ FONDLY
BOULANGER

૱   ૱   ૱

Stravinsky Family to Boulanger

Paris

Mademoiselle Nadia Boulanger
36 rue Ballu
E.V. 9th
March 19, 1938

Our thoughts and love are with you, dear one.

The Igor Strawinsky family

૱   ૱   ૱

---

42. Mildred Woods Bliss, wife of Robert Woods Bliss, was a highly influential patron of the arts in the United States and a supporter of Stravinsky's. For a discussion of the Blisses' relationship to Boulanger, their *Dumbarton Oaks* home, and the connection to Stravinsky's work, see Brooks, *Musical Work*, 224–9. For more on women patrons of the United States, see Locke and Barr, *Cultivating Music in America*, especially Brooks, "Mildred Bliss Tells Nadia Boulanger to Think of Herself for Once," in Locke and Barr, 209–13.

Boulanger to Stravinsky

Garden Street
Cambridge Mass.
Via "Queen Mary"
Sailing April 6

M. Igor Strawinsky
25 Faubourg St. Honoré
Paris, France
April 5, 1938

Dear Friend,

I am arriving from Washington—the performance can only take place in the first week of May—rehearsals begin on the first. I have sent you a wire, because the program with the *Thèmes du concerto* must be given to the printer before the 20th because of the Blisses' trip. I am also anxious to work through the finale—because of my eyes, I must know it almost by heart.

Mrs. Bliss has asked me to handle all expenses for you—and yours [your family's]? I would very much like news!

With deepest affection,
Nadia

❧   ❧   ❧

Boulanger to Stravinsky

NADIA
63 GARDEN STREET
CAMBRIDGE, MASSACHUSETTS

(IGOR) STRAWINSKY
25 FAUBOURG ST HONORE
APRIL 5, 1938

BLISS MAY 1 STOP NEED YOU TO SEND THE MANUSCRIPT WE WILL COPY IT HERE

FONDLY

❧   ❧   ❧

Stravinsky to Boulanger

Paris

Mademoiselle Nadia Boulanger
63 Garden Street, Cambridge, Mass. U.S.A.
April 6, 1938

Very dear friend,

Received your cable this morning. Last night I received, on engraved proofs from Strecker, pages 27–37 (inclusive) of the last movement of my Concerto in E-flat. I have just finished correcting them and am sending them to you on the SS Europa.[43] There are still some seven to eight pages yet to come and I will send them to you as soon as I have them (next week). You can therefore create the parts from what you have because [if you were to] work from the manuscript—which has many missing bowings (and also quite a few mistakes that I have not had the time to correct)—you would have serious difficulty establishing correct parts. I will try again to obtain a special printing from Strecker *for you*.* Refer only to the copy (for the orchestral parts) that you've already received from me (that being the corrected proofs of the first and second movements) and which I'm sending you today.

It was very unexpected, this obsession with having our concert on the first of May, and has taken us by surprise. I am hopeful that everything will sort itself out, especially when I think that it is you who will be handling everything.

With deepest affection,

Your
Igor Strawinsky

[P.S.] Have you been able to speak to Mrs. Bliss on the subject of our last conversation?[44]

*because you will be returning your own [current copy] in order to complete the parts.

---

43. Willy Strecker was Stravinsky's representative at the publishing company, B. Schotts Söhne. For Boulanger's correspondence with Strecker, see N.L.a. 109 (97–108), F-Pn.
44. This statement is an allusion to the final payment for the *Concerto*, which Stravinsky had not yet received. He mentions the issue again in his letter from April 25, 1938.

Stravinsky to Boulanger

Paris

Miss Nadia Boulanger
63 Garden Street
Cambridge, Mass.
U.S.A.
April 11, 1938[45]

Attached are some errors identified after having sent you the first pages of the third part of the Concerto. I hope that this package reached you and that you sent back a copy.

I am sending you today (on the SS Aquitania that only leaves on the 13th—no ship before then) the final pages of the movement. So now you have the entirety, and I hope you'll have the time (too short, in my opinion) to finish the copying and to rehearse it with the musicians. All the same, what madness to move ahead the date (May 1!) so suddenly without finding out if it would be physically possible to have the time for the copying and rehearsals. It was just discovered that my manuscript was with the engraver, Schott, who sent it back April 9 (the SS Deutschland left on the 8th—think of the bad luck, and no ship until the 13th) with the final pages (*) that I'll send you after tomorrow.

Yours,
I Str.

*proof engraving

❧   ❧   ❧

Boulanger to Stravinsky (original in English)

NADIA BOULANGER
63 GARDEN STREET
CAMBRIDGE, MASS. U.S.A.

STRAWINSKY
25 FAUBOURG-SAINT HONORÉ, PARIS
APRIL 19, 1938

WORRIED, HAVE NOT RECEIVED MATERIAL FROM YOU [FOR] FIRST TWO MOVEMENTS (STOP) COPYING FINALE MATERIAL HERE

---

45. Boulanger signed for the material referenced here by Stravinsky. The receipt remains in the Stravinsky collection, Paul Sacher Stiftung.

NADIA[46]

❧ ❧ ❧

Boulanger to Stravinsky

63 Garden Street
Cambridge, Massachusetts
Special Airmail to the SS *Aquitania*
Cunard-White Star Line
Sailing April 20, A.M.
Pier 90, N.R. N.Y.C.

Mr. Igor Strawinsky
25 Rue du Faubourg St. Honoré
Paris, France
April 19, 1938

Dear Friend,

I just sent you a wire because I am very worried about not having received the material for the first two movements.

The final movement, which I know well now, is so beautiful.

The copying will be done very carefully and I think that all will be well.

I believe that Mrs. Bliss counts on having the manuscript for the performance. Would you please send it to me? I will deliver it to her. Or would you prefer to send it to her directly? Excuse my meddling in something that does not concern me—but . . . have you thought to have the dedication printed?[47]

Another thing:

I do not know if you should come here next year—but could we draft an agreement saying that you reserve—for you firstly, and then for me should *you* be unable—the performance of the *Concerto*, for one year? I am writing to Strecker to say the same thing, but naturally, only what suits you can suit me.[48]

But, it seems to me that I have *so connected* my life with your work this year that I would give anything—*if you do not come*—to have the remarkable privilege of making the concerto known here.

---

46. This telegram dates from April 20, but Boulanger references it in her letter from April 19.

47. The dedication to the Woods-Blisses for their thirtieth wedding anniversary does not appear today in the published score. Stravinsky, *Dumbarton Oaks: Concerto in E-flat for Chamber Orchestra* (London: Ernst Eulenburg, 1939).

48. Boulanger did write to Strecker about the matter. Strecker, in turn, approached Stravinsky about Boulanger's request on April 30, 1938, CH-Bps.

Forgive me if you find this request indiscreet, [and] know that I am guided only by my deep affection for what you mean to all of us, and not foolish ambition. It is a matter of pride in *knowing* what this concerto represents. Last night, again, at Wellesley, it was such a wonderful time with *Le Sacre*. Today with the *Duo concertant*; the day before yesterday with the *Concerto for Two Pianos*; Saturday the *Ave Maria*; next week, *Mavra*; and so forth . . .

How can I thank you? My thoughts go much further, because a work of art, to a certain degree, is an image of God. I cannot express it, but I know the *proof* flows from what is *beautiful*, from what *is*.

With great affection,
Nadia

❧   ❧   ❧

Boulanger to Stravinsky

Nadia Boulanger
63 Garden Street
Cambridge, Mass. U.S.A.

Strawinsky
25 Faubourg Saint Honoré, Paris
APRIL 20, 1938

(DON'T) WORRY HAVING RECEIVED FROM YOU TWO FIRST PARTS STOP HAD THE FINAL PART COPIED HERE[49]
NADIA

❧   ❧   ❧

---

49. The night before sending this telegram, Boulanger signed a receipt for the third movement. The French in this telegram is ambiguous as to whether she means "Worried. Have not received" or "Don't worry, have received." The ambiguity is compounded by Boulanger's use of "avoir." Stravinsky interpreted this to be an urgent call for the material once again and within the hour had sent along another copy. That said, the chronology of these two telegrams is also ambiguous, and the events may have occurred the other way around.

Stravinsky to Boulanger

BOULANGER
63 GARDEN STREET
CAMBRIDGE, MASSACHUSETTS, U.S.A.
APRIL 20, 1938

STRECKER IS SENDING YOU THE COMPLETE SCORE [on the] EUROPA

STRAWINSKY[50]

❧   ❧   ❧

Stravinsky to Boulanger

Paris
Via Cherbourg,
SS Europa

63 Garden Street
Cambridge, Mass.
United States of America
April 25, 1938

Very Dear Nadia,
    Tomorrow the *Europa* will leave from Cherbourg, bringing you this note along with the music that Strecker placed on board in Bremen (with a letter for you). This music (complete parts for the *Concerto in E-flat*) will be sent in rolls (three, if I'm not mistaken) *by mail* and . . . Strecker hopes that there will not be any difficulties with customs that could slow the arrival of this music in time for rehearsals—something which would be truly dreadful.[51]
    In my first letter to you (of April 6), I had asked if you had seen Mrs. Bliss and if you had spoken to her on the subject of our last meeting here—which is to say the question of the second and final payment. You never responded (I can only imagine everything you have going on inside your head!). If you think of it, would you be so kind as to speak with her about it to speed up the payment, which would do me a great service (especially now—God knows what the sickness of my daughter and wife are costing me).

---

50. There are three copies of this particular telegram in the Sacher archives.
51. Boulanger's copy of these drafts are still extant in her collection. See Stravinsky, "Dumbarton Oaks Concerto," F-Pn, Rés Vma Ms 315. The paper still curves up at the edges.

I impatiently await news of rehearsals and of the scores, if they arrive in time.

Fondly,
Your
I. Str

[P.S.] Excuse the hasty scribbling

❧   ❧   ❧

Boulanger to Stravinsky

Monsieur I. Strawinsky
25 Faubourg St. Honoré
Paris, France
May 15, 1938

Dear Friend,

I have not been able to write you, because the life I lead is an impossible problem. But I must, all the same, tell you what a joy the concert was at the Blisses' on the 8th. I knew, but *did not know at all*, the joy I would find in performing the *Concerto*—and upon listening to it, I have understood once again [things that] I wouldn't know how to tell you. I can't express it, but such loneliness is a certainty in my life.

And, after all the courses dedicated to your music, I believe that I understand all the better.

The *Concerto* was played honestly, *well*, very well—and was *understood*, I believe. There remain many mistakes—and a few problems—I hope that you can wait for my return before printing it, because it seems to me that a few passages should be modified in places (insufficient repeats, the notation, etc.) and I cannot formulate the list at this time—I work almost *night* and *day*.[52]

How can I thank you? And how can I prove to you such great devotion? You have clarified everything, not only through your works, but also by the clarity they project onto all music.

You have given us ears and a conscience! I cannot tear myself away from the *Concerto*—everything has such an unexpected sound!

---

52. The materials in Boulanger's archives (F-Pn) pertaining to the *Dumbarton Oaks Concerto* offer some indication of changes she wanted made to the score. This is particularly true of her copy of the two-piano reduction. See Stravinsky, "Dumbarton Oaks Concerto," autograph of the two-piano reduction, Ms. 17945; *Dumbarton Oaks Concerto*, two-piano reduction (Schott Publishing, 1938), Vma 4002; and *Dumbarton Oaks Concerto*, full score (Schott Publishing, 1938), Vmg. 22935.

I think of you and your family with deep affection, and am close to you through these heavy, anxious times. May God be with you and bring peace. This helplessness in the face of sickness is so frightful.

Your
Nadia

[P.S.] You *must* know that the Blisses were deeply moved by the *Concerto* and are so thankful.

❧   ❧   ❧

Boulanger to Igor Stravinsky

Gargenville S.O.

August 25, 1938

Dear Friend:

Here is, finally, my small payment.

You must know, don't you, that it shames me . . .

You must also know that I would quite like to show you my gratitude in this material fashion as well as in my heart and mind.

From the bottom of my heart, with deep affection, I am your
NB

Chapter Two

Toward America

January 1939–June 1940

Though brief, this chapter is one of the most emotionally moving in the entire collection of the Stravinsky–Boulanger correspondence. Boulanger completed her final tour of the United States in the early months of 1939, while Stravinsky toured, composed, and watched as his wife's tuberculosis worsened. Boulanger's triumph with the *Dumbarton Oaks Concerto* in May 1938 encouraged her to engage in far more ambitious projects on Stravinsky's behalf, including attempting to secure a commission for Stravinsky's Symphony in C. She also began to advocate for his nomination to the post of Charles Eliot Norton Chair of Poetry at Harvard University. Unfortunately, as the letters from 1939 reveal, Boulanger's optimistic zeal was no match for the crushing economic realities of the Great Depression, and the Symphony in C project fell through, though the Norton Chair project was a success.[1] Stravinsky's distracted letters, though few in this chapter, speak of his need for money. No doubt anxieties over his wife's health made matters worse. Boulanger was abroad when news reached her of Catherine's death (March 2, 1939), and I have included in this edition five of Boulanger's letters to the family in response (March 4–15, 1939). Her concern over the Stravinskys' welfare, especially the children, is quite profound, and subsequent letters to Igor Stravinsky wove sympathies alongside business affairs. Denise Strawinsky appears in this chapter twice, informing Boulanger of the state of the family after March 1939. At that point, the Stravinskys had been cleft in two. One group remained in Paris while the others recuperated at the Sancellemoz sanatorium in Eastern France. Indeed, in this uncertain time, it became difficult for Boulanger to contact Stravinsky, with one of her letters

---

1.   For more details about Boulanger's negotiations concerning the Symphonie en ut, see Francis, "A Most Unsuccessful Project," 234–70.

(May 11, 1939) requiring redirection three times before finally reaching the composer. On September 3, 1939, France declared war on Germany. Three months later, Soulima Stravinsky wrote to Boulanger from Cosne, France, where he had been stationed after being mobilized as part of the French Army (December 21, 1939).

On September 23, 1939, Stravinsky left France by way of Le Havre and emigrated to the United States. With this voyage, and with Boulanger back in France following the conclusion of her 1939 tour, the Atlantic Ocean again serves as a dividing point. Stravinsky's lover, Vera Sudeikina, soon joined him in America, and in a strained letter of April 18, 1940, Stravinsky revealed he had remarried—just over a year after Catherine's death. His letter reverberates with a desire for Boulanger's blessing. From France, Boulanger wrote to sanction the union thirteen days before Stravinsky's letter was sent, but her text did not find its way to him until later.

This chapter contains within it two of the new, recently catalogued letters held by the Paul Sacher Stiftung. The first dates from December 13, 1939, and sees Boulanger writing candidly about her distaste for nineteenth-century music and how she held it responsible for "even the deformation of the physical [body]—eyes that [couldn't] see, ears that no longer [knew] music was about sound." The second is also the last letter in this chapter. Though brief, it is a deeply moving text dashed off as Boulanger fled Nazi-occupied Paris. Boulanger's letter makes her priorities clear. Fearing for her own safety and that she might never see Stravinsky again, she wrote to him first that she could not "learn . . . about the children," that it was impossible at this point to "do anything for them." She then concluded by writing to Stravinsky: "If it is God's will that we never see each other again, know that you have been one of the greatest lights of my life" (June 22, 1940).

1939

Boulanger to Stravinsky

January 3, 1939

Dear friend,

Copley has just left.[2] I cannot tell you how moving his attitude is. Not only does he understand but he tells me that everyone here shares in your pain with a deep affection.

---

2. Richard Copley was Igor Stravinsky's New York agent at this time. Walsh, *Second Exile*, 89.

At his office, the orchestra, the staff, the musicians, the managers; everyone understood—and we are truly looking forward to your coming next year because we need you, Igor Strawinsky. Because then we will know—your presence will prove that your worries have passed and that your wife is better.

I knew it would be so, [but] I didn't think to such an extent—all the better for them! Arrived yesterday morning and am struggling amidst so many things [to do]. How foolish this is becoming—but my heart remains there, and you know what a large place [you hold in it]!

Fond wishes to you and your mother, Catherine, and I am, Dear Friend, your Nadia

[P.S.] Sorry for the haste, but the *Aquitania* leaves tomorrow morning.

❧   ❧   ❧

Boulanger to Stravinsky

Gerry's Landing
Cambridge

February 21, 1939

Dear Friend,

I think of you every day I have news, but the unbelievable life I lead has not really allowed me to write to you. Do not believe me inactive, though. I saw the Blisses, the Carpenters, and Mrs. Lorimer, and things seem finally to have taken shape this week.[3] I hope for a letter from Mrs. Lorimer in Washington this Friday, when I will be at the Blisses', and if all procrastination finally ceases, I will be able to give you detailed news. Such patience is necessary! The Carpenters and the Blisses truly *want* to act,, but everything depends on Mrs. Lorimer, because without her, the amount is incomplete. All this is to say that

---

3. Boulanger and Ellen Carpenter knew each other because of the latter's husband, John Alden Carpenter. See Letter from John Alden Carpenter to Nadia Boulanger, 1937, F-Pn, N.L.a. 59 (223). A Philadelphia socialite, Mrs. George Horace Lorimer (née Alma V. Ennis) chaired the Philadelphia Chapter of the Metropolitan Opera Association and was the widow of Mr. George H. Lorimer, editor of the *Saturday Evening Post* from 1899–1936. See "George H. Lorimer Noted Editor, Dies," *New York Times*, October 23, 1937, 1; "Lorimer Gave Art and Park to Public," *New York Times*, October 28, 1937; "Opera Leaders Plan Philadelphia Party," *New York Times*, November 13, 1938, 50; On George H. Lorimer's career see Cohn, *Creating America*.

a lovely letter will head your way, but you know, don't you, that I live in the thought of your fears, your hopes, and your work.

Harvard is preparing *Oedipus* with an indescribable enthusiasm and it is good to know all that you represent to them.[4] I send both Catherine and you all my deepest affection and remain your

Nadia

❧   ❧   ❧

Stravinsky to Boulanger

Paris

Miss Nadia Boulanger
c/o Miss J. A. Carpenter
1020 Lake Shore Drive
Chicago, Ill.
U.S.A
SS *Aquitania*
Via Cherbourg
January 12, 1939

Dear Nadia,

How can I thank you for such kind wishes?

Now Sam has also left on the *Ile de France* (on the 11th).[5] He saw an American woman to whom Miss [*sic*] Bliss[6] is sending letters and a copy of your cable (the one to Mrs. Bliss) to let her know what remained to be done to secure the premiere of my Symphony in the United States next season. Do you

---

4.   Two of Boulanger's concert programs from early 1939 reference concerts containing excerpts from *Oedipus Rex*, including Jocaste's air (April 14, 1939) and "Non eubescite, reges" (April 26, 1939), "Programmes," F-Pn, Rés Vm Dos. 195 (639 and 648–9). There is no conference program referencing a complete performance of *Oedipus Rex* from this time.

5.   The "Sam" mentioned here is Samuel Dushkin, violin virtuoso for whom Stravinsky wrote his violin concerto. Dushkin and Stravinsky toured America together in 1937 and concertized together regularly in Europe during the 1930s. For Stravinsky's words on Dushkin, see Craft and Stravinsky, *Dialogues*, 47. For Dushkin's on Stravinsky, see "Working with Stravinsky," in *Igor Stravinsky*. For more, see Walsh, *Creative Spring*, 507–13 and 527–28; ibid., *Second Exile*, 4–12, 38, 58–61, 91, and 125.

6.   The Blisses had no children. It is unclear if this was simply a typo on Stravinsky's part or if perhaps there was another member of the Bliss family whom he is referencing here.

believe there is a possibility of success? My God, I would be so grateful if the steps you have taken were to have the results we are hoping for.*

Here continual flus keep delaying our trip with Catherine to Pau.

Heartfelt wishes to you, my very dear Nadia. My kindest thoughts to the Carpenters.

Yours,
I Stravinsky

*If this thing becomes a reality, I would very much like to *give my manuscript* (of the Symphony) *to Mrs Bliss.*

[P.S.] Best regards to Sister Edward.[7]

❧ ❧ ❧

Boulanger to Stravinsky

CAMBRIDGE, MASS

IGOR STRAWINSKY
25 FBG ST HONORE
[ca. March 2, 1939]

DEVASTATED BY THE TERRIBLE NEWS AM DEEPLY DISTRESSED TO BE SO FAR AWAY KNOW I AM WITH ALL MY HEART YOUR

NADIA

❧ ❧ ❧

---

7. In 1935, two Dominican nuns from the Sinsinawa Convent in Madison, Wisconsin, came to study with Boulanger. After their experience at Fontainebleau, the two women—Sister Edward Blackwell and Sister Ignatia Dorney—sought and received special permission to stay on for the year to study with Boulanger in Paris. These three women became lifelong friends: Rosenstiel, *Nadia Boulanger*, 261. Both nuns also provided entries for Boulanger's student directory; see Boulanger, Student Directory, F-Pn, Rés. Vm. Ms. 1198 (1).

Boulanger to Stravinsky

Gerry's Landing
Cambridge

Monsieur I. Strawinsky
~~25 Fbg St. Honor.~~
Sancellemoz, France
Haute Savoie
March 4, 1939

Oh . . . how I weep for you—I am so sad! I knew all too well that you were living in increasing anguish, but I wanted to hope, at all costs . . .

Dear Catherine, she was here, so full of life, and now she, too, is gone. It is better, of course, for those who have passed, but how can we bear their absence?

I can only imagine the state you are in, yet perhaps Catherine has given you strength that will continue to support you beyond her passing. This is what happened to me with my sweet Lili who, knowing she was dying, would often speak to me about this future in which I would have to live without her. And when I wanted to stop her, she would tell me: "You will love, afterward, to think back to when we spoke of this time when I would be far away and yet always remain with you." In several days it will be twenty-one years since she died, and the wound remains the same, yet so does the deep feeling of the constant presence of the child who was and remains an example [to me].

May God give you His light, His peace in the face of this dreadful new ordeal that has deprived you of someone who was, without a doubt, the light of your life. May God allow your aching heart to turn toward Him, and to wait for your own time when you will enter into eternity and finally find rest yourself. But may He also grant you the certainty that we *need* you, and that this certainty gives us the strength to complete your work despite everything. When we are all gone, this work will remain to grant unto those who are worthy a nourishment of the spirit and heart without which everything would be intolerable.

I know that I know nothing, but this taste of death, I have tasted it—and taste it still on my tongue since *all* of mine have passed away.

But carrying on is the only way to deserve one day attaining that same peace.

Can you understand—or even tolerate this idea? Can you even think about anything but your pain? I doubt it is possible, because I know.

If you would allow it, I would take you in my arms like a sister who loves you tenderly and hold you. I am so sad to be far away.

Thinking of ~~Milène~~ Mika and Catherine, I cherish you more than ever, and ask you to believe in my deepest affection for you.[8]

---

8. Boulanger first wrote the name of Stravinsky's living daughter, Milène, by mistake. Boulanger's effort to strike out the error was insufficient. Mika was the

With all my heart,
Nadia

[P.S.] Give your mother and the children a kiss for me.

ᵂ   ᵂ   ᵂ

Boulanger to Soulima Stravinsky

CAMBRIDGE, MASS

STRAWINSKY 25 FAUBOURG, ST HONORE

MY LAST LETTER SENT BY MISTAKE, PLEASE RETURN IT TO ME
UNOPENED. A LETTER FOLLOWS
YOURS

NADIA

ᵂ   ᵂ   ᵂ

Boulanger to the Stravinsky Family

Gerry's Landing
Cambridge
Manhattan
New York

Mademoiselle et Messieurs Strawinsky
25 Fbg St. Honor [*sic*]
Paris, France
March 6, 1939

My Dear Friends,
   I am with you at each moment and am saddened to be so far away. What can
be said at such a sad time? I know well that there is no consolation, and that
only God can support you. As well as thinking of those whom you mourn—
these are the anniversaries of the deaths of Mother and my dear Lili, who,
before her death said to me: "I offer my sorrows to God so that they will return
to you as joy."

---

nickname for Lyudmila Stravinsky, Stravinsky's older daughter who had died
just months earlier on November 30, 1938. For Boulanger's reflections on the
event, see "Agendas," 1–5 September, F-Pn, Rés. Vmf. Ms. 102 (4–5).

I know that this was your Mother's wish. Could you still feel, despite your grief, that She is forever with you? With deepest affection, I am, more than ever, alas, your old and faithful friend,

NB

‽   ‽   ‽

Boulanger to Soulima Stravinsky

March 15, 1939

My dear Sviétik,[9]
   I can tell you the reason for the wire that I had to send to your Father. By some shocking absentmindedness I spoke of Mika while writing Milène, and I did not want to let him read such a mistake. If you can, find my letter and strike out the error, then give it to him, and please forgive me.
   I received the letter from Souvtchinsky and R. Bernard only on Monday, before April 1 and before June, even I do not know how I could write anything.[10] I lead a life that nothing can describe.
   What's more, I am so unworthy of such an honor—*for* or *against* who *can*, who has the right to stand up and attack or defend? Isn't trying to understand all we can allow ourselves to do?
   And yet, in such a situation, I would like to forget my scruples, my weakness, and express my uncompromising conviction, which, at the moment, seems quite impossible. I would be sick of it if I did not feel with equally great conviction that there is no greater cause than to serve this work that is in and of itself so very important, and that also projects a light upon all music.
   How sad it is to be foolish, to not know how to express oneself, and yet each day I speak of your Father's work, and am met with enthusiastic understanding. If humanly possible, I will try, but I work *so much*.
   I do not need to tell you that I am with you every moment. I have so much pain myself—I loved your mother very much. It is truly awful, and yet I know She has finally stopped suffering.

---

9.   Boulanger addressed the envelope: "To Monsieur Sviataslaw[*sic*] Strawinsky."
10.   Boulanger's correspondence with Pierre Souvtchinsky, close friend of Stravinsky's and a composer and writer himself, dates from 1935–75, F-Pn, N.L.a. 105 (76–83). The letter Boulanger references here was not retained in the archives. The only reference to a letter from a R(obert) Bernard dates from 1948, N.L.a. 55 (115). Boulanger's biographer makes no mention of any such event. I hypothesize Boulanger is referencing an invitation to speak in defense of Stravinsky or make a political statement against European Fascism.

With deepest tenderness,
NB

❧   ❧   ❧

Boulanger to Stravinsky

March 15, [1939][11]

My dear Friend,

I received a telegram from Mildred Bliss—finally everything has been done for the Symphony. How [helpful] she and Ellen Carpenter have been, I *can never* tell you. Everything was complicated by the fact that so many possibilities were available, and in our opinion none offers you enough of a guarantee. Therefore, Mildred Bliss will write you with the details. The manuscript goes to the Library of Congress and the first performance is booked in Chicago, with you conducting. I have suggested this be non-negotiable.

I just received the telegram and do not know how you will read the situation—such as it is, it is the result of a very admirable effort, you will surely say—and I quite agree it is a pleasure to promote the work of such a man as yourself. But with regard to financial questions everything has become difficult, unfortunately. And the persistence, the determination to succeed shown by the Blisses and the Carpenters is really moving.

Must I tell you, I think of you *incessantly*? But I am getting over a bad flu, and with such a crazy work schedule—I have literally not had a moment to myself. It is very cruel at a time when I would only like to think of you, of Catherine, of Mika. How could you possibly be doing? It is twenty-one years ago today that my little sister died, four years on Sunday since Mama passed, and my heart remains wounded as ever. And yourself, after these past months—which I have suffered with you—these two departures from which there is no return, how do you physically withstand it?

Undoubtedly, you are at the end of your courage and strength—and yet—our need for you is immense. You would feel it strongly here amongst these young people who depend on you. But would you be able to see, understand, listen to it at this moment? I send my love—and say this affectionately, just as Catherine would have wished it.

Your
Nadia

❧   ❧   ❧

---

11. Originally dated as 1934.

Denise Strawinsky to Boulanger

Sancellemoz
Haute-Savoie
France

March 23, 1939

Dear Mademoiselle,

If I dare write to you it is because my father-in-law, who has been horribly taxed by the terrible misfortune that just befell us, is not in a state to be able to write and has asked me to do so in his place and to tell you how deeply he was touched by your letter.

We have just settled in in Sancellemoz, because, unfortunately, my father-in-law, given his generally weakened state caused by the dreadful days he had just endured, had another pulmonary embolism, like the one he had two years ago in America. The doctors said he needed to treat it most seriously, and to be rested and well [he must] submit to this isolation.

He has therefore moved his headquarters here, where he can work in the greatest tranquility without the thousand worries and preoccupations there are in the city—He will promote his European tours from here.

As for my sister-in-law, Milène and myself, we both greatly needed rest and have come to live close to him. Théodore is also with us. Now he is in the best condition for his work. Just think, dear Mademoiselle, how hard it was to cut the family in two, but there was no other solution. So Nini stayed in Paris with his grandmother and Madubo. They are understood to be leaving the Faubourg apartment which is linked to too many dreadful memories (and would also be too expensive).[12] All three of them are going to go live in our small apartment on rue Antoine Chantin.[13]

My father-in-law finds himself forced to abandon his American tour for next December, even though this has resulted in many weighty concerns for him, but this time it is necessary that he follow the doctor's orders completely in order to recover fully. I know how precious your time is but I also know how happy my father-in-law would be to have news from you, if that were possible, and I ask you to believe, Dear Mademoiselle, in my deepest and most respectful affection,

Denise Strawinsky.

---

12. Nini was another nickname for Soulima. Mina ("Madubo") Svitalski was the Stravinskys' governess and had been in the family charge since the children were young. In April 1947, she along with Milène and Milène's husband, André Marion, moved to the United States. This arrangement failed to work, and so Madubo returned to Switzerland in 1954 and died in 1957. Walsh, *Second Exile*, 340–41; Craft, *Dearest Bubushkin*, 180.

13. This was Denise's mother's apartment.

P.S. As a matter of course, as far as Durkheim's concerned, to whom I have just written, my father-in-law is not telling anyone he is obligated to take a restorative break . . .

❧ ❧ ❧

Boulanger to Stravinsky

Gerry's Landing
Cambridge

Mr. Igor Strawinsky
Sancellemoz
Haute Savoie
France
April 12, 1939

I think of you every hour of the day and am saddened not to be able to prove it to you even a little bit.

Denise wrote me the most moving and tender letter you could imagine. Thank her for me. What a heart she has!

These words are improper, and I cannot say anything to you. But every day I understand your importance a little more, and I pray to God that you understand it, too. Perhaps you will find the courage to fight on. But . . . I know, and I know that time cannot heal such wounds. However, it seems to me that the memory of Catherine, her dear soul, will remain around you. Like a blessing, without a word, I would like to comfort you and cry with you.

Time now moves so terribly slowly with work and wears on my heart, but I will be there in July. Then I will come to you.

To have succeeded with the Harvard plan would have been a joy—maybe next year![14] May God give you strength—we are all praying so fervently for you, and I remain connected to you by the deepest sentiments of which I am capable,

Your
NB

---

14. I believe Boulanger is here referring to efforts to have Stravinsky selected as the Charles Eliot Norton Chair of Poetry. In her correspondence with Forbes, she advocated for either Paul Valéry or Igor Stravinsky as excellent candidates. The position was eventually offered to Stravinsky. Walsh, *Second Exile*, 91, and Rosenstiel, *Nadia Boulanger*, 310. For Boulanger's correspondence with Forbes, see F-Pn, N.L.a. 70 (222–50).

❧   ❧   ❧

Boulanger to Igor Stravinsky

Gerry's Landing
Cambridge, Mass.

Mr. Igor Stravinsky
Sancellemoz
Haute Savoie
France XIV
May 11, 1939[15]

Dear, Dear Friend,

I cannot tell you the feeling here now that it is known that you're coming. For me, it is a thing of momentous importance, because I know what you will do for them, and more important, because I know you will have peace in which to work—this is in the foundation's mandate. This is why, I tell you, I had such a desire to see you be next year's "Norton's Lecturer."

I live in such a rush that I don't even dare to speak to you. This is not good, but I am always thinking of you.

The business with Chicago still isn't sorted out after everything seemed arranged. But I'm going to Washington next week before leaving for the West to have, finally, a definitive resolution. The forced departure of Mrs. Carpenter seems to have called everything into question, it is really disappointing.

Know at least that I will do everything so that things turn out for the best. Sorry![16]

Fondly, I am your
Nadia B

❧   ❧   ❧

---

15. The letter was sent on May 12, 1939. The address had to be rewritten three times before it actually arrived in Sancellemoz. (It was sent first to the Saint Honoré address, then to rue Antoine Chantin, and then finally to Haute Savoie.)
16. Her apology is in reference to a smudge in the ink.

Denise Strawinsky to Boulanger

Sancellemoz
Haute Savoie

April 6, 1939[17]

Dear Mademoiselle,

My father-in-law thanks you very much for your letter of March 15, and you can just imagine how happy he was at the news that everything is ready concerning the Symphony and again he thanks you very warmly for all the trouble you have taken and for all the effort you have put into it. He is still waiting impatiently for Mrs. Bliss's letter, which has not yet arrived.

I am very happy to be able to give you better news about my father-in-law today. I would not hide from you that, after arriving here, following the painful misfortunes we have had, we were a bit frightened to learn of his illness, because the doctor has not hidden from us that he foresaw the possibility of an operation (either for a pneumothorax or a more serious procedure) if he did not see rapid progress and then just today (we go to the clinic every week for X-rays). Today, the doctor saw that the sick lung has cleared up and that he has gained 1.2 kg since our arrival here, which is an excellent sign. It was hugely important for the doctor to see his natural resistance and defenses. All of this has given us great confidence and allowed us to consider the future with greater clarity.

My father-in-law thus thinks he will be able to do his American tour, leaving here in the first half of January. There is one point that needs clarifying. I have therefore written to Dushkin asking him to find out what has become of the Copley agency that took over my father-in-law's interests.

Dear Mademoiselle, my father-in-law would like to write you personally to tell you again how grateful he was for all you have done, but he spends these days in bed, resting as much as possible. One day soon, when he is able to resume his normal work, he will write to you.

With deepest and most respectful friendship,
Denise Strawinsky.

Φ Φ Φ

---

17. Denise Strawinsky to Boulanger, June 6, 1939, F-Pn, N.L.a. 108 (104–5). Denise Strawinsky wrote three separate versions of this letter, two of which are at the Sacher Stiftung and a third that Denise actually sent to Boulanger: F-Pn, N.L.a. 108 (104–5). I have published the version Boulanger received. Denise Strawinsky is lying in this letter. Instead of convalescing, Stravinsky had left on a concert tour against doctor's orders.

Boulanger to Stravinsky

Gerry's Landing
Cambridge, Massachusetts

Mr Igor Strawinsky
Sancellemoz
Haute-Savoie
June 4, 1939[18]

My Dear Friend,

I imagine what June 18 will be like for you this year. Know that my thoughts always accompany you, and particularly those of the happy times that have passed! Following Denise's and Mrs. Forbes's letters, I presume that you are feeling better, taking care of yourself, whatever it takes. We need you so much.

I will stop in Chicago on Wednesday to "try" and fix the Chicago business—these hesitations, these difficulties explain things a little, but they are so difficult to tolerate. And what can be done? Everyone knows the importance of the awaited decision, but people are so preoccupied with financial matters that they daren't move anymore.

With heartfelt fondness, I am,

Your
NB

[P.S.] I'll be in Paris the 2nd or 3rd of July and will do all that I can to see you as soon as possible. I leave on the *Normandie* on June 28.

ﾞ   ﾞ   ﾞ

Boulanger to Stravinsky

July 4, 1939

Dear Friend,

I read and reread Copley's letter but can't, don't want to believe it.[19] I was thinking of going to comfort you, but on leaving yesterday, I was greatly

---

18. The envelope connected to this letter was post-dated June 15 from Place Victor Hugo, mailed with a French stamp, suggesting Boulanger did not mail the letter until she had returned to Paris.

19. Boulanger's letter is in reaction to learning of the death of Anna Stravinsky on June 7, 1939.

distressed by my own awful news—our oldest friend, Mr. Bouwens, is getting sicker. I spent the night there and could do nothing.[20]

I am in pain for you, but for myself as well. I loved your mother very much. It is with the most profound emotion that I am with you, in thinking of *them*.

NB

≈ ≈ ≈

Boulanger to Stravinsky

Les Maisonettes
Gargenville
S.O.

December 13, 1939

Dear Igor,

I am with you in such emotion and tenderness in these days of memorializing. I wanted to go and bring flowers to Mika's grave on the 30th but I was unsuccessful, I couldn't go out. But how I think of Her, of Catherine, of your Mother—and how I love you in Them, [as] I love them in you.[21]

It is necessary, so as to honor their memory, that you carry on yourself. It was in understanding God's will, finding strength still, even in your pain. But your heart's fatigue felt itself carried away by your spirit, by it alone. It's so beautiful to *act*, again and until the final hour.[22]

I know what you did there. Your radiance and that which you brought to this young girl, anxious to understand you, wishing to be guided by you, illuminated the clarity of your spirit. Good will creates such utopias—and even more ideology. The nineteenth century played with people's minds by creating false values. The most absurd conception of art, and from there, even the deformation of the physical [body]—eyes that couldn't see, ears that no longer knew that music was about sound. Your role is limitless. Your action—because through works and words you've brought the house back into order. On the one hand sometimes roughly, but . . . the reaction will only be better.

---

20. Richard Bouwens is believed to have been Boulanger's biological father. See Francis, *Teaching Stravinsky*, 101–2.
21. Boulanger's own capitalization is inconsistent in the original.
22. This paragraph is another instance where Boulanger's prose is convoluted. I have made an effort here to transmit the meaning as clearly as is possible.

I have just written to Miss Holl (Longy School) to confirm to her my desire to come next year.[23] This year I do not wish to leave France. I hope this will happen—and that you will still be there.

I'm going to Paris next week and count on seeing Vera.

Fondly and wholeheartedly,

Your
Nadia B.

🐦 🐦 🐦

Soulima Stravinsky to Boulanger

Cosne[24]

December 21, 1939

My dear Mademoiselle,

I knew that you would be with us on this day of cruel and tender memory.[25] You understand that on this sorrowful anniversary I have felt an infinite affection and it is through this feeling that we are connected to one another.

To tell you that I am unhappy wouldn't be the truth. I've settled quickly, I will even say instantly, to this difficult life that I didn't know before. It's a curious thing—it makes you discover certain neglected feelings, unexpected reactions. Good health sustains me, without which I doubt I could do the harder exercises. My superiors are attentive and intelligent, which is so important. So, I cannot complain about anything and I thank God for that.

As always, with affectionate thoughts and a faithful heart, I am with you more than ever Dear Mademoiselle. I am fondly,

Your Sviétik

---

23. Attached to this letter is a program for a lecture at the Longy School of Music relating to performances by the Boston Symphony Orchestra on January 16–18, 1941. The title of the lecture was "On the Music of Igor Stravinsky," and the event took place at the home of Mrs. Bartlett Hardwood on January 15. Tickets were $3.00 and proceeds went to scholarships to study with Boulanger. Minna Franziska Holl was then the director of the Longy School.

24. Soulima was undergoing military training, having signed up to serve with the French Army. When the armistice between Nazi Germany and France was signed on June 22, 1940, France was demilitarized, thereby ending Soulima Stravinsky's service.

25. This is a reference to the anniversary of the death of his sister.

[P.S.] You would give me such pleasure by sending me a book.[26] Thank you a thousand times for having suggested it to me.

1940

Théodore Strawinsky to Boulanger

Le Mans

January 1, 1940

Dear Mademoiselle,

It's already been two weeks since I ought to have answered your very kind letter that brought me once again an account of the pain we have suffered over the course of this past year that just came to a close. Telling you how much Denise and I are touched by your friendship is useless; you already know. Thank you with all my heart. As we enter 1940, let me offer you the greetings we all send one another, to which I add much more personal wishes for you, for your health, and for your very precious work.

Allow me, dear Mademoiselle, to send you my love and my deepest and most faithful friendship,
Théodore

⅍   ⅍   ⅍

Boulanger to Stravinsky

36 rue Ballu Paris

April 5, 1940[27]

Dear Igor,

Where will this note find you, I don't know, but I'd like you to know that I am wholeheartedly with you both. It was necessary that your union take this definitive form, and I know that it's what Catherine would have wanted.

---

26. Which book is unknown. A list of books Boulanger purchased as gifts during her first years in America provides a glimpse of authors she enjoyed. See Boulanger, "Biographie," F-Pn, Rés Vm. Dos 124.

27. Unsure of how to reach Stravinsky, Boulanger sent this to the Hotel Hemenway, by way of the Forbeses. Her mention that she knew of the marriage already suggests that Stravinsky's earlier telegram had already arrived or that word of the union had reached her from other channels.

I seem far away, but I followed with a profound joy your winter, your activity, and its great results. There are those who will never understand, there are those for whom you have provided guidance. And, by being yourself, you illuminate for them the past and guide their future.

It was so beautiful, so good, and so necessary that you gave this concert. We were, for example, overwhelmed by Preger's case who, having wanted at all costs to serve, has fallen ill, both lungs to be reopened after several weeks in the barracks.[28] He must spend a year in a sanatorium, and without your help, we could not insure him.

Mrs. Loudon is the president of our small committee. No meetings, no publicity, but true, active support.

We have given concerts to armies with orchestras made up of professional musicians brought together through the officers' efforts, an admirable initiative that did so much good for those who command so humanely, as well as for those who performed.

All this said too hastily, but I haven't a minute. With great fondness for Vera and you, I am, with all my heart, your
Nadia B.

❧   ❧   ❧

Stravinsky to Boulanger

Igor Stravinsky
Hotel Hemenway
Boston, Mass. U.S.A.

Mademoiselle Nadia Boulanger
36 rue Ballu
Paris 9th, France
April 18, 1940

My very dear Nadia,

I am feeling an irresistible urge to write you, be it only a couple of lines. I hope that you are aware of the news of my marriage to Vera (civil for the moment, in observance of the Orthodox Lent) about which I had sent a telegram to Paris, but I wanted to announce it to you personally. We had to celebrate it earlier than first planned, but the tactlessness of the press since Vera's arrival in America and my terrible solitude (despite my numerous occupations)

---

28. Léo Preger (1907–65) was a Boulanger pupil during the 30s. He would later become a composer and organist of some renown. For Preger's correspondence with Boulanger, see N.L.a. 97 (10–78).

made me decide to have her come from Charleston (where she was staying at some friends') to Boston* to get married—which was done on March 9 in Bedford, 30 km from here, at the house of some Russian friends (a Harvard professor), in the country.[29]

A month ago, under the auspices of our ambassador, with the skillful and influential aid of Mr. and Mrs. Bliss, I succeeded in giving a chamber concert in New York benefiting French musicians affected by the war that was successful both from a financial and an artistic point of view.[30]

You and Mme Loudon should already be in possession of the large sum of $2,640 that was collected and that the good Mrs. Bliss told me about.[31] I am very proud of this and very happy that it is you, along with Mme Loudon, who are responsible for the distribution, as I was able to understand it from Mrs. Bliss' letter.

We are very distressed by the events, although fully confident in the outcome of this gigantic struggle with evil. I very much want to have some news from you, dear friend—direct news. Sister Edward whom I saw in Chicago had some and *not me!* We leave for *Los Angeles* (143 So. Gramercey C/O Dr. A. Kall) in May where we will spend the summer and probably the autumn. Word from you would fill me with joy.

Your
I. Str.

*Where we are living at this moment—the Hotel Hemenway—until the end of my work at Harvard (May 5)
[P.S.] Hugs and kisses, dear Nadia—Vera

❧   ❧   ❧

---

29. The Professor mentioned here was Timothy Teracuzio. Walsh, *Second Exile*, 112.

30. This was a "Town Hall" concert held in New York and in part arranged by the Blisses. Walsh, *Second Exile*, 113.

31. Lydia Loudon, referred to by Boulanger elsewhere as "Tante Lydia," was the wife of the Dutch Ambassador to Paris and friend of the Boulanger family from at least 1905 until 1957. Boulanger–Loudon Letters, Don Campbell Private Archives. Loudon was living in Holland at the time Stravinsky wrote this letter. Only a month later, the country was invaded by the Nazis.

Boulanger to Stravinsky

Faugeras
41 Uzerche
Corrèze [Letterhead]

Mr. Igor Strawinsky
c/o Dr. Alexis Kall
143 South Gramercy Place
Los Angeles
California
June 22, 1940

My Dear Friend,

No doubt this is the last chance to write to you.

I could learn nothing about the children. Could do nothing for them—impossible to communicate.

If it is God's will that we never see each other again, know that you have been one of the greatest lights of my life.

My love to you and Vera,
Nadia B.

[P.S.] How I thought of you on the 18th! What a sad birthday you must have had, so far away.

Chapter Three

The American Years

November 1940–January 1946

If the 1930s were a time when Boulanger and Stravinsky learned how to dialogue as colleagues, 1940–46 marked the time when they came to respect and care for each other as friends. Boulanger arrived in the United States on November 5, 1940, on the SS *Excambion* to assume teaching duties at the Longy School of Music in Boston, Massachusetts. Her first text to the Stravinskys dates from November 19, 1940, in which she wrote of seeing Soulima Stravinsky in Vichy, France, prior to her departure and of how disappointed she was to learn she had missed performances of Stravinsky's new Symphony in C in Chicago by only two days. Igor and Vera, in turn, wrote to Boulanger, asking if she could intervene on their behalf with Sergey Koussevitzky, conductor of the Boston Symphony Orchestra. Moreover, Boulanger and the Stravinskys sought ways in which all three could reunite.

This chapter presents Stravinsky at his most candid and charming. In letters from March 31, 1941, and July 29, 1941, for example, Stravinsky writes to Boulanger of his sincere worries about her health. Elsewhere, he playfully squabbles about money and the cost of copies of his latest compositions (May 18, 1943, February 28, 1944, and June 29, 1943). In this chapter, Stravinsky gives Boulanger a copy of Mussorgsky's *Boris Godunov* (November 14, 1944), and elsewhere he writes to share with her newspaper clippings of musical and nonmusical matters to "amuse" or "distract" her (February 28, 1944, for example). In a rather touching exchange from 1945, Stravinsky arranged to have copies of his latest work, the *Symphony in Three Movements*, sent to Boulanger for her fifty-eighth birthday (letter from September 20, 1945). This was the last birthday she would spend in the United States. When Boulanger replied to ask if she could pay Stravinsky for the copies, the composer responded: "Why do you bring up money . . . I can give you a gift, too—it's true, it's nothing big, all the more reason to—why talk about it? You owe me nothing save a few 'love and kisses' in your next letter" (November 16, 1945).

The texts from November 1940 to January 1946 contain references to several other of Stravinsky's works and publications. Two such examples include a discussion of the correction of Stravinsky's Symphony in C (May 30, October 13, and October 29, 1941), and Boulanger's vexing work with Harvard University Press to publish Stravinsky's *Poétique musicale*, the publication of which she oversaw independent of Stravinsky's input. Elsewhere Boulanger references the correction of a Sonata, though to which specific score she is referring remains a mystery (November 28, 1942, December 14, 1942, and March 16, 1943). Perhaps the most complex tangle of letters involves the premiere of the *Sonata for Two Pianos*, with letters presented in this chapter in chronological order despite the fact that they read better in the order shown in table 3.1.

Beyond copyediting scores and assisting with professional affairs in Boston, Boulanger enjoyed a vibrant social connection with the Stravinskys while in America, especially when doctor's orders required her to take a leave of absence from teaching duties in Boston and Washington for the 1941–42 school year. Forced to be idle, she settled with friends, Arthur and Georgette Sachs, in Santa Barbara, California, close to the Stravinsky's home in Hollywood. When her leave of absence ended, and Boulanger headed to the East Coast again, she wrote to the Stravinskys that, "truly, if not financially, it was a marvelous thing to be sick last year!" (August 22, 1942).

Boulanger's correspondence during the war years shows her at her most open and intriguing. In a deeply poignant letter of March 17, 1941, she pours out in broken, nonsensical French the deep pain she felt in abandoning her friends and country. Elsewhere, she excoriates Olin Downes and rails against "self-proclaimed intellectuals' 'complete' materialism" (August 19, 1944). And in a tantalizing reference from December 22, 1943, Boulanger writes to the Stravinskys of a Hogarth painting she gave them for Christmas, urging them: "If you don't like it, please tell me. I will take it back. I don't know if I'd like to give it to you anymore or not." Which painting and how, or even if, it relates to Stravinsky's *The Rake's Progress*, remains open to conjecture.

Table 3.1. Order of letters, July 15, 1944–August 19, 1944

Initial letter		Response	
Author	Date / Initial phrase	Author	Date / Initial phrase
Boulanger	July 15, 1944 "Since yesterday"	Stravinsky	July 18 "Can we play?"
Boulanger	July 28, 1944	None	
Stravinsky	July 16, 1944 "Read This"	Boulanger	August 19 "Why, Dear Igor"

At the end of the chapter, Stravinsky and Boulanger anxiously await news of France's liberation. Stravinsky expresses deep gratitude to Boulanger for sending care packages to his children throughout the war years; and on November 27, 1944, Boulanger writes to him that she shares his concern about his granddaughter, Catherine (Kitty), whom they have learned was orphaned by her father's death in a concentration camp. The first letter from Soulima Stravinsky to Boulanger does not appear until June 14, 1945, but in it Soulima reassures Boulanger that he is well. He also writes of his new wife, Françoise Blondlat; of the reception of his father's works in war-torn France; and that he and Françoise are expecting a child. When Igor Stravinsky learns of Boulanger's decision to return to Paris, a departure she secured for January 3, 1946, he writes to her of his sadness while also begging her to use her influence when back in Paris to convince his children to relocate to the United States (December 19, 1945).

❧   ❧   ❧

Boulanger to Stravinsky

November 19, 1940

Dear, Dear Igor,

Sorry for not having written yet [and] not telling you that I had seen Sviétik in Vichy, that they all are as well as possible, courageous, and that he, Sviétik, has a sort of confidence in himself.[1] And then I received your telegram, which was so nice, so good, so necessary.

But . . . limited time and above all, personal difficulties. Everything is still so hard! How I would like to see you, you and Vera both. I need to build up my strength again, [I need] to see you.

To think that no one had told me: the Symphony in Chicago.[2] I found out two days after! Completely ridiculous.

I hope the Forbeses will agree to keep me. The need to be "home," which I can satisfy a little here, is so great. My God, my heart is heavy, but one *must* hope, and fight on!

I send my love to both of you, and am with all my heart,

---

1. Boulanger had been in the city of Vichy to process a travel visa with which to leave France for the United States.
2. Symphony in C. The work premiered in Chicago on November 7, 1940, performed by the Chicago Symphony Orchestra with Stravinsky conducting. Boulanger arrived in the United States two days later. See Francis, *Teaching Stravinsky*, 119–21.

Your
Nadia

❧   ❧   ❧

Stravinsky to Boulanger

December 4, 1940

My very dear Nadia,

I was so happy to have your letter. We hope to see you soon in January, when we will be in Boston for the week of my concerts.

The Forbeses have invited us to come down to their place—it's very kind on their part. I am writing them a letter to thank them. I'll accept their invitation [if] it also allows us to see you for a little longer.

How I missed your absence in Chicago (or in Cincinnati) where I had some beautiful performances of my Symphony! In Boston, where Koussevitzky wanted me to conduct as well (for rehearsals of *Oedipus Rex*, too), they asked me to supply the orchestral material, i.e., to pay for the rental [of the parts].[3] I am quite afraid that this very unexpected condition will make the performance nearly impossible. I have never paid for the rental of my compositions, never, anywhere. It would be all the stranger for me to do this at the Boston Symphony, i.e., *chez* Koussevitzky where I have always been considered a "member of the family." Someone has probably made a mess, imposing this ludicrous condition on me behind Koussevitzky's back, and I want to hope that he will intervene to cancel it.

See you soon, Nadia, with sincere affection.

Yours,
Igor Stravinsky

[P.S.] We are here until December 13, then in Minneapolis for a week, then coming back here for January 10.
[P.P.S.] With tender thoughts, I am very impatient to see you soon.—Your Vera

❧   ❧   ❧

---

3. These letters reinforce Boulanger's connection with Koussevitzky, whom she had reviewed glowingly as early as 1921: Boulanger, "Concerts Koussevitzky," *Le Monde Musical*, nos. 23–24 (December 1921): 401. Boulanger mediated Koussevitzky and Stravinsky's relationship on several occasions, including her writing of Stravinsky's speech for the Koussevitzky Testimonial Dinner in 1944. See Boulanger, F-Pn, Rés. Vm. Dos. 124 (103–10). For Boulanger's correspondence with Koussevitzky, see F-Pn, N.L.a. 78 (109–19).

Boulanger to Vera Stravinsky

December 10, 1940.[4]

Dear Vera,

Thank you—the 23rd at Dick Hammond's—got it.[5]
In Washington on the 4th at Miss Winslaw's—all of *us*.
Thank you for the lectures.[6] I can do nothing for the program.
K[oussevitzky] has left for a week. But it seems *impossible* this can't be arranged.
So the 23rd—I will attempt to see you before "our" dinner.

With all my heart to you both,
NB

1941

Stravinsky (postscript by Vera Stravinsky) to Boulanger

Hollywood
Chateau Marmont

March 3, 1941

My dear Nadia,

It's been a bit less than a month since we have had word from you. Would you be so very kind to send us something, if only a postcard? I know that it is not always easy. All the same, we await news and hope that everything is more or less as usual for you.

We have already been here for three weeks. My concerts here and in San Diego (after some very hard work, about the same as in Boston but complicated

---

4.   This is a direct response to Vera Stravinsky's earlier letter wherein she implied that Boulanger should intercede with Koussevitzky about a program for the Boston Symphony Orchestra. Vera Stravinsky wished to see *Oedipus Rex* performed on the concert, but Koussevitzky would not respond to her entreaties. Vera Stravinsky to Boulanger, December 9, 1940, F-Pn, N.L.a. 109 (64).

5.   The Stravinskys returned to New York from Minneapolis on December 22. Letter, Vera Stravinsky to Boulanger, December 9, 1940. Richard (Dick) Hammond was a Boulanger pupil and an event promoter in New York. He lived close to the Stravinskys in Hollywood, and they became close friends in the 1950s.

6.   Most likely a reference to a copy of Stravinsky's Harvard lectures.

by a bad head cold) were a great success. Now I won't conduct my symphony again until July, in Mexico City.[7]

With regards to the latter: I spoke with Mr. Ernest R. Voigt about this (Associated Music Publishers, Inc., 25 West 45th Street, New York City) and he promised me that he would send you (as soon as he receives the material from here) a part for each instrument as well as the orchestral score. The parts will be untouched, i.e., full of errors, and the orchestral score will be the grey one with which you already are familiar. If you need mine (the black one) I will send it to you, but I prefer to keep it here (I may need it.)[8]

There are lots of people here and we are having great difficulty finding a house as a permanent residence—everything is taken and the horrors leftover are priced very high. It is more advantageous to buy one with a nice little mortgage. That's what we'll probably do.

When will we see you again? Is it completely impossible to see you again here this year?

With sincere affection, dear Nadia,
Your,
I Strawinsky

[P.S.] If you have my *Ave Maria*, my *Pater*, and my *Credo*, I would be infinitely grateful if you could send them to me. I am going to make photostats (photocopies) and give them back to you. Thanks in advance.[9]

---

7. For more on Stravinsky's trips to Mexico, see Levitz, "Igor the Angeleno," 141–76.

8. The *fonds* Boulanger of the Bibliothèque nationale still holds these scores in its collection: Rés Vma Ms 1218, 1 à 3. Stravinsky's own copies of the *Symphony in C* score date from 1948 and 1949 respectively, Stravinsky, *Symphony in C* (Mainz: Schott, 1948), CH-Bps, IMD and 2MD. His printed scores are annotated with performance markings, but do not contain substantial revisions such as those discussed in this correspondence. Indeed, I have yet to locate the score for the Symphony mentioned here. See Francis, "A Most Unsuccessful Project," 258–9.

9. Boulanger owned two sets of scores for Stravinsky's choral prayers. One set of choral parts dates from the early 1930s and was published by Édition Russe de Musique: *Pater Noster* and *Credo* choral parts, 1932, F-LYc, UFNB 525 STR. Boulanger also owned both an autograph and a photostat of the autograph of the 1934 *Ave Maria*: autograph, F-Pn, Rés Vma Ms 980; photostat, F-LYc, UFNB M 525 STR. Boulanger's set of choral parts for the *Ave Maria* is also located in Lyon: UFNB 525 STR. The remaining scores for the works mentioned were all purchased in 1949. It is possible Stravinsky was asking Boulanger to copy her 1930 scores, but her response suggests that she, too, was looking for a published version of these works.

[P.P.S.] Please give best regards to the Forbeses from the two of us.
[P.P.P.S.] With wholehearted and fond affection for you, dear Nadia—Vera.

❧   ❧   ❧

Boulanger to Stravinsky

Gerry's Landing
Cambridge, Massachusetts
Throwbridge 78–89

Monsieur Igor Strawinsky
Chateau Marmont
3221 Sunset Boulevard
Hollywood, Los Angeles
California
March 17, 1941[10]

My dear friend, I'm ashamed not to have written you earlier, but, if I am very busy, I am also dealing with a heavy moral crisis. It was twenty-three years ago on Saturday that my little Lili died—it will be six on Wednesday since Mother has been gone—it is impossible to do here what we always did in Paris, but at least I had believed it possible. All of this, the feeling of shame I have for having left at such a time, has filled my heart with pain. I should have known, but on the other hand, what else can be done. To help them over there, it was truly necessary to carry out this other work. Ultimately, as you see, it's not going very well. And it's not really necessary that things work, if we want to find a balance again. These past few years have been filled by our lost ones and today we pay for it; it's only right. And it has to be so, because if remorse acts as a springboard for us, we can create new strength in ourselves from it. The trick is to figure out what it is we are ready to give our lives for. And we have several things to give, because even if it is hopeless, we must all still prepare for the end. But just imagine how my despair is paired with an indescribable hope. And I offer my strength to that which requires all of it, but for the time being I have lost my strength, which is absurd. But I didn't know how much I loved France, how I need her, and how, in her weakness, I feel she is great. How badly we have served her, we other French men and women whose flesh and spirit were crafted by her, her traditions, and her faith. We are suddenly reminded that we descended from those who fought with Joan of Arc, who prayed with Saint

---

10. My transcription of the original, found on the companion website, reproduces this text exactly as it appears in the original. Boulanger wrote this letter on a typewriter (incredibly unusual for her) and the original contains a tangle of typos and incorrect punctuation.

Louis, who witnessed the construction of Chartres. And such memories will permit neither weakness nor treason.

What have we done with this heritage that was our honor and demanded our responsibility? We suddenly realize when waking up from such an awful nightmare—because that has been our collective existence—that we do not have enough tears to offer up to God. It has nothing to do with sentimentality, but rather the awakening of the conscience—it is well worth going through a serious crisis. So if it takes cruelly seeing one's self in an unsympathetic mirror, the result is worth the suffering. I do not like to be ashamed, and, thank God, I have not had much shame in my life. I have been selfish, like almost all humans, but haven't had too many irreparable faults. (I believe in the forgiveness of sins, certainly, but for the past to be erased, it must remain the past.) As for life in general, there are so many concessions to let go of. And the result doesn't allow us to blame our neighbors—the "guilty ones" (the "guilty ones" are easy to blame)—but it forces us to judge our own actions, our own efforts. And it is not a pretty picture. Everything gets forgotten, it's that simple. As if we didn't have parents to whom we must show respect and be accountable. The time has come—but a great country that radiated glory has lost everything in a few wretched days by the mistakes accumulated over such a long time. We have to think about this first, then next, and for always; we must understand it from every angle, and then—and only then—with our house put back in order— we will (perhaps) be able to set out on a new course, or be left to sleep in the peace of God, having measured [our] faults, and though forgiving [them], fearing them still.

Please forgive all of this, which makes no sense other than to me. But I am so alone with this that I must open my heart. And who can understand it like you? What bad luck to be honored by such an overwhelming trust. It doesn't matter. It is worth something, because how many men, at this very moment, are beating their own breasts?

As for the score, I hope that it will not come right now because we are giving a concert for the Polish on April 4 in New York, with Schütz's Resurrection. . . .[11] One set of parts had to be completely redone since I did not have them anymore, and although Barbara is making copies, that has taken a long time. One would not think, to see this endless and useless letter, that I am short on time. But it is easier to say everything in a jumble than it is to choose, eliminate, reject, and craft.

I have not yet found a copy of the prayers. I have just sent a letter on this subject and will keep you informed.

---

11. Reference to a gala performance at Carnegie Hall in support of Ignacy Jan Paderewski. Spycket, *Nadia Boulanger*, 109; Rosenstiel, *Nadia Boulanger*, 318.

Give Vera my love, and, rest assured, I am finished. I send my love. I miss you both terribly, and I hope that we will meet again . . . one day.

Yours,
Nadia

❧ ❧ ❧

Stravinsky to Boulanger

Chateau Marmont
8221 Sunset Boulevard
Hollywood, Los Angeles, California

Mlle Nadia Boulanger
c/o Mrs Forbes
Gerry's Landing
Cambridge, Mass.
March 31, 1941

My dear Nadia,
With all my heart I have been with you this whole time. Your letter touched me greatly.

Affectionately yours,
Your
I. Str.

❧ ❧ ❧

Stravinsky to Georgette and Arthur Sachs

April 31, 1941

Very dear friends,
Two words to ask you how things are going and if you've had troubling news regarding Nadia. I did not write to her, not wishing to tire her with the obliga-tion of responding if she still feels weak right now. I would absolutely like to see her again before her departure, which is why I would be infinitely grateful if you could let me know what has been decided with respect to her.
I received a letter from my son, Théodore. Indeed, it is as I had told you the other day: he is asking me to find someone in France who would help him in his very difficult situation—he finds himself like a prisoner in his town (Villemur, Haute-Garone) without being able to do the least sort of work to

feed himself or [to acquire] the basic necessities of life, which is already hard enough.[12] May his sense of liberty remain as it was before his internment. Would you know, my dear friend, whom I might contact, either the Minister of the Interior or of Justice? Maybe Nadia, who also wanted to intervene to help Théodore, could give you some useful advice?

Thank you, and thank you again to the both of you for the lovely days spent at your home with you,

Your
I. Str.

❧   ❧   ❧

Stravinsky to Boulanger

2160 North Wetherly Drive
Hollywood, California
May 19, 1941

My dear Nadia,

Once again it has been a long time since I've heard any news of you. Are you still in Cambridge, are you on vacation (rather implausible)? It has been an eternity (March 17) since you sent me your (unfortunately sad) news. Since then, the Associated Music Publishers, in their letter from April 1, spoke to me about you, letting me know that "the material of your Symphony was sent to Miss Boulanger . . . she wrote us in the meantime that her corrections would be delayed as she is rather busy at this time." Is *this time over?* I'm wondering about this with a certain degree of concern for two reasons: (1) My concert in Mexico City, where I am playing my symphony, is approaching and I am wondering if I will be able to count on this newly corrected material from you. (2) If we had sent you the unchanged piece from which I had conducted along with the unaltered material (in order to help you with the corrections), I am scared that the Associated Music Publishers, having to deliver this corrected material to the Mexico Philharmonic (it is necessary to allow 10 to 14 days to send it from New York to Mexico) for my concerts (beginning of July), will be obliged to take [the score] away from you, thereby interrupting your precious work. Unless you will be able to continue correcting it according to the corrections written partially in the gray score and on the bottom of the paper. As you see I am completely ignorant of what is going on. A note from you would settle my nerves, providing the letter is reassuring.

---

12. Villemur-sur-Tarn, Haute-Garonne, a municipality in southwestern France, north of Toulouse.

I received a letter from Mr. Forbes letting me know about his "Committee's" refusal to publish my lectures in two languages. I thought as much. They are now proposing to publish them only in their original language, i.e., French. I consented. Their reasoning is incomprehensible to me. If the edition, with the two combined texts, frightened them—a higher cost for the volume without any great hope of a good run—what would be the advantage of publishing in French, I wonder?[13]

All my affectionate and faithful thoughts, my very dear Nadia,

Your
I. Str

[P.S.] The troubling news from Vichy scares me.[14]

     ❧   ❧   ❧

Boulanger to Stravinsky

Gerry's Landing
Cambridge, Massachusetts
Throwbridge 78–89

May 30, 1941

Dear Igor,

Forgive my silence, but everything justifies it—first, the worrying preoccupation we all share, then the student who was to help me work for you was ill, and finally my arm has made writing very difficult all these past months (while falling, I horribly bruised my muscles and my nerves are still very sore).

I only had one new score, the second one—and this makes the work more uncertain, because I have the feeling that I'm forgetting piles of

---

13. Boulanger served as an intermediary between Stravinsky and Harvard University Press with this publication (referenced in further detail in later letters). Stravinsky eventually sent Boulanger a first edition copy of the text. She annotated it heavily, most likely while helping Stravinsky draft an English version of the lectures to present in Chicago on January 20, 1944. *Poétique musicale* (Cambridge, MA: Harvard University Press, 1942), F-Pn, Mus. Vmc. 9362.

14. Possibly Stravinsky was referencing events relating to the recent surrender of Yugoslavia to the German forces (April 17) and Greece to the German and Italian armies (April 20). 22 June 1941 also marked the German assault on the Soviet Union and a decided shift in the war to the "eastern front." See Weinberg, *A World at Arms*, 264–309; and Murray and Millet, *A War to Be Won*, 91–142. The question remains exactly what news Stravinsky and Boulanger managed to receive from France at this time.

details—moreover, I've had to accept, with much gratitude, to go teach at Sister Edward's Convent where I'll be from June 18 to June 26—going afterward to Santa Barbara (assuming this is still possible!)[15]

I would have to find the right score here with the already corrected parts, around the 15th or 20th of August (I have to go to Canada again for my visa to be changed to a Professor Visa) and I will do everything that is possible. But the truth is that new parts must be created, and this I cannot take on. The student who wanted to do it will not be here *for months*, unfortunately, and Barbara does not have the means to assume such work. Ultimately, I will do *all* that I can—if you knew how painful it is to write, you would understand why I've really not been able to do it.

It is peculiar, I was convinced I wrote to you several weeks ago, when I spoke with you about the house, about this summer—was it actually a dream? I suddenly have doubts, and yet I can even remember what I told you. I don't know myself, anymore! My love to both of you,

NB

[P.S.] I hope to give you the *Ave Maria* next week. But . . . so many promises have already been made to me that I don't believe anything anymore—still, I have *Noces, Apollon, Symphonie de psaumes, Sérénade*, etc. . . .[16]
[P.P.S.] Am distressed.

ᴥ   ᴥ   ᴥ

15. Sinsinawa Mound, Madison, Wisconsin, home of the Sinsinawa Dominican Order. St. Clara is a reference to the academy connected to The Mound.
16. Boulanger's archives still hold these scores: *Noces*, piano/vocal reduction (J. W. Chester & Co, 1922), F-LYc, UFNB M 531 STR. Boulanger numbered every measure up until the fourth tableau, perhaps in preparation for rehearsals; *Noces*, Miniature score (J. W. Chester & Co, 1923), F-LYc, UFNB MEp STR 530. She acquired this score in Chicago at Rosary College; *Apollon Musagète*, piano reduction (Édition Russe de Musique, 1928), F-LYc, UFNB M 111.01 STR P, acquired in 1942, according to the cover annotation; *Symphonie de psaumes*, miniature score (Édition Russe de Musique, 1941), F-LYc, UFNB MEp STR 530 1941; and *Sérénade* (Édition Russe de Musique, 1926), UFNB M 111 STR. The *Sérénade* score sold for 30 cents and contains performance markings throughout.

Stravinsky to Boulanger

June 12, 1941

Good Lord, my dear Nadia! Your letter deeply distressed me! A single thing remains constant—that is, your plan to come to Santa Barbara. So long as events don't make you change your mind. With deepest affection,

Your
I Str.

[P.S.] How is your arm? Have you been able to arrange your trip to Canada?
[P.P.S.] Warm wishes to Sister Edward, please.

                                    ❧   ❧   ❧

Stravinsky to Boulanger

1260 North Wetherly Drive
Hollywood, California
July 29, 1941

Dear friend,

I received your letter of June 29 in Mexico City and am just responding to you today with a couple of words to thank you for it. *Reply quickly by return mail* if you are coming here (or to Santa Barbara where Mrs. Bliss is waiting for you) since in that case it would be simpler to look at things concerning my symphony together and to make decisions face to face. It's so complicated to correspond on such subjects. I am so grateful to you for taking care of this, thank you with all my heart! I am back from Mexico City with the two orch[estral] scores, mine and the grey one that I want to try to correct according to my own. Can you believe those idiots at the Associated Music Publishers sent (for some potential performances) a complete version of my symphony to London before they had received your corrections!!!!!! So I await your response doubly impatiently.

I'm sorry to hear that you're in a poor state of health and beg you to give me details, if only as an exception [to what you would usually do]. Is it your nerves, insomnia, or something bigger yet? I am very worried.

I've just received a letter from Théodore who, the poor boy, was taken away by two policemen to a concentration camp close to Toulouse where he spent four horrible days dying of hunger, a result of measures taken by the government against all Russians *without exception* (Red or White), following the break in diplomatic relations with the Soviets. If it wasn't for the Swiss Consul at Toulouse who acted as guarantor for my poor Théodore, he would still be imprisoned like the others. Such noble measures are taken, probably to please Hitler, against refugees deprived of all their rights. And [to think] Théodore offered his services to the French army at the beginning of the war! The other day in Mexico City someone asked if I was for Pétain or, like many French here, a "Degaullist," I responded to them that I am "Dis*gueul*sted."[17]

Very affectionately yours,
I. Stra

❧ ❧ ❧

Boulanger to Stravinsky

Chicago, Illinois [stamp]

c/o Mrs. Arthur Sachs
Ra Ben Farm
Hope Ranch Park
Santa Barbara Cal.
Mr. Igor Strawinsky
1260 North Wetherly Drive
Hollywood
California
August 1, 1941

Dear Friend,
    Thank you for your letter—I will be in Santa Barbara on Monday, but will be resting for at least ten days. I just finished my courses at the Convent, and . . . I don't have a choice. It is nothing, and it is not important. But an old, tired heart does not bear it—in addition to the daily effort, the remorse—and *I cannot* get used to the idea of having left them there, suffering, oh what suffering.[18] I know that certain tasks can only be accomplished this way, and I have the dearest friends here like you couldn't imagine—the most faithful. I have *understood* the value of these weeks at the Convent, the work demands all of my

---

17. In the original French, Stravinsky is making a play on the name of general Charles de Gaulle, leader of the French Free Forces during the Second World War, and the colloquial word *dégueulasse*, which translates as "disgusting." Henri Philippe Pétain was chief of the Vichy government from 1940–44. See Williams, *Pétain*; and Curtis, *Verdict on Vichy*.
18. Boulanger understates the severity of her ill health. In fact, her doctor ordered her to take a leave of absence, and that was why she traveled to the East Coast at this time. Rosenstiel, *Nadia Boulanger*, 320–6.

attention—but . . . something stronger than all that haunts my thoughts: "You left everything." [Even] if I were to face hardship here, everything is easy—and despite all that I have, my conscience is troubled and that is greater than any reason, even the serious, concrete [ones], that I have to pursue my work here. And I know this is all that one can do.

See you soon, I hope. We will arrange something, because we must settle these parts once and for *all* (if that is even imaginable!).

You told me nothing of Milène, of Sviétik, but I guess there is the world between you, and Théodore, harder again for you than for him!

To Vera and to you, with all my affection,
NB

❧ ❧ ❧

Stravinsky to Boulanger

1260 North Wetherly Drive
Hollywood, California

August 5, 1941

My dear Nadia,

Happy to know you [are] so close. May this stay with the good Sachses do you some good and may this short vacation give you new strength—you need it since you give it away left and right so generously.

The more you spend your energies thus, the more troubled your conscience will become. I know that you have nothing to blame yourself for. These troubles are part of your nature and they will torment you less when your heart's strength returns to you. May God come to your aid.

Yours,
I Str.

[P.S.] Mr. Bliss was operated on last Saturday. We sent a telegraph to Mrs. Bliss to ask for news.

❧ ❧ ❧

Stravinsky to Boulanger

1260 North Wetherly Drive
Hollywood, California

October 13, 1941

My dear Nadia,

A note to remind you not to forget to bring with you (when you come to see us this Friday) the Harvard University Press form letter—I need to respond to him and I can't even remember his name!!! Also bring with you, if you think they'll be useful, the letters and notes concerning my Symphony.

We're looking forward to seeing you, dearest,

Your
I St.

[P.S.] My fondest regards to the Sachses. I do not believe that it will be possible for us to come to Santa Barbara this weekend—too many things are stalled and there are so many letters to write.

🕿   🕿   🕿

Boulanger to Stravinsky

Avon Old Farms
Avon, Connecticut
Gerry's Landing
Cambridge Mass.

7 Nov. 1941

Finally found a Littré, Dear Igor. But $60.00—$28.00 is better.[19] I didn't dare take it—but if you want it, say the word[20]—because the new copy is $100.00 and it seems improbable that we'll find others.

I'm taking the train in a few moments which explains my somewhat frantic letter. But know that I think of you both all the time.

Fond regards,
Nadia

---

19. A four-volume French–English dictionary edited by Émile Littré. Stravinsky later relays that the bookstore was asking $60 for it (which today would equal approximately $900).

20. Boulanger writes "dire" which is an antiquated structure for the imperative.

❧ ❧ ❧

Boulanger to Igor and Vera Stravinsky

Gerry's Landing
Cambridge
Massachusetts
Trowbridge 7339
Studio
197 Coolidge Hill

Mr. & Mrs. I. Strawinsky
1260 North Wetherly Drive
Hollywood
California
December 19, 1941
(Mother's birthday)

Dear Vera and Igor,

Christmas will be here soon, and my thoughts are dedicated to reuniting with you, mixed with the memories, the hopes, of those present and those absent. It is too emotional to try to say what is felt, what is thought, and what is desired. But you know that there is not a day when I do not feel you close to me, when I do not feel close to you.

And in the certainty of this very old and sure affection, I send my love to you both, and I am wholeheartedly your

Nadia

1942

Boulanger to Stravinsky

Gerry's Landing
Cambridge, Mass.

Mr. Igor Strawinsky
1260 North Wetherly Drive
Hollywood, California
March 6, 1942

Dear Friend,

We are gambling with misfortune, really, and I don't know what to think, because, to tell you the truth, I find your silence . . . long and sad.

I have written you two letters, first of all:

Nov. 7 from Avon to tell you that my bookshop has found a Littré.

Nov. 15 from Washington to inform you of my visit with Mr. Malone's assistant who told me he wanted to do away with the summaries—which, given the manner in which they were to be kept in, seemed the best solution to me. I told you that if you didn't agree, I would ask you to write to Mr. Malone directly. I also asked if you thought removing the abstracts would change the text, which I don't think to be the case.[21]

At first I thought you had written to Mr. Malone and that things were moving along. But, I began to have doubts in my mind, and on December 9, I wrote a second letter to you from Providence regarding this, telling you that, having reread everything, I found that the summaries of the essays were unnecessary, that the clarity of the presentation made them superfluous in print, as opposed to in a lecture.[22] Furthermore, I asked you when you would be able to have another look at the corrected proofs so the book can finally be published, which seems essential to me. Nothing, still nothing.

Then a small card in December for Christmas, and that was it. I know your meticulous organization—find my letters and give me instructions.

It is sad not to see you, above all in these times when courage is running out, but you have better things to do, for you and for us, than to exchange letters! Thus I don't expect anything from you, and am happy and surprised when you take the time to express your thoughts. This time, I beg you, help me to complete this business, because at the heart of it . . . I'm the one Mr. Malone and Edward blame. And yet, admit it, I am innocent. I was going to say as innocent as a newborn child, but, to be entirely honest, even more so—because in this case I have fought for and earned my salvation.

We live with and *for* your music. Because you are there, it seems to us that the road is not so dark. Or, at least at the end, there is a light that eliminates the shadows.

Have you read Saint-Exupéry's book?[23] It is a great book, and it influences young men in the same direction he is going himself.

My love to both of you with the most profound affection,

---

21. Further discussions of the publication of Stravinsky's *Poétique musicale* with Harvard University Press.

22. Boulanger's original French is rather convoluted in this instance; this translation is an attempt to capture her essential idea.

23. Most likely a reference to Saint-Exupéry's, *Pilote de Guerre* (*Flight to Arras*), published first serially in *The Atlantic* (trans. Lewis Galantière), January 1942. It was then published in French and English in February 1942. The novel depicted the brave actions of the French military, particularly the air force, before France surrendered to the Germans in 1940.

Your
Nadia

🐦   🐦   🐦

Stravinsky to Boulanger

BEVERLY HILLS
CALIF

MISS NADIA BOULANGER
C/O MRS FORBES
GERRYS LANDING, CA[MBRIDGE]
12–13 MAR 1942

YOUR NOVEMBER DECEMBER LETTERS NEVER RECEIVED. BECAUSE
FOR ME OTTERLY [*sic*] IMPOSSIBLE PLEASE TAKE ALL NECESSARY STEPS
TO RUSH PUBLISHING MY LECTURES HAVE ENTIRE CONFIDENCE IN
YOUR JUDGMENT THANKS WARMEST GREETINGS=

IGOR STRAVISKY.

🐦   🐦   🐦

Boulanger to Stravinsky

Gerry's Landing
Cambridge
Mass.

Mr. Igor Strawinsky
1260 North Wetherly Drive
Hollywood, California
March 16, 1942

Dear Friend,

We will never convince one another, so . . . let's agree to disagree! It has to
be said that it is a singular story that in the end appeared very simple to me,
when everything was unanswered. So, there's really nothing to understand.

Be that as it may, to save time I will take the steps that seem the most favorable to me and will get the publication of the lectures started. Therein lies the
question. Elimination of the summaries, corrections, proofs, they are all problems too minor to continue occupying your time.

No doubt they will draw up a second set of proofs, but I won't send them to you, either. Is there a way to have a score of your new work?[24]

Excuse these horrible scribbles, but I wrote all night and can no longer feel my hand, can no longer see.

This is almost better [though]—because when one isn't overwhelmed one is yet more anxious. How can I fight against this old, frustrating heart!

Kiss Vera for me, and have her give you one, too,
NB

[P.S.] Would you be *an angel* and send me a small thank you note for my student Mme Raphaël Salem who has reviewed all the proofs and annotated them.[25] It's quite the project.

❧   ❧   ❧

Stravinsky to Boulanger

1260 North Wetherly Drive
Hollywood, California

March 24, 1942

My very dear Nadia,

Here is a photo with a couple of words of thanks for Mme Rafaël [*sic*] Salem, just as you asked.[26]

I am really embarrassed: it's not just you who are my victim—I must bother your students again, too! May they forgive me generously for this.

The two letters of which you speak (the one from Nov. 15 from Washington and the one from Dec. 9 from Providence) never reached me. Whose fault, ours (wrong address) or the post office's? God knows. It is most unfortunate!

---

24. Boulanger's only copy of the *Danses concertantes*, the work referenced here, was given to her on September 20, 1944, by Igor Stravinsky. *Danses concertantes* (New York: Associated Music Publishers, 1944), F-Pn, Vma. 4001.

25. I can find no other reference to Raphaël Salem in Boulanger's correspondence or archival materials.

26. Stravinsky recorded on his copy of this letter: "Responded on March 24, [19]42 with my deepest thanks for Mme Rafaël [*sic*] Salem" ("Repondu [*sic*] le 24 mars/42 avec mes profond [*sic*] remerciements pour Mme Rafaël [*sic*] Salem."), CH-Bps. Also attached to this document in the archives is an envelope addressed by Boulanger to a Mrs. A Raphaël Salem (April 10, 1942). The envelope was posted with a 2-cent stamp that includes the text "Army and Navy, for Defense," and an image of a Scott 900 anti-aircraft gun pointing skyward.

As for the $60 Litré[*sic*]—it's too much money at this moment, though I don't find this to be an exaggerated price.

Wait a bit for an orch. score of my new composition *Danses concertantes* (are you satisfied with the title?): I need it here (radio project) and also eventually for the editor of the Associated Music Publishers. The score is very carefully corrected. The performance gave me great joy.*

I want so much to see you.

With all my heart,
Your
I. Str.

*I've had five rehearsals with excellent musicians.

❧   ❧   ❧

Boulanger to Stravinsky

Gerry's Landing
Cambridge
Massachusetts
Trowbridge 7339
Studio
197 Coolidge Hill

Monsieur I. Strawinsky
1260 North Wetherly Drive
Hollywood
California
For June 18, 1942

Dear Friend,

Once again we will be separated on the 18th—and at this time, all separation is doubly cruel, because we must at all costs gather together at every opportunity. I will be in Sinsinawa, at the Convent, and a Mass will be said for you. If only wishes could mean as much.

I could send you a volume—I have so many things to talk to you about again—but I leave the day after tomorrow. I have to move everything because the Forbeses cannot keep me, and . . . this is not the moment for effusions. If you could see what has happened to what used to be a room!!

With deepest affection to Vera and you, I am once again

Your
Nadia B.

[P.S.] Would you and Vera be so kind as to autograph these two photos, because I need you both so much, and send them back to: St. Clara's Convent, Sinsinawa, Wisconsin.

Are you going to Tanglewood???[27] Are you coming to [Lake] Tahoe???[28]

❧   ❧   ❧

Boulanger to Stravinsky

Glenbrook Lake Tahoe
Nevada
Glenbrook, Lake Tahoe, Nevada

Monsieur I. Strawinsky
1260 North Wetherly Drive
Hollywood California
August 22, 1942

Dear Friend,

To see you when one is at the height of exhaustion seems a folly and a crime! But now that you are not coming—and that I risk not seeing you for many months, I am very simply, but deeply, sad.

I am going to try to spend a few days in Santa Barbara before going back to Boston, but . . . will this be possible?

Truly, except for financially, it was a marvelous thing to be sick last year!!

Hugs to both of you, I am with all my heart

Your
Nadia B

❧   ❧   ❧

---

27. Tanglewood, Massachusetts is a summer performance space for the Boston Symphony Orchestra in Lennox, Massachusetts. For a history, see Pincus, *Scenes from Tanglewood.*

28. Lake Tahoe, Nevada, referenced in the following letters, was where the Bliss family had a vacation home.

Stravinsky to Boulanger

1260 North Wetherly Drive
Hollywood, California

August 25, 1942

My dear Nadia,

Do whatever you can to come to Santa Barbara since for me, unfortunately—there is no chance I will be able to go to Glenbrook.*

Your note greatly touched and encouraged me in the hopes of seeing you again soon. I am sure that if you are going "*to try* to spend a couple of days in Santa Barbara" you will come here and we will see you.

Hoping to see you soon.

With great affection,
Your
I Str.

*I must stay here to make some important decisions.

ঌ   ঌ   ঌ

Boulanger to Igor and Vera Stravinsky

122 Bay State Road
Boston

Del Monte Lodge
Pebble Beach, California
Ashton Stanley, Manager
September 29, 1942

Here we are, in view of Boston, and the train is bouncing along enthusiastically. That does not mean all that much to you. But I know how these coming days will be, and I must, my dear Igor and Vera, tell you what the visit to your place this Thursday meant. It was so nice for me, did me much good, and I thank you with all my heart. [This note is] not very interesting, but I would not have peace of mind without telling you. You are so *good* and I love you dearly.[29]

---

29. Boulanger sent a telegram on September 26 as well, thanking the Stravinskys for their hospitality that "Thursday morning." Boulanger to Stravinsky, September 26, 1942, CH-Bps.

Your
NB

❧   ❧   ❧

Boulanger to Stravinsky

122 Bay State Road
Boston, Massachusetts
Kenmore 7277

Mr I. Strawinsky
1260 North Wetherly Drive
Hollywood
California
November 28, 1942

Dear Friend,

I'm ashamed by my long silence—it is not my fault, please believe me. Work is crazy, [I am] extremely stressed about whether a glimmer of hope has appeared.[30] The terrible sacrifices, the endless suffering, demanding superhuman courage to have been submitted to the worst moral torture for two years, [torture that] grips the heart and no longer allows freedom of thought. I know, one must trust in God, and I bow my head without a whisper, but how can I not fearfully think about what awaits those whom we love. How I pity you—because the silence that walls them in leaves us only room to worry.

You will tell me "it's far too easy to worry," but—we know well that our hearts tremble if they hope and withdraw to pray more fervently. Oh, how I miss Vera and you. Your presence is such a necessity for the heart and mind. But, unfortunately, California is far.

Saint-Exupéry has been a great comfort. He is so strong, so good, but he leaves any day now to join Giraud, and now, having found peace for himself, he will finally have the opportunity to act.[31]

Excuse me for not having corrected the *Sonata* still. If you knew my life, you would understand.[32] I will get to it, *I promise you*, after the 20th.

---

30. The Allies had some notable victories by November 1942, including the defeat of the German army's attack on Stalingrad on November 22 and further successful campaigns in northern Africa. See Williams, *A World at Arms*, 264–310
31. Henri Giraud, a French general fighting in the North-African arena.
32. Boulanger is either referencing Stravinsky's solo sonata of 1924 or his *Sérénade* of 1926. He had not begun to compose his *Sonata for Two Pianos* at this time. The only annotations included in Boulanger's copy of the Sonate concern the insertion of changes indicated by the score's accompanying errata sheet: Igor Stravinsky, Sonate (Paris: Éditions Russes de Musique, 1924). F-LYc, M. 111.01

Another thing, *very pressing*, the Lili Boulanger fund has a prize of $500 to distribute. The young Alexï [*sic*] Haïeff has written a *very good* symphony in the right direction.[33] Will you trust me and vote for him? You will be doing him a great service, which he deserves for his talent, his work, his seriousness—and his solitude. He lives only to write, and to earn a living, gives lessons, and he is not one of those who knows how to overdo things.

I would not allow myself to ask you this if I did not know for *sure* you would be in agreement if you saw the symphony.

It is—almost morning, and I can no longer find my words. With fondness, I am wholeheartedly,

Your
Nadia B

ﾞﾞ   ﾞﾞ   ﾞﾞ

Stravinsky to Boulanger

1260 Wetherly Drive
Hollywood, California

Mademoiselle Nadia Boulanger
122 Bay State Road
Boston, Mass.
December 3, 1942

Just this signature that you asked of me, dear Nadia, and which I give to Haïeff with joy.

But are you sure that I am a member of Lili Boulanger's Memorial Fund [*sic*]? I *most wholeheartedly don't object*, but since when?

Forgive me for not having written you more—impossible right now, and I send you all my faithful affection.

Yours
I Str.

ﾞﾞ   ﾞﾞ   ﾞﾞ

STR P. Her copy of the *Sérénade* contains performance markings throughout. Stravinsky, *Sérénade en la en quatre mouvements* (Éditions Russes de Musique, 1926), F-LYc, UFNB M 111 STR.

33. In March 1939 Boulanger established the Lili Boulanger Memorial Fund as a means of promoting her sister's music and memory. It was intended to assist young, promising composers in their studies. Stravinsky was sent his last voting ballot in 1970; see Letter, Boulanger to Stravinsky, February 8, 1970, CH-Bps.

Boulanger to Stravinsky

122 Bay State Road
Boston, Massachusetts
Kenmore 7277

December 14, 1942

Dear Igor,

Finally—a promise kept—I am sending you your *Pater* and *Credo* in the same package! Sorry about the *Sonata*, it is not really my fault, but I hope [to send it] next week. Thank you for Haïeff. Yes, you are a part of the Fund. I asked you when you were still living in Paris, in 1936, I think.

Give my best to Vera, and know both of you that I am there where you are, with all my heart. My God, what I would not give to see you again,

Yours,
Nadia B

1943

Boulanger to Stravinsky

January 3, 1943

[Postcard inscription:
Art is born of constraint, lives of struggle, dies of liberty. André Gide][34]

You cannot know the pleasure that you brought me, Dear Igor, and . . . what a lesson in this score![35]

Koussev[itzky] is putting on *Oedipus* and "is thinking" about doing it on the same day as the Symphony—we are so delighted, but . . . you will not see it!

Many warm wishes, and with very deep affection. A kiss for both of you,

Nadia B

---

34. Boulanger taped this quote over the card's original text, two stanzas of Victor Hugo's *Patria* ("C'est l'ange du jour.") Boulanger wrote of her addition: "This to hide V[ictor] H[ugo]." ("Ceci pour cacher V.H.")

35. A gesture of thanks for Stravinsky's Christmas gift to her that year: a copy of the autographed score (printer's fair copy) of his *Circus Polka*. "Circus Polka," autograph, F-Pn, Vmb 4452. Inside annotation: "For you, dear Nadia, this little Christmas present, 1942" (Pour vous, chère Nadia, ce petit cadeau de Noël, 1942.)

❧   ❧   ❧

Boulanger to Stravinsky

122 Bay State Road
Boston, Massachusetts
Kenmore 7277

Monsieur I. Strawinsky
1260 N. Wetherly Dr.
Hollywood
California
March 16, 1943

Dear Igor,

How dear your thoughts are to me. How I miss you, you and Vera. It is so silly, we have so little time, [it is] fleeting, and we make such poor use of it! I do, at least. Undoubtedly, in facing this dreary, mundane work, one makes a living, but . . . that which we're given passes quickly, and we miss our only true opportunities by losing contact with those we love.

When will you be in NY? Can you not come as far as here? I'll doubtless see you, at least I will do my best. But I would so like for my students to speak to you, or rather, to listen to you.

I'm sending you the *Sonata* in the same package. Sorry to be so late. You couldn't imagine the dreadful, absurd life I lead. It's ridiculous, and inexcusable, but one cannot escape the system. And yet . . . one really must!

This week is my week of reflection, a good twenty-five years since my little sister died, [and] on Friday it will be eight years since Mother is no longer [with us]. I ask myself: Which is greater, the inconsolable pain of having lost them, or the enduring joy of having lived in their shadow and their light? You know, don't you, that I never forget your mother, nor Catherine, nor Mika[36]—and in my memories, they hold a very real place. I see them, and it is my consolation, this certainty of neither being able nor wanting to forget.

A thousand questions run through my mind—I would like very much to know what you have done, how you are, etc. etc. All this winter, I have lived with your work, and every day I understand better all that, though knowing it note by note, one never completely understands. What the works, *the true works*, contain is inexhaustible.

---

36. Boulanger uses both Mica and Mika throughout the correspondence. I have retained the variations here.

But excuse all these excessive and awkward words—one alone would have sufficed—*see you soon.*

You are going to receive a note from Tom Whittemore.[37] He is arriving from Turkey where he was working in [Hagia] Sophia and is a great friend of the Princesse de Polignac. I would be happy if he were able to see you. He truly hopes to, and deserves it, because he is one of those *really good* people.

Kiss Vera, and know that I am always wholeheartedly yours.
Nadia B.

[P.S.] Is there a way to have the Scherzo and the end of the symphony (orchestral [part])?

❧   ❧   ❧

Stravinsky to Boulanger

1260 Wetherly Drive
March 20, 1943

My dear

Just a word to tell you my joy at receiving your letter, so affectionate as always.

Thank you as well for sending me the *Sonata* that I was waiting so impatiently for.

We have to be in NY on March 31 (Ritz-Tower). Happy at the possibility of seeing you again soon

Your
I Str

P.S. The Scherzo and Finale of my Symphony are as difficult to obtain as the rest of the score—it is not printed—it does little good to complain, as you know.[38]

---

37. This is a rare instance of Boulanger presenting a non-student. Tom Whittemore (1871–1950) was a scholar and archeologist specializing in Byzantine art. He founded the Byzantine Institute of America and helped rebuild the Hagia Sophia mosaics in Turkey. His work was also connected to the Dumbarton Oaks Center for Byzantine Studies. See Byzantine Institute of America, *The Mosaics of St. Sophia at Istanbul* (1933 and 1950).

38. Stravinsky's original French is fairly casual/convoluted. "Le Scherzo et Final de ma *Symphonie* est tant aussi difficile de procurer que la reste de la partition—ce

❧   ❧   ❧

Boulanger to Stravinsky

122 Bay State Road
Boston, Massachusetts
Kenmore 7277

April 7, 1943

Dear Igor,
    I'll be in N.Y. *Friday—if possible,* keep your evening free for me. I do so need
to see you.
    Phone in the morning between 10 and noon Pl. 3 1880.

Warm wishes for you both,
NB

[P.S.] Useless to apologize for this frightful haste.

❧   ❧   ❧

Boulanger to Stravinsky

122 Bay State Road
Boston, Massachusetts
Kenmore 7277

Monsieur I. Strawinsky
Ritz Tower Hotel
New York City
April 26, 1943

Dear Friend,
    I will be there on the 9th, for sure. Could you arrange it so that we have
seats together (Marcelle, Haïeff, my godchild and his fiancée) Vera and me?[39]
In other words, *I will take* five seats next to Vera. It will be so good to meet up
for such an occasion. Would Vera truly take care of it *for me?* The *Concerto* went

---

n'est pas gravé—c'est très mal protesté, comme vous le savez."
39. Guests listed here are: Marcelle de Manziarly (1899–1989), one of Boulanger's
     first pupils and also a friend of Stravinsky's, and Alexei Haïeff, a former
     Boulanger student and also the person Boulanger tasked with correcting
     the Symphony in C. It is unclear who Boulanger means by "godchild and his
     fiancée."

well, and seems clearer, more beautiful to me after this new work.[40] The musicians were all happy to work with such *diligent* care. It is so good to see them understand it and to find therein a calm and dignity too often forgotten.

How I wish I were able to tell you all that I *know*—but I express myself so poorly—and besides, your music does not need us to "speak" about it, thank Heaven.

I am sending you a program. I believe you would have loved the whole thing, and this is a source of courage for me, to have lived in your shadow, [and] by your truth.

My love to both of you, with much tender affection,
N

[P.S.] On this Easter Day, I am close to you both.

❧   ❧   ❧

Stravinsky to Boulanger

1260 North Wetherly Drive
Hollywood, California

May 18, 1943

My very dear Nadia,
    In the next few days you'll receive the photostats (negatives and positives) of the orchestral parts for *Oedipe* and *Apollo*, as agreed, from the Economy Blue Print Co.[41] They'll send you this music C.O.D.—in other words, paid on delivery. Despite the exceptionally low price (25¢ per page of *Oedipe* and 16¢ for *Apollo**) the total sum is considerable given that all [the pages] appear twice (positive and negative). Let's hope this enormous expense doesn't turn you away from my music for a while. Word of honor—I had nothing to do with it, it was you who wanted this.

---

40. Reference is to a performance of the *Dumbarton Oaks Concerto* as part of a War Savings Concert at the Sanders Theatre, Cambridge, Massachusetts, on April 22, 1943. For a copy of the program, see Boulanger, "Programmes," F-Pn, Rés Vm Dos. 195 (718). Boulanger sent a copy of the program to Stravinsky. According to her thank-you letter, it was Stravinsky's idea that she conduct the work on the concert. Boulanger to Stravinsky, n.d. [ca. April 22, 1943], CH-Bps.

41. Boulanger's archives still hold both photostat scores of the autograph orchestral material: *Apollon-Musagète*, F-Pn, Vmb 5461 and *Oedipus Rex*, F-Pn, Vma 4006.

A hot wind is blowing from the desert—after forty days in New York with its spring showers, this makes one meditate on the imperfections of human physiology, and it is difficult to get back to work.

How happy I was to see you again and to know you were in the room when I was conducting *Apollo*. I'm in the process of rehearsing the *Dumbarton Oaks Concerto* for the First Congregational Church of Los Angeles' Modern Music concert. Today we are missing the two horns and a contrabass, tomorrow probably others and the concert is May 22—how nice!

Merritt wrote me a very kind letter regarding my concert at the Fogg Museum.[42] Have you had any news?

Love and kisses,
I Stravinsky

*Approximately

﹖   ﹖   ﹖

Boulanger to Stravinsky

122 Bay State Road
Boston (15), Mass.
Tel. Kenmore 7277

Monsieur Igor Strawinsky
1260 North Wetherly Drive
Hollywood, California
June 18, 1943

Dear Friend,

Everything has arrived, has been bound, and I am delighted. Sad to be incoherent—you should receive a very nice letter regarding these two scores. But you know, without my proving it in words. I understand them, I believe, and I love them as much as I am able to love and admire [anything].

Only . . . one complaint, are pages 58 and 59 of *Oedipus* supposed to be hidden from me? *They are missing*, negative as well as positive. Would you please go to the trouble of having them printed and sent to me: N.B., c/o Dominican Sisters *Edgewood Madison* Wisc.?[43]

---

42. A. Tillman Merritt, chairman of the Music Department at Harvard from 1942 to 1952 and then from 1968 to 1972. Ramey, *Irving Fine*, 64. The Fogg Museum is the principal art museum on the Harvard University campus.

43. On June 23, 1943, Igor Stravinsky sent a telegram to the Economy Blue Point and Supply Company, Los Angeles, requesting that Boulanger be sent the two

Today is your birthday. I have just sent you a sad little telegram. You should receive a "pretty" letter with flowers all around. But, I send fondest thoughts, and I know that you know how much I love you.

To you, to Vera, with all my heart,
NB

❧   ❧   ❧

Stravinsky to Boulanger

1260 Wetherly Drive
Hollywood, California
June 19, 1943

My dear,
    So happy for your telegram—sending most affectionate thoughts,

Your
I. Str

[P.S.] Were you satisfied with the photostats? It was a real extravagance, this expense—forget about it if possible.
[P.P.S.] And Birti? Has he finally taken his course in Baltimore? I received a kind note from Reginald Stewart thanking me for my letter and telling me he was going to see Birti—a month ago.[44]
[P.P.P.S.] I am sending you this clipping—if it can reassure you.[45]

---

missing pages 58 and 59 in negative and positive in the same size as before, and to return to him the original score, CH-Bps.

44. Reginald Stewart, pianist and music director of the Baltimore Symphony Orchestra from 1942 to 1952.

45. There are three clippings connected to this portion of the correspondence. One from the *Los Angeles Times* about the Peabody Opera Company that also mentions Boulanger, the "internationally known music scholar," as a new professor of interpretive analysis at Peabody Conservatory. (Most likely the "letter" referenced in the June 29, 1943, letter). The second article, from no known source, announced that Southern Californians could now send food packages to France. Each package cost $2.50 Canadian and the shipments were sent via Montreal. The third article, Rudolph Elie Jr., "Music" *Symphony Concert*, was a review of a January 15 concert of Stravinsky's music with the Boston Symphony Orchestra. It was an unfavorable review. "Two hours of Stravinsky . . . is the apotheosis of rhythmic frustration . . . it is to be questioned if any person in

❧   ❧   ❧

Stravinsky to Boulanger

1260 North Wetherly Drive
Hollywood, California

June 29, 1943

Dear Nadia,

A few days ago I read this letter in the *Los Angeles Times.*

Have you received the photostats (negative and positive) of pages 58 and 59 of *Oedipus* that you were missing? The Blue Print should have sent them to you 5–6 days ago. Very upset at this oversight.

Sincere affections,[46]
I Str.

❧   ❧   ❧

Boulanger to Stravinsky

Dominican Sisters Convent
Edgewood College
1000 Edgewood Avenue
Madison, Wisconsin

Monsieur I. Strawinsky
1260 North Wetherly Drive
Hollywood 46
California
July 3, 1943

Dear Friend,

Received the letter, the pages from *Oedipus*, the newspaper clipping—*thank you.* Will arrive *August 5* at 11:43 on the "Chief," truly hoping we will have lunch together.[47] I miss you greatly. In the peace of this convent, in the midst of these women whose conviction makes them smile, close to Sister Edward, I forget a little what makes everything more and more intolerable: false values,

---

the auditorium . . . came away with any feeling whatever of fulfillment." F-Pn, N.L.a. 108 (160–2).

46. An example of Stravinsky playing with expressions in writing "Tendresses Affections." "Tendres affections" is the typical construction here.

47. The "Chief" was a passenger train that connected Chicago with Los Angeles.

false ambitions, false ideas. What can I say: the lack of values, the absence of ideas, and satisfaction with this emptiness, not too foolish, not too sad.[48]

Even here, where we are not as isolated as we were in Sinsinawa, the air still carries with it a dust that nothing can stop.

But it is enough to go back into the Chapel, to pick up once again one of the books that remain a mainstay, then reread one of your works, to say to one's self that after everything, this *alone* shall remain of our miserable time, deserves to endure, and will overcome our errors, our blindness, our weaknesses.

I am so happy you are there, and what luck that the Sachses are staying in Santa Barbara! I hope that you will come often. I need you greatly.

All my affection for Vera and for you,
Much love,
Nadia

[P.S.] Sister Edward sends you her thoughts. She prays for you every day.

❧   ❧   ❧

Boulanger to Stravinsky

Featherhill Ranch
Montecito
Santa Barbara, California

Monsieur I. Strawinsky
December 12, 1943

Dear Igor
    1) Sister Edward Blackwell Edgewood College, Madison Road
    2) have written to Neff[*sic*][49]
    3) have written to Olga[50]

---

48. Boulanger contradicts herself oddly in this prose. Most likely she miswrote the text, though the translation here is exact out of respect for the original.

49. John Nef, Professor of Economics at the University of Chicago and chairman of the Moody Foundation Lecture Committee, requested that Stravinsky present his lectures in English. Boulanger's archives show Nef corresponded with her from 1942 to 1979, F-Pn, N.L.a. 91 (6–75). She spells his name incorrectly twice in this letter. For more on John Nef, see Walsh, *Second Exile*, 151.

50. Possibly Olga Sallard, a friend of Vera's living in Europe, who passed on information and money from Stravinsky (and it would appear also from Boulanger) to Soulima, Théodore, and Milène Stravinsky. Walsh, *Second Exile*, 119. There is no record of letters from Sallard to Boulanger in the Boulanger archives.

4) Here are three ex. from the lecture in English[51]

5) To type them in French, she asks 8 to 10 dollars. She must do it by the hour, because she types slowly in French. What do you think? I will keep the French in the meantime.

6) Will pass all the arrangements on to you, arrival and departure times for Madison.

7) Would you like me to keep the third copy of the lecture? I will send it to you immediately if you'd prefer to have it. You can give it to me on your way back, as always, if it suits you.

8) Here is the telegram from Neff[*sic*]

9) Have nothing from Sister E. on the matter. I told her that you agreed to come for a fee of $250 plus expenses. Of course, she simply told me that would be fine.[52]

I hope I haven't forgotten anything. I send you my heartfelt affection and am sad not to see you before Christmas, but . . . I am always with you,

Nadia

❧   ❧   ❧

Boulanger to Vera Stravinsky

Featherhill Ranch
Montecito
Santa Barbara, California

December 22, 1943

Dear Vera,
    First, business:
    1) Do you want to give this package here to Elizabeth?[53]
    2) Do you want to give to the Bolms . . .?[54]

---

51. Reference to the adaptation of his *Poétique musicale* for a lecture he gave in Chicago and later at the convent in Sinsinawa, Wisconsin. Walsh, *Second Exile*, 151.

52. Stravinsky participated in a lecture recital at the Santa Clara Convent, tacking it on to the end of a tour that also brought him to the University of Chicago at the end of January 1944. Walsh, *Second Exile*, 154; 170.

53. An uncommon name among Boulanger's correspondents. Only three Elizabeths date from the time of this letter: Elizabeth Ames, Élisabeth Chavchavadze (née Breteuil), and Elizabeth Park. None of these names appears in the Stravinsky literature.

54. Adolph and Beata Bolm. Adolph Bolm (1884–1951) was a Russian-born ballet dancer who came to America with the Diaghilev Ballet in 1916 and 1917. In America, he worked with the New York Metropolitan Opera House, the Chicago

3) Here is the photo—I couldn't find a frame here, or, [they were] too "beautiful." In my opinion, that would hardly suit [it].

4) I'll send you the exact itinerary for Madison–Chicago.

5) The Hogarth—if you don't like it, please tell me. I will take it back. I'm not sure anymore whether I'd like to give it to you or not.

6) I couldn't find what I wanted for you. I still hope to before your departure. If gloves, what size?

Do you prefer a scarf, white or pink? Handkerchiefs?

What do I want . . . who knows anymore?

7) Thank you for the pencils, I look forward to [using] each in order.

8) Don't forget you're dining at Mrs. Smith's on the 11th. Her sister is Miss Johnstone—Boston, 122 Bay State Road.[55]

I'll write to you—fondly—I think of you all the time. May Christmas be kind to you.

With all my heart,
[unsigned]

1944

Boulanger to the Stravinskys

Featherhill Ranch
Montecito
Santa Barbara, California

Mr and Mrs I. Strawinsky
1260 N Wetherly Drive
Hollywood
Cal
January 15, 1944
My Dears,

We are awaiting the concert with impatience—oh, what this week will have been for you: the rehearsals. Have you heard any news about Koussev[itsky's]'s project? All of us would finally like to know—we miss you a lot.

Civic Opera, and then the San Francisco Opera, founding its ballet school. Bolm choreographed the first production of *Apollon Musagète* in 1928. See Walsh, *Second Exile*, 116–17; and Debra Craine and Judith Mackrell, "Bolm, Adolph," in *The Oxford Dictionary of Dance* (New York: Oxford University Press, 2010).

55. Winnifred Hope Johnstone, administrative assistant for the Lili Boulanger Memorial Fund. Spycket, *Nadia Boulanger*, 98; and Rosenstiel, *Nadia Boulanger*, 276. Her sister's full name was Ann Smith.

I hope that all is in order for Madison.[56] You will find your tickets to Chicago. I also wrote to the University [asking] for the cheque, saying you are a resident.

Fond and heartfelt wishes to both of you,
NB

&   &   &

Boulanger et al. to Stravinsky

SANTA BARBARA, CALIFORNIA

IGOR STRAWINSKY
HOTEL HEMENWAY BOSTON MASS
JANUARY 15, 1944

HAD MOST WONDERFUL HOUR PERFECT TRANSMISSION EVERY DETAIL SO CLEAR MADE US FEEL ABSOLUTELY WITH YOU ALL DEEPLY THANKFUL SO ANXIOUSLY AWAITING YOUR RETURN LOVE

NADIA DIANE GEORGE BERMAN LEFEVRE[57]

&   &   &

---

56. Santa Clara Convent-University of Chicago tour. Walsh, *Second Exile*, 154; 170. See also n. 52.

57. Diane; George(ette Sachs); (Eugene) Berman; Lefevre. Eugene Berman was a Russian-emigré painter and designer (1899–1972). He, too, fled Russia for Paris after the Revolution and relocated to Los Angeles in 1940. After moving to America, Berman became known for his stage designs for ballet and opera. Boulanger may have met Berman when the artist approached Stravinsky about the possibility of designing a balletic version of *Danses concertantes* in the summer of 1944. See Walsh, *Second Exile*, 160; and Edwin Denby, "Balanchine's 'Danses Concertantes,'" *New York Herald Tribune*, September 17, 1944. There is no reference to anyone by the last name of Lefevre or Lefebvre in the list of Boulanger's correspondents. Diane is also a difficult figure to pinpoint. It is likely that the radio transmission referenced here was a broadcast of one of three concerts held at the Sanders Theater in Cambridge, Massachusetts January 13–15. The program included concert premieres of the *Circus Polka*, *Four Norwegian Moods*, and the East Coast premiere of Stravinsky's arrangement of "The Star-Spangled Banner," alongside performances of his Symphony in C and *Jeu de cartes*. Walsh, *Second Exile*, 152.

Boulanger to Stravinsky

SANTABARBARA CALIF
MR AND MRS IGOR STRAWINSKY=
25 JAN 1944

JUST NOW REALIZED YOU ARE ON THE SAME TRAIN AS ARTHUR
THRILLED AT YOUR RETURN CAN HARDLY WAIT LOVE

GEORGE AND NADIA.

ꙮ   ꙮ   ꙮ

Boulanger to Stravinsky

Featherhill Ranch
Montecito
Santa Barbara, California

Mr. I. Strawinsky
1260 Wetherly Drive
Hollywood 46
California
January 26, 1944

Only a small hello, so happy that you are finally coming back. We [tried] in vain not to show it, [but] to feel you so close changes everything.

If you realize what you have given to so many people, you ought to return [a happy man]. The letters [we've] received and the news from the orchestra do [us] good. [There is] an enthusiasm that [makes] those keenly [want] to thank you but dare not. [It has been] an event in Bostonian life. This must seem typical, obvious, but . . . and we are so happy to see that despite everything, you are good for them, for *many*, as you are in life.[58]

We feel better since your visit—and we once again want to fight on.

Give Vera a kiss, may she give you a kiss for me, too, and may you both know the deep tenderness I feel toward you,

Nadia B.

---

58. This letter contains very abrupt, and in some places incomplete, French. I have taken some liberties with the translation to smooth out the syntax.

[P.S.] Still no news from Chicago, nor from Madison except a telegram over-
flowing with joy.[59]

❧   ❧   ❧

Stravinsky to Boulanger

                                                                    Hollywood
February 28, 1944

My dear Nadia,

As promised, I am sending you a package with four copies of my *Sonata*.
One of these copies is intended for you "with compliments of the author,"
which is to say in French, "à l'œil" (for free).[60] As for the other three, which
are not for you, nothing can be done—we have to pay for them and the cost is
$7.86. Here's a good opportunity to finally settle up my debt of $4.50 (I believe
that's it—for the copies of the lecture) that you have been stubbornly refusing.
Yes, $7.86 minus $4.50 makes $3.36, a sum that you unquestioningly owe me.

To entertain you, [here is] a letter that'll amuse you.

Love Kisses,
I Str.

❧   ❧   ❧

---

59. Boulanger awaited news from Chicago about Stravinsky's lecture, "Composing,
     Performing, Listening," the hour-long digest of his *Poétique* that Boulanger had
     helped him construct, as well as a concert he gave on January 21 with Remi
     Gassman of the *Duo concertant* and *L'histoire du soldat*, put on at the University
     of Chicago. From Madison, she awaited reviews of his concert on January 23,
     where he repeated his concert from two days earlier. Walsh, *Second Exile*, 153–4.

60. Reference to copies of "her sonata," the *Sonata for Two Pianos*, that Stravinsky
     had finished on February 11. The *Sonate pour deux pianos* is the first piece
     Stravinsky wrote for Boulanger. Her copy of the autograph, complete with
     many corrections, is held in the Lyon archives. Stravinsky, "Sonate pour deux
     pianos," ph. a., ca. 1944, F-LYc, M 111.02 STRAV S. Fingerings and expressive
     markings are indicated throughout.

Boulanger to Stravinsky

> Featherhill Ranch
> Montecito

Santa Barbara, California
March 1, 1944

What happiness, Dear Igor, to have the *Sonata* soon. Here is $15.00,[61] because
. . . $3.00 is not enough!

With all my affection for both of you,
Nadia B.

❧ ❧ ❧

Boulanger to Stravinsky

> Featherhill Ranch
> Montecito
> Santa Barbara

For March 3, 1944

Dear Friend,
    May I place some flowers in front of Catherine's portrait? When I received
here the telegram announcing that she had finished suffering, I knew that I
would never console myself at having lost her—or at least [at having] to finish
the voyage without her.[62]

In her memory, wholeheartedly fond wishes to you,
Nadia

❧ ❧ ❧

---

61. In 1944 $15 would equal approximately $200 today.
62. This is another instance where Boulanger's French is missing essential por-
    tions of the syntax. In this sentence, she omits the negative participles. I have
    taken some liberties with this translation to reflect the spirit of the text.

Boulanger to Stravinsky

Featherhill Ranch
Montecito

Santa Barbara, California
March 4, 1944

Dear Igor,

What Happiness to have the *Sonata*—how I love it, how balanced it is and how *correct* it is.

I cannot write to you, *nor write* about your music, because crushing humility overwhelms me and my ridiculous attempt, but I know with unmistakable certainty that I love and understand it as it *must be*, as it is. What pretension! I know . . . but this is the pretension I have, and every day I thank God for having given me the dignity to measure my weakness, and furthermore the privilege to know *what it is*.

THANK YOU

This is a "flippant" letter from a certain point of view, and absurd. This comes from being taught to question and abolish all distance and to assume all liberties. But it's a child who's writing it, and undoubtedly there is more [to this] than it seems, but . . . poor little one! And a few stamps to settle the debt. Having stolen $4.36 of the $7.50 from you, I therefore steal from you $0.72 from $15.00, and so as to not alert the police, here is what will spare me further complications.[63]

With heartfelt affection,
Nadia B

ॐ   ॐ   ॐ

---

63. In addition to this exchange about money, in another letter from April 30, 1944, Boulanger wrote to reconcile a debt to Vera and Igor Stravinsky (I. F. Igor Fyodorovich) of $43.52. Boulanger does not state in the letter what the money was for, although this is a substantial sum. This is also the only time in the correspondence that I have found Boulanger referring to Stravinsky as "I. F."

Stravinsky to Boulanger

Hollywood

March 18, 1944

My dear Nadia,

I don't have a memory for dates but it seems to me that it was in March 1935 that your dear mother died, nine years ago . . .

I will not forget her in my prayers. I am thinking of you and send you my fondest wishes.

Your
I Str.

[P.S.] Tomorrow is the *centenary* of my dear Rimsky Korsakov.[64]

❧   ❧   ❧

Boulanger to Stravinsky

Edgewood College
1000 Edgewood Avenue
Madison, Wisconsin

Mr. I. Strawinsky
1260 N. Wetherly Drive
Hollywood 46
California
July 2, 1944

Look what I received, Dear Igor—what do you suggest?[65]

Too occupied since my arrival here to write, but between the lecture this winter, the memories of each of your gestures, setting to rights what I said, sorting out the *Sonata*, and the *Circus Polka*, the lecture on *Babel*, on *Scherzo [à la] Russe*, on *Perséphone*, and then my heart "that beats only for you" as the song says, and it doesn't lie.[66] Truly, you are always here and present in Madison!

We live, quite tensely, somewhat somberly, with some relaxation, [illegible word] in the calm of this place.

---

64. This is one of three instances in the entire correspondence where Stravinsky writes in Russian, writing Rimsky-Korsakov in Russian characters first.

65. Reference unidentified.

66. Paul Verlaine's poem "Green" set by, among others, Claude Debussy in his 1888 song cycle, *Ariettes oubliées* (New York: International Music Co, 1951).

My best to Vera and you, my Dear—and already I say with impatience: When am I going to see you again.

Your
N

[P.S.] Abbot Fortier . . . *thrilled*.[67] But does not want to thank you before he has read—read and understood everything. He's not used to these combinations and so [he] struggles!!

❧   ❧   ❧

Boulanger to Stravinsky

Edgewood College
1000 Edgewood Avenue
Madison, Wisconsin

July 15, [1944]

Dear Igor,

Since yesterday, a struggle between despair and rage! As I had told you, I wanted to give an informal performance at Indiana University, Bloomington. And upon informing my student of this, I told him: *private* performance, insisting that he publish *nothing* before I gave him an *exact* text for the program. In his excessive joy, the idiot in fact published nothing except for the only thing that he ought not have—and announced the premiere of your *Sonata*. I just sent him a livid note that, barring a miracle, we could no longer play the *Sonata* thanks to his "disobedience"—what do you think about this? I'm upset, but, how could I have foreseen that these precautions would be inadequate. If you confirm my decision—place an (X) on the slip of attached paper following "no." If, given that it is a music school, you choose to overlook it—an (X) following "yes." But, I will understand (despite my despair), if it is rage that you choose and refuse in a fit of anger.

Am proud of my honesty, because . . . You would undoubtedly never have known of his gaffe otherwise. This is not blackmail—I am consoling myself over the fury I've felt since yesterday! So terrible!

I'll write Vera another day—first I'm going to confession!

With heartfelt affection for both of you,
NB

---

67. A priest from Montréal, Monseigneur Elzéar Fortier, corresponded with Boulanger from 1943 to 1978. F-Pn, N.L.a. 70 (273–323) and (330–44). Walsh provides some context in *The Second Exile*, 170.

ﹶ   ﹶ   ﹶ

Stravinsky to Boulanger

July 16, 1944

My dear,

Read this—Mr. Tangeman sent me these two articles with this remark: "Professor Guido Stempel is a retired professor of philology without musical training.["] The other article is from the "student paper" in which the "musical training" does not appear to me to be clear.[68]

What is the point of making this effort to receive such a reaction?

When will I see you?

Personally, I cannot yet travel.[69]

Love Kisses,
I. Str.

ﹶ   ﹶ   ﹶ

Stravinsky to Boulanger

July 18, 1944

Can we play the *Sonata?*

~~NO – NO~~

Don't worry yourself about this. There are more important things. *Of course:*
"Yes."
With fondness, my very dear Nadia

Your

---

68. Robert Tangeman (pianist) and Nell Tangeman (soprano) were both professors at the University of Chicago. Nell Tangeman would later premiere the role of Mother Goose in Stravinsky's *The Rake's Progress*. The articles sent along by Robert Tangeman included rather uncomplimentary comments about Stravinsky's music (particularly its use of "upsetting metres"). See Jean Tabbert, "Wisdom's Return to Music Cited," *The Indiana Daily*, August 9, 1944, 1 and 3; and Guido H. Stempel, "C-Sharp Minor," *The Star Courier*, August 11, 1944.

69. "Bouger" literally translates as "to move (about or around)." Stravinsky leaves it ambiguous as to whether he means he cannot travel or if his health rendered him incapable of physically moving. I have chosen the former translation here.

I Str.

❧   ❧   ❧

Boulanger to Stravinsky

Edgewood College
1000 Edgewood Avenue
Madison, Wisconsin

Monsieur I. Strawinsky
1260 North Wetherly Drive
Hollywood 46
California
July 28, 1944

How kind and good you are. Thank you with all my heart. We are working on the *Sonata* here for the Sisters and it is such a joy. We're preparing Palestrina's St. Dominic Mass, and the Mass and the *Sonata* illuminate one other—they present the same problems, fundamentally—and the material is so beautiful. Oh, how the two pianos sound . . .

No need for effusions, you know what I think better than I do!

To both of you, with all my heart,
Nadia

[P.S.] Everyone here is talking about you! Sister Edward and Sister Ignatia send many thoughts to you.

❧   ❧   ❧

Boulanger to Stravinsky

Edgewood College
1000 Edgewood Avenue
Madison, Wisconsin

Arrowhead Woods

Lake Arrowhead
California

Monsieur Igor Strawinsky
1260 N. Wetherly Drive
Hollywood 46
California
August 19, 1944

Why, Dear Igor, would you think me better able to measure their incurable stupidity? And [how deep] my remorse—because it is a dead-end argument. Each day we plunge a little deeper into this terrifying, all-too-self-satisfied mediocrity. Everyone judges everything, has the right to "express themselves," and shares their ignorance, with a simple: "Stupidity is not my strength," [as] says M. Teste.[70] Yet they haven't the faintest sense that intelligence isn't, [either]. But . . . enough, let's not talk of all that. I am alternately shocked and discouraged by the complete lack of humility that can only be explained by the "integral" materialism of these so-called intellectuals.

Without a doubt, [illegible] the present is always troubling to the mass of idiots who hide exactly what is worth being seen. While we're mentioning it, the other day, because of what these two articles represent so well and what one sees first-hand everywhere—when it seemed to us that our time has been so tremendously troubling, all of a sudden, Couture, one of my Canadian students, said: "It's true, but it's enough for me that Mr. Strawinsky's works are there for me to be happy and proud that I live today."[71]

And he is right. The *Sonata* is there. No one seems to notice it—it has already taken its place. They may vomit. They will not vomit for long. Olin

---

70. Monsieur Edmond Teste was a character meant to represent a "pure intellectual" created by Paul Valéry and later believed to be Valéry's depiction of his own alter ego. M. Teste's goal was to discover the inner workings of the human mind, especially the nature of the creative intellectual. Paul Valéry, *Monsieur Teste* (Paris: Gallimard, Editions de la Nouvelle Revue Française, 1927).

71. Jean Papineau-Couture was one of Boulanger's most famous Canadian students. He won the Lili Boulanger Memorial Fund Award in 1944. For his correspondence with Boulanger, see F-Pn, N.L.a 92 (144); (147–83) and (186–8). For Papineau-Couture's biography, see Milot, *Jean Papineau-Couture.*

Downes has been attacking J. S. Bach again—this has been going on since 1720 and J. S. doesn't find himself any worse off.[72] But the anger, the daily anger, will cost us.

*You can go directly to the (X).[73]

[P.S.] (X) Would you consent to having six copies of the *Sonata* made: two for Abbot Fortier, two for Couture, and two for Johnston who played at Madison—(and so *honestly*)—(at their expense, but you will tell me how much. I do not have the checkbook here to tell me.).

Thank you for telephoning, these are such tense days that we marvel at the heart's resilience. To be far away, tranquil on the shores of this beautiful lake, while over there . . . It has taken these four years for me to understand completely the weight of remorse. How I pray for them. But how I pray for them to pray for me! Saint-Exupéry's disappearance is a great sorrow for me.[74] From the bottom of my heart, my love to Vera and you, Dear Igor.

Nadia

❧   ❧   ❧

---

72. Possibly a reference to Olin Downes's "Walter Conducts Matthew Passion: Westminster, Pius X School Choirs." *New York Times*, April 7, 1944, 23, wherein Downes characterizes the *St. Matthew Passion* as "a very great deal of music, and not music of uniform inspiration, and more than once music in which Bach becomes enmeshed in formulas and redundancies."

73. The markings (as well as the reference to "thanks for telephoning") added to this letter suggest that the bulk of its content had been covered in a previous telephone conversation. Boulanger added a "coda" marking of sorts to the letter to indicate Stravinsky could skip to the end of the text where new, undiscussed material, could be found.

74. Saint-Exupéry disappeared on July 31, 1944, while flying a reconnaissance mission for the French Resistance in the south of France. Remains of his plane and identifying materials have since been recovered, though there is some disagreement about whether or not he was shot down. Tanase, *Saint-Exupéry*, 388–420.

Boulanger to Stravinsky

Arrowhead Woods
Lake Arrowhead
California

Mr Igor Strawinsky
1260 North Wetherly Drive
Hollywood 46
California
August 21, 1944

Dear Friend,
Here is what Abbot Fortier wrote to me:
"I am sending you two copies of Bossuet's *Elévations sur les mystères*. I probably found the last two copies in [all] Quebec.[75] I am sending you a copy of one of those; the other is mine. You will surely want to offer it to Mr. Strawinsky. It is from the same collection as the *Méditations sur l'évangile*. It is my pleasure to offer it to him, and this time, I will not deprive myself of the text, as I'll be keeping the other copy. The pleasure I felt recently listening to his *Sonata for Two Pianos*, and of course the other music I'd already heard, inspired me to respond in kind with this text that will be equally the deepest source of inspiration."
Not yet received the sent item, will expedite it as soon [as it arrives].
I told you the Abbot was struggling with the reading of *Scherzo*[76]—he was not familiar with the notation for the saxophones and does not want to thank you until he is able to read it properly . . .
Another thing:
Germain Prévost (violist Pro Arte), a *good* musician, a good man, charged me with a request for you that he does not dare ask himself.
He took part in my lectures in Madison. Sister E. gave him a small cheque of $100 as a stipend. He at first refused, then said: "I'll accept it, since I just had a vision for this money."
"Would you, he said to me, explain this story to Mr. Strawinsky, and tell him that I permit myself one truly audacious but very humble [request]. I know it's ridiculous to dare to offer him $100. I know, but I know he will understand

---

75. Jacques-Bénigne Bossuet (1627–1704) was a French theologian during the seventeenth century. Part of his duties as bishop included sermonizing for King Louis XIV. Fortier is referring here to a collection of Bossuet's religious ruminations: *Elévations sur les mystères*, written from 1694 to 1695.

76. Boulanger only owned one copy of the work's score, *Scherzo à la russe*, F-Pn, Vma 4018, though this letter shows she possessed and shared with her students earlier versions of the work.

that this is all I can part with at the moment (his wife and his daughters are in Belgium, he has a *very difficult life*, mentally, practically, because, the quartet is here . . .). Would you, if you judge that you can pass along such a request, see if he might write me a small piece dedicated to the memory of Alphonse Onnou, or to you? I am not worth the trouble.[77] I would be so happy, so proud."

He reminded me of the day when you gave them the manuscript for the *Concertino*.[78] So here you are, I have passed along his request. If you had seen his devotion to your entire body of work and his enthusiasm for the *Sonata*, you would understand why I feel obliged to share this with you.

See you soon I hope. I think of you often, and always work with renewed joy on the *Sérénade* that I will never play well, but that I want my fingers to know as well as my head does.[79]

With love for both of you.
Nadia B.

[P.S.] Today is the anniversary of my little sister's death. It is sad that you did not know her. You would have liked her.

ೞ   ೞ   ೞ

Stravinsky to Boulanger

Hollywood

August 24, 1944

My Dear,

Forgot to tell you yesterday that regarding the *Sonata* it is necessary to contact Hugo Strecker (Associated Music Publishers, Inc 25 West 45th St. NY City 19, N-4) because he is the one who has my manuscript on transparencies, thus he is the *only one* who can make the necessary print run for you.

---

77. Alphonse Onnou was the founder and original first violinist of the Pro Arte Quartet, a Belgian ensemble that toured the United States regularly under the patronage of Elizabeth Sprague Coolidge, only to be forced to remain in the country when the Second World War broke out. They served as resident musicians for the University of Wisconsin–Madison. Germain Prévost was the original violist. Robert Philip and Tully Potter, "Pro Arte Quartet," *Grove Music Online.*

78. Likely this is a reference to the first version of Stravinsky's *Concertino* for string quartet, which was finished in 1920. Boulanger's copy is of the reorchestrated version. She acquired it in Boston in 1962. F-LYc, UFNB MEp STR 402.

79. The *Sérénade en la* is an early work (1926) for solo piano. See also n. 29.

It's a rather difficult day after these twenty-four hours of worldwide madness.[80]

Fondest wishes,
Your
I Str.

☙ ☙ ☙

Boulanger to Vera Stravinsky

Featherhill Ranch
Montecito
Santa Barbara, California

Mrs. I. Strawinsky
1260 N. Wetherly Drive
Hollywood
California
November 14, 1944

Dear Vera

Just a note, to thank you for all that you do for me—with such *tenderness*. It is the only word that matches what you give to me, and to express the kindness I have experienced. You and Igor give so much of your hearts to me. I am thankful and happy.

To break up these effusions [which are] at once both fleu-fleu, fleu-fleu, fleu and very exact. Here are the accounts:

Paris City Books: $16.11
Mendelssohn's Symphony: $1.40
Mozart: $0.35
Mozart: $0.40
Total: $18.75
Moussorgsky, which I already have: $15.00
Total: $33.75

---

80. Allied troops liberated Paris from August 23–24, 1944. The previous day, King Michael of Romania also led a successful coup to overthrow the government of Romania. Romanian forces then joined the Allies and ceased fighting the Soviet Union. Moreover, on August 21, the Dumbarton Oaks Conference took place, where American, Chinese, French, and Soviet officials met to discuss what would later become the United Nations. Weinberg, *A World at Arms*, 587–665.

But it will still be Igor who has given me *Boris*, because I'm going to keep his copy and give mine away so as to keep the one he bought for me. Impossible to accept it without paying him. [But] I would be rejecting a gift that was given . . . well, *intentionally.*

Fond and heartfelt wishes to you both.
Your
NB

🙚   🙚   🙚

Boulanger to Stravinsky

Featherhill Ranch
Montecito
Santa Barbara, California
November 21, 1944

Thank you—the things to say about these pages! Dear Igor—
    But we will be together soon. Have received [word] from Haïeff, everything is his fault, and not his fault. (Winter's fault, primarily). He has been sick, at the mercy of terrible difficulties. I will bring you his letter. *Forgive him.* He needs it.[81]

With all my heart,
Nadia B.

🙚   🙚   🙚

---

81. Haïeff failed to complete the corrections for the Symphony in C as he was supposed to. See Francis, "A Most Unsuccessful Project," 258–59.

Boulanger to Stravinsky

Featherhill Ranch
Montecito
Santa Barbara, California

November 27, 1944

Dear Igor,
    Here is the letter from Beveridge—you will want it from me. Tell me if I can do something.[82]
    Naturally, the $200 is guaranteed. I told Beveridge that again.
    You know, don't you, that not being with you on Thursday is a *profound sadness*. But, [I'm] leaving Friday for nearly a week, and *I cannot* leave before because of the students. How I think of you, of Them, of the little girl alone there. You know that, too.

I love you so much,
Your
Nadia B.

[P.S.] See you Friday

1945

Boulanger to Stravinsky

Featherhill Ranch
Montecito
Santa Barbara, California

January 31, 1945

Dear Friend,
    You are always in my thoughts, I am with you hour after hour these days, in a very self-centered manner, full of regret and *envy*, ferocious envy, which it is nice to admit to.
    But I received a letter from Mrs. Bliss, who awaits an urgent response. This concert is a very high priority for her. Sam has requested a fee of $300, she

---

82. For Boulanger's correspondence with Beveridge Webster, see F-Pn, N.L.a. 116 (4–15).

believes the orchestra will cost $750. Personally, I say $1000. You should have $1000, and it would give her great joy [to do so].[83]

I cannot go anymore, *truly*, but hope with *all my heart* that you will accept. In my opinion (and if you don't say I'm getting on your nerves by expressing it) *you must.*

Arrange things with her. I have written her, sending my regrets, which are much greater than either you or she can imagine. (There are no seats available to reserve for the trip anyway.)[84] Give her some hope: she knows all too well that you *want* to do what she wishes, in a state of profound attachment to you and your work. May God grant that the concerts in NY bring you all that I hope for and expect of them musically. Because critics who are understanding . . . that is another thing. Playing the role of Mother is going better for me than expected, and I am happy. But [I am] sad not to be with you. To Vera and to you,

With love,
NB

❧   ❧   ❧

Boulanger to Stravinsky

February 1945
[Never sent]

Dear Igor,

I have not yet written to you, because . . . I was absorbed by my new position, because I exaggerate, unfortunately, everything that I do—and also, and perhaps especially, because I do not know how to write to you. If I *could* tell you what this concert meant, I would be proud with a peaceful yet arrogant pride. But while we listened to this music where I know every note by heart, but where each note, each time, becomes new—I knew already that I wouldn't write you, because my mind and my ears, my heart and my hand were truly incapable of finding the right words. And I thanked you, just as I thank you today, for these works that year after year bring us the joy of which Bergson spoke: "Crazy, it is completely crazy . . . I understand you here."—"And this lyricism, too many

---

83. It is unclear to which concert Boulanger is referring here. There is no mention of a Bliss concert or a concert with Samuel Dushkin elsewhere in the literature until April 1947. Walsh, *Second Exile*, 201.

84. Transport was limited almost exclusively to military personnel at this time.

instruments, too many notes, too many rich harmonies."[85] And so, it's because I share your opinion that . . . from time to time I succeed.

Wednesday—only the Abbot heard vague, far-away notes [quotes nonsensical excerpt, likely from *Apollo*]. We didn't even hear that and missed *Apollon*. On the 4th everything was so clear. And if you could have seen us Saturday, going over once again step by step all the scores with such impatience, and the next day, the surprise of finding them again, of "replacing" each note, we were ecstatic with this order, this evidence, this freshness. Then . . . on Sunday. We ought to know, and me more than anyone. But no—everything is again unexpected, again exhilarating—and the thought that everything is *inevitable*—but always "discovered," as if never heard before.

When you are here again, with the scores in hand, I would so love to walk the path again with you—these admirable *Scènes de ballet*—so necessary.[86] And . . . so simple—all that one ever has to do is just look—there is but one man in millions who finds it—and not many in a hundred who understand what they have found. What solitude. Without a doubt, provided by God to protect you from other horrors and from yourself. In this austere solitude, no comfort, no intrusion, no distractions—what [a] severe treatment.

Back to Paris

Boulanger to Stravinsky

Featherhill Ranch
Montecito
Santa Barbara, California

March 21, 1945

Dear Friend,
   Would you please sign this and send it back to me straight away? I trust that you will agree.[87]

---

85. Henri-Louis Bergson (1859–1941), a French intellectual famous for his description of time. For Boulanger's engagement with Bergson, see Brooks, *Musical*, 60–62 and 197–98.

86. *Scènes de ballet* was the piece Stravinsky was working on while also listening to reports of the Allied forces liberating the French capital. On the final page of the autograph score he wrote: "France is no longer in the hands of the Germans." "France n'est plus aux Allemands," Walsh, *Second Exile*, 161; See also Craft and Stravinsky, *Dialogues and a Diary*, 50. Stravinsky gave the autograph sketches for the "Étoile, Adantino" movement to Boulanger. Stravinsky, "Scènes de Ballet," a. (excerpt), F-Pn, Ms. 17942.

87. Reference to that year's ballot for the Lili Boulanger Memorial Fund Award.

1) Arthur[88] is the one who gave the sum so that Couture can work here.

2) This is the bursary awarded last year (you had already signed).

3) Bursary to be shared between these two young Poles with real talent (they have written good quartets, symphonies) [and] are *dying* of hunger in France.[89]

4) *Preger?* I did not recommend him to you.

I have received many letters from France. It is a tragic situation. Annette works at the Conservatoire—thirty and more than thirty at my place.[90] They are all hungry, and [have] nothing to wear, money is less useful than supplies. I am deeply unhappy, but this is fair, punishment will come . . . we don't know when, but it surely will. Forgiven, yes, God forgives. I believe it very strongly, but if He wasn't [actually] punishing us, it [is] enough to have given us a *conscience*!

I am thinking of you and love you, both of you,

Fondly and with love to you both,
Nadia

❧   ❧   ❧

---

88. Arthur Sachs.

89. Michal Spisak (1914–65) and Antoni Szalkowski (1907–37) were both awarded the prize in 1944 and 1946. Léo Preger was a student who studied with Boulanger in the 1930s, and attended some of the classes co-taught by Boulanger and Stravinsky at the École normale de musique. For more on the experience, see Perrin, "Stravinsky in a Composition Class." See also: White, *Stravinsky*, 110. Preger won the Lili Boulanger Memorial Fund Prize in 1945.

90. Annette Dieudonné (1896–1990) was a pupil of Boulanger's beginning in 1910. After her studies, Dieudonné worked as Boulanger's assistant and grew to become a close friend. Dieudonné taught solfège courses at Fontainebleau for many years and served as executor of Boulanger's estate after Boulanger's death. Rosenstiel, 89; Spycket, *À la récherche*, 16. I am uncertain about the meaning of the numbers Boulanger has inserted here; it may be a reference to the number of pupils Dieudonné had been teaching or to the hours she was teaching a week. Certainly the "chez moi" reference implies that Dieudonné kept on teaching private pupils in Boulanger's apartment during and directly after the war.

Soulima Stravinsky to Boulanger

56, rue de Bourgognue, Paris

June 14, 1945[91]

Dear Nadia,

How can I tell you all that your very kind letter brought to us? What you wrote about yourself, my father, and Vera moved me so deeply . . . And what happiness to feel that despite this abyss of six terrifying years we still speak the same language, and we understand each other implicitly despite the distance.

It is so nice to know that you are often close to my father and Vera. In each of their letters, they speak of you to me, of their happiness to have you at their place. I know what you mean to them and what they mean to you.

I received a package from you and am embarrassed despite all the joy that I had in opening it. Embarrassed to have caused you daily chores, because I know that over there nothing is easy either. Let me express my deepest gratitude for your great kindness and for everything. And you tell me that you've sent other things as well as some letters. It is disheartening—I never received anything, at least nothing beyond this package some weeks ago from Mrs. Sachs, to whom I wrote.

You make us hope for your coming return among us. I don't dare believe, and yet Vera wrote to me again that you are leaving them for Boston and probably Paris. You will find here all those who cherish you, worship you, and await you. But I fear you will face great disappointment in seeing what all these years of horror and misery have produced: pettiness, selfishness, and meanness. As for our poor music, as for everything that we hold dear, let us not speak of that. It is chaos. It would seem that the most elementary of values has been lost.

We are involved in some distressing performances, whose echoes, perhaps, have already reached you. A "Strawinsky Quarrel" that has no other pretext than to enhance certain mediocre artists; they have trouble camouflaging their desire to take Strawinsky's place (anything but that!).[92] It is ridiculous, but the flippancy, the impudence of possible demonstrations is significant and worrisome.

---

91. Though written on June 14, the letter was not mailed until June 30.
92. On January 11, 1945, Manuel Rosenthal began a concert series with the Orchestre national dedicated to music that had been banned during the war. The concerts of Stravinsky's works, particularly the Parisian premiere of his *Four Norwegian Moods* on March 15, 1945, were met with sirens, whistles, and catcalls. Pierre Boulez and Serge Nigg were among the students responsible for the outcry, and many believed Olivier Messiaen was the instigator. Sprout, "The 1945 Stravinsky Debates," 85–131; and Sprout, *Musical Legacy*.

The monthly radio festivals should have brought us joy in hearing pretty much the entirety of his work. Unfortunately, it is nothing more than a series of shaky, tiresome, pathetic, and most often inexcusably poor performances. And to think, Mr. Rosenthal, to whom we owe all this, had the nerve to violently oppose the committee's initiative when they wanted to invite Strawinsky to conduct all these festivals himself!

You have felt, very dear Nadia, that happiness has returned to me, you understand so well what Françoise means to me, what our life is. And it is with a grateful acknowledgment that we welcome the kind, warm words you sent for our child.

I still have so many things to tell you, one letter does not suffice. Give us the pleasure of seeing you soon and being able to continue a bond that all these draining years could not break.

Françoise joins with me to tell you how deeply moved she was in reading your letter, I am most fondly, and with deepest and most devoted affection.

Your
Sviétik

❧   ❧   ❧

Stravinsky to Boulanger

1260 N. Wetherly Dr.
Hollywood, H6, Calif

Miss Nadia Boulanger
c/o Mrs. Shortell
339 Berry Ave
Chicago, Ill.
June 15, 1945

My dear
    Nothing to tell you, save that all I do is think of you and of your absence which I believe will be unbearable to me.
    Send news, please. You write so elegantly.

Yours,
I Str.

❧   ❧   ❧

Boulanger to Igor and Vera Stravinsky

Featherhill Ranch
Montecito
Santa Barbara, California

From 20–26 c/o Baroness R. Boël
1675, 31st Street
Washington, DC
Thereafter: 122 Bay State road, Boston 15 Mass.

June 17, 1945

It is not easy to leave you, dear Igor, darling Vera, and I do not know what to say, because . . . I do not want to whine.

Once again the page turns. I am reunited with very dear Friends here,[93] their welcome touches me, but . . . I will not see you again for a long time, and that disappointment occupies all my thoughts.

Thank you for everything, you do not know the good that your affection does me.

For both of you, very fondly,
Nadia B

❧   ❧   ❧

Soulima Stravinsky to Boulanger

56 rue de Bougagne, Paris
August 27–September 14, 1945

Dear Nadia,

We have recently had good news from Léo Preger. It seems we will see you this winter; I don't need to tell you how delighted I am and how great my need is to see you and to speak to you. So many things to tell you . . . and so, just the other day I received a wonderful package that I must, I think, thank *you* for, because it was sent by a certain Moreys Southern Sea Shop from Santa Barbara.[94] Thank you with all my heart, dear Nadia. I am moved to see that with all you have to do you still find the time to think of us.

---

93. On the East Coast; she had not yet returned to France.
94. See also n. 48.

Despite the end of the war it is not yet ideal here. Without being pessimistic, I fear that this winter will again be a bit harsh. We will try to be patient, but pray that it will be the last of its kind!

The Léo Preger competition was such a joy for us. He is a serious musician, modest to such an extent that his marvelous talent goes unnoticed by all those here who should be interested in helping him. I find it very beautiful and meaningful that this encouragement brought him here. Did you know that he is currently writing a piano concerto, the premiere of which he was kind enough to promise to me?

My father was able to send along some of his recent compositions. Imagine what it has been like for me to discover the *Circus Polka*, the *Scherzo à la Russe*, the extraordinary *Sonata for Two Pianos*, and finally the *Tango*, from which I have not yet recovered![95] Truly, I cannot find the words to tell you all that I [illegible], all that I find and rediscover in the works, and how much all of this impresses me. And how is it we were not reunited with you and him around these marvels? In this inestimable collection is also the *Danses concertantes*. Désormière conducted them twice this winter, I must say, impeccably so.[96] Personally, I played them innumerable times on two pianos with François Michel.[97] Remembering how they sound and feel to play, I attempted to write a version for two hands. My effort seems to me to have been rather successful. I am going to send it to my father and, with his adjustments, maybe he will have it published.

My father wrote that he had just finished a symphony and will give the premiere at the New York Philharmonic at the beginning of October. How I envy your being there to hear it. He also asked me in his last letter how the Symphony in C was received. Unfortunately, the performance of it was so flawed one couldn't really hold it against the audience for, on the whole, having understood nothing. For my part, I had to attempt a veritable reconstruction of the piece upon hearing it along with what I could guess, because it truly did not even remotely come through. But what did materialize seemed to me beautiful and of a stunning grandeur.

To speak of other things, Françoise and I were able to escape to the seaside for a month, close to Arcachon. This vacation was marvelous and did a world of good for both mother and child. Still nothing to tell you regarding the baby.

---

95. Boulanger did not acquire copies of the *Tango* score until 1962 and 1963; see F-LYc, UFNB M 111.02 STR, and F-LYc, UFNB M 111.02 STR.

96. Roger Désormière (1898–1963) was a French conductor who supported many modern composers. He was also lauded as a part of the Resistance during the war.

97. François Michel (1916–2004) studied with Boulanger in 1934, writing in his diaries about learning Stravinsky's *Perséphone* in her classes. He corresponded with Boulanger from 1932 to 1977. F-Pn, N.L.a. 86 (237–56).

Of course we will keep you informed of the birth that will likely happen at the end of October. In the meantime, Françoise has asked me to pass along her fond regards.

Dear Nadia, I must stop, I truly abuse your patience with this unending chatter. I am fondly and with my most faithful affection forever your

Sviétik Str.

[P.S.] Nika Skarjinsky has returned from a remarkable imprisonment, marvelous morale.[98] I have been so happy to see this excellent friend and comrade once again.

❧   ❧   ❧

Boulanger to Stravinsky

122 Bay State Road
Boston, Mass.
Tel. Kenmore 7277

Mr Igor Strawinsky
1260 Wetherly Drive
Hollywood 46
California
September 20, 1945

Dear Friend,
What a magnificent surprise, what happiness, and what satisfaction.[99] You are *an angel!*

I cannot tell you about this exceedingly beautiful piece. I feel unworthy. This is the sixth letter I've started. My praise seems to me so small, so awkward—courage will soon return to me, I hope, but not today. I read, I reread. What success on the whole and in each detail, and . . . and again I don't know [what to say]. I am not going too fast! But I know what this symphony represents. I love it and you. It is just too sad to not see you anymore, to not be near

---

98. Nicolas Skarjinsky. Reference to him and to his internment in France during the Second World War can be found in Bourne, *La Divine Contradiction*, 1.

99. Marcelle de Manziarly arranged with Stravinsky to send Boulanger a copy of the newly-composed *Symphony concertante* for her fifty-eight birthday. For the sketches, see Stravinsky, "Symphonie concertante," ph. a. (sketches), ca. Sept. 1945, F-Pn, Gr. Vma. 475. For the full score, see Stravinsky, "Symphony in Three Movements," ph., a., orch. (ins.) September 16, 1945, F-LYc, UFNB ME STR 400.

you at the piano, to not have you hear *me* play it for you. This separation is awful. It weighs on me heavily.

Leaving for Montreal. Will write you upon my return. Jealous of all who have seen Vera's boutique, they tell me it is so stunning—not being able to go to Hollywood is a death sentence.[100]

Received an interesting, kind letter from Sviétik. He seems happy, everyone writes to me about him with much musical confidence. Everyone finds Françoise so kind. Saturday is his birthday. I hope that my package will be there for that day. I really want to speak with you about the finale. I cannot think of more to tell you about other things and yet, I do not see how I might demonstrate to you that I understood! But I have understood, I believe, and heard—and I feel very proud of myself!

You are too great for me to forget it, especially when I am not close to you and my old incorrigible shyness is as strong as ever.

Thank you. You have given me the nicest double-present you could imagine, and the two aspects of the score follow the same line of thinking[:] an order established by one is definitively expressed by the other.

I love you so much, admire you, and miss you. To you, to Vera, very fondly,
NB

❧   ❧   ❧

Boulanger to Stravinsky

MONTREAL, QUEBEC

IGOR STRAVINSKY
1260 NORTH WETHERLY DRIVE
HOLLYWOOD, CALIFORNIA
SEPTEMBER 22, 1945

TENDER WISHES FOR SVIETIK SENDING HIM WOOL FOR BABY THINKING CONSTANTLY OF YOU THANK YOU AGAIN FOR FINALE ALL MY LOVE TO YOU TWO

NADIA

❧   ❧   ❧

_____

100. Vera Stravinsky opened a small gallery called *La Boutique* in August 1945 along with her partner and friend, Lisa Sokolov. The focus of the gallery was modern art, but Vera also exhibited her own works. Walsh, *Second Exile*, 185; and Vera Stravinsky, McCaffrey, and Craft, *Igor and Vera Stravinsky*, 104.

Boulanger to Stravinsky

122 Bay State Road
Boston, Mass.
Tel. Kenmore 7277

15 Oct 1945

1) Thank you for Leyssac's address, Dear Friend.[101]

2) Thank you for your speed.

3) Have I told you that I found wool undergarments, a waistcoat, boots, and gloves for Milène and André,[102] and baby clothes for Sviétik's baby in Montreal?

4) At last, just found wool undergarments for Milène here. It was too early, they did not yet have them when I looked in Montreal.

5) Would you like to have a copy made (I ask you very timidly) of the orchestral score of the new symphony, movements I and II, of which I only have sketches? I cannot begin to write to you about this symphony. I feel ridiculous and insignificant, but . . . I believe that I know *what* it is. And I am very happy.

6) Have you taken my old car? If you do not need it or want it anymore—tell me. I'm glad that it has been useful to you, but doubtless you do not want it anymore

7) Will leave at the end of December. It is sad not to see you before, but I must go back. I will speak to you again about all this very soon.

I think of you two all the time. You cannot imagine the sadness of not seeing you anymore. It was so wonderful . . . you are always with me, but . . . a bit of your real presence would do me good.

To you, with all my heart,
Nadia B.

❧   ❧   ❧

---

101. It is possible Boulanger is referring to the contact information for Paul Leyssac, a well-known Dutch-American stage actor who sometimes performed the narrator roles for Stravinsky works and was connected to Boulanger. Paul Leyssac sent Boulanger two letters in 1945, N.L.a. 81 (130–31).

102. André Marion, Milène's husband.

Stravinsky to Boulanger

[no date]

Nadia dear, you too, now?—too bad.[103] When are you leaving? Received the program for the Fauré Centenary, Nov. 27. So, you will leave in December, perhaps with Arthur Sachs?[104] I am unable to tell you how disagreeable this surprise has been to me (you know my selfishness) especially as all this takes place on the eve of my symphony in Boston. Better not to think of it.

I'm sending you the photostats of the first two movements of my symphony, as you asked me.

Details, please, on the topic of your appointment to the Paris Conservatoire. George, who saw Nini and Françoise,* told us that you were named professor of "accompaniment." What does this title mean?[105]

Useless to tell you how touched we both were by your gifts to our [loved ones] in Paris. How can I thank you! And for your car—all our gratitude. It has been here for a week. Vera has desperately needed it and your present will be a great relief to her, for her little shopping trips especially, and also during the inevitable repairs on our Dodge, as it is becoming a little old and a little tired after five years of continual work.

I'm composing a little concerto (working title—*Ebony Concerto*) for Woody Herman's band (in New York). Decently paid and will be published according to our contract by their ASCAP editor. The music will be recorded by W. Herman[106] himself under my direction (February) and will be placed on two sides of a single disc: side 1: Moderato (2 1/2 min.) and Andante (2 min.); side

---

103. Boulanger had written to say she had decided to return to Europe.

104. Boulanger organized and participated in a festival in honour of Gabriel Fauré on November 27, 1945, a hundred years after the composer's birth. For the concert program, see "Programmes," F-Pn, Rés Vm Dos. 195. See also Boulanger, "Documentation sur une partie de l'activité de Nadia Boulanger en 1945: Séjour aux Etats-Unis," F-Pn, Rés. Vm. Dos. 150. Elsewhere, her archives contain numerous items concerning Gabriel Fauré, including her letters to him, N.L.a. 296 (7–11) and his letters to her, N.L.a. 69 (255–70).

105. Boulanger was hired as *professeur d'accompagnement*, which encompassed sight-reading, transposition, and improvisation at the keyboard. She had first applied for a position at the Conservatoire in 1910. She was required to retire from the Conservatoire in 1957 when she turned seventy. Rosenstiel, 334, 371; Spycket, *Nadia Boulanger*, 138.

106. Woodrow Charles "Woody" Herman (1913–87) was a jazz performer (clarinet, saxophone, voice) and big band leader. The groups he led called themselves "The Herd" and became known for experimental music. See Kriebel, *Blue Flame*, and Lees, *Leader of the Band*. Stravinsky employs an Anglicism here, writing "recordée" [sic]. The correct French would be "enregistrée."

2: Theme and Variations (3 min). The ensemble consists of: oboe, clarinet, 5 saxophones, 5 trumpets, horn, 3 trombones, contrabass, harp, piano, guitar, and percussion. The whole thing has to be composed by around the end of December '45. A little irritated given how little time I have in front of me and the fact that I am not familiar with this type of thing.

Send me even the briefest news of what you are doing.

*We are awaiting their telegram announcing the birth of the child. Madubo has gone to Milène's to join Nini for Françoise's labor and recuperation.

ᔍ ᔍ ᔍ

Boulanger to Vera Stravinsky

122 Bay State Road
Boston, MA

November 7, 1945

What a great letter. What a delightful announcement. Were I only there![107]

There is a cost for certain joys. Dear Vera! I could not find a way to delay my departure, but I am also sad.

And to not see you again is a heavy sorrow. I will try to have Sezna do the musical phrase for Igor—I am exhausted.[108] Have lessons from morning till night, all the rehearsals, parts to correct, things to buy for France, etc., etc., etc.

This is all to say that I pray to God not to collapse. It is very difficult, but that's *all right.*

I embrace you both with
the tenderness you know.
I am happy that I will soon see
little Jean!
This birth and all it represents is marvelous!

Your
Nadia

ᔍ ᔍ ᔍ

---

107. The baby had been born.
108. I could find no reference to a Sezna amongst Boulanger's correspondents. Judging by previous letters, this most likely references a student charged with copying material for Boulanger.

Stravinsky to Boulanger

Beverly Hills California
1260 Wetherly Drive
Hollywood H6 (46?), Calif

Miss Nadia Boulanger
122 Bay State Road
Boston, Mass.
November 16, 1945

My very dear Nadia,

Moved by your words, moved by your departure. I wonder, however, if this departure is truly permanent in view of the upheaval created by de Gaulle's leaving.[109]

Have you heard Prokofieff's [*sic*] Symphony no. 5 (what are the other four that we have never heard)? Unfortunately, at the same time as the broadcast, I had my rehearsal for *Babel*, conducted by Werner Janssen[110]—less helpless than the *Dumbarton Oaks Concerto* last year. I don't think that this indicates progress on his part, simply that the piece is less difficult to conduct

They say that Koussevitzky is having Shostakovsky [*sic*] come from Russia in March and it's also been said that Koussevitzky is retiring and giving up the baton at the beginning of the next season to Mitropoulos.[111] Sounds so exciting, but is it true?

Why do you bring up money (photostats of my *Symphony*). I can give you a gift, too—it's true, it's nothing big, all the more reason to—why talk about it.

---

109. On November 13, 1945, Charles de Gaulle was elected President by the newly appointed assembly. His unwillingness, however, to grant any notable positions to members of the Communist Party, then the largest group within the assembly, caused untenable conflict. De Gaulle resigned over the matter. Roussel, *Charles de Gaulle*, 510–22.

110. Werner Janssen (1899–1990), an American composer and conductor. Most likely the ensemble performing the work was the Janssen Symphony Orchestra of Los Angeles.

111. Stravinsky had fallen victim to gossip. Koussevitzky retired in 1949 and recommended Leonard Bernstein as his successor. Instead, the Boston Symphony Orchestra hired Charles Munch. Dimtri Mitropoulos's American conducting premiere was with the Boston Symphony Orchestra, but he was first associated long term with the Minneapolis Symphony Orchestra and then, in 1949, was appointed conductor of the New York Philharmonic. For more on Koussevitzky and the Boston Symphony Orchestra, see Horowitz, *Artists in Exile*, and Horowitz, *Classical Music in America*.

You owe me nothing save a few "love and kisses" in your next letter. (Pencil please—to erase)[112]

Your
I Str.

Who loves you, who loves you, who loves you.

[P.S.] Received very kind words from Abbot Fortier (for the birth of little Jean)—don't even have time to respond to him. Tell him how touched I was. Thanks.

❧   ❧   ❧

Stravinsky to Boulanger

I.S.
1260 N. Wetherly Dr.
Hollywood, Cal.

Miss Nadia Boulanger
122 Bay State Road
Boston, Mass.
Los Angeles
California
December 19, 1945

Nadia dear,
    I wonder if it's [worth] the trouble of writing to us. When are you leaving? I wait for even the slightest word from you.
    How good you are to have thought of me on the day of my grief. Thank you.

Always yours,
I. Str

[P.S.] Kyriena told me about the death of her father. Ziloti died at age 83. The poor old man had a very weak heart after successive cases of pneumonia.[113]

---

112. This is, again, an example of Stravinsky being playful and flirtatious. The original handwriting of the parenthetical content is quite difficult to read.

113. Alexander Ilyich Siloti (1863–1945) was a Russian composer, pianist and impresario. His concerts of modern music were the vehicle by which Diaghilev learned of Stravinsky's music. Siloti died in New York. His daughter, Kyriena Siloti, was also a musician (piano and pedagogy). For more on Alexander

Milène and André received your precious presents from Canada. They suppose it's your doing (the name of the exporter as well of the giver were missing) and both want to write with their gratitude and enthusiasm. Our plan is to have them come here. I think that you approve of that and if so—please exert all your influence when you are down there.

Perhaps ask our dear friend Winifred to take care of the reservations at the Hotel Hemenway in Boston for the week of my concerts (February 18 to 24—days of our departure to and from Havana)?[114]

Is it as difficult as in N.Y.?

❧ ❧ ❧

Boulanger to Igor and Vera Stravinsky

BOSTON, MA

MR AND MRS IGOR STRAWINSKY
1260 NORTH WETHERLY DRIVE
DECEMBER 25, 1945

SO SAD BEING FAR AM SAILING DECEMBER 31 WILL SEE AT ONCE SVETIK HOPE MILENE WILL SOON BE WITH YOU WISHES DEAR VERA LOVE TO BOTH

NADIA

❧ ❧ ❧

Siloti's career, see Barber, *Lost in the Stars.* For more on Stravinsky and Siolti, see Taruskin, *Stravinsky and the Russian Traditions,* vol. 1.

114. Winifred Hope Johnstone, member of a prominent Boston family, met Boulanger in 1937. She later studied with Boulanger and would eventually serve as administrator for the Lili Boulanger Memorial Fund. Rosenstiel, *Nadia Boulanger,* 276 and 376.

Igor and Vera Stravinsky to Boulanger

BEVERLY HILLS, CALIFORNIA
NADIA BOULANGER, C/O MARCELLE DE MANZIARLY
304 EAST 66 ST, NEW YORK
DECEMBER 30, 1945

MAY YOUR RETURN FRANCE BE NUCH [*sic*] HAPPINESS TO YOU
DEAREST FRIEND. TELL NINI AGREE ENTIRELY CHRISTEN JEAN
CATHOLIC
    HAPPY NEW YEAR BON VOYAGE LOVE KISSES=

IGOR VERA STRAVINSKY,

1946

Boulanger to Igor and Vera Stravinsky

122 Bay State Road
Boston, Mass.
Tel. Kenmore 7277

Mr. Igor Strawinsky
1260 Wetherly Drive
Hollywood 46
California
January 3, 1946

Dear Igor, Dear Vera,
    These last few hours I have been so sad to leave you that after having asked
for your number, I hung up, not having the courage to hear your voices.
    But I will soon kiss the cheeks of Jean, Sviétik, Françoise, maybe Milène.
Who knows, [perhaps] I will return sooner than I think. Finally, may God
keep you, my dearest ones. I love you, and when I consider just how much, the
thought of this long-awaited return costs me very dearly.
    And to miss the *Symphony*!
    Know all that these last-minute lines bring to you, and speak of me often. I
need to feel you close by my side.

Your
Nadia B.

[P.S.] I will speak to Sviétik and Françoise about the baptism. Again, *all my love*,
Dear Igor, Dear Vèra!

Chapter Four

After the War

1946–1951

Boulanger returned to Paris in January 1946, joyfully reuniting with friends in France while painfully separating from those back in the United States. Boulanger's letters provide a glimpse of life in Paris in the immediate postwar years. She writes of the lack of heat in her apartment, during the middle of one of Europe's coldest winters in years (January 27, 1946).[1] In April 1946, Boulanger references purchases acquired through the black market (April 27, 1946). Here, she briefly describes how difficult it was to carry out daily activities and the bravery of those who attempted to meet people's needs through illegal measures. And yet, although Boulanger's optimism outshone the inconveniences of her reality initially, her outlook began to sour by 1950, amid the uncertainties brought about by the onset of the Cold War. Indeed, by fall of 1950, her optimism had turned to anger, as she wrote to Stravinsky on September 14, 1950: "I cannot hope that you'll come to Europe, a Europe that everything threatens. What savages, what fools we are who, no matter what, want to find nothing more than perfect ways to destroy everything." Boulanger's letters bear witness to the extensive postwar struggle to establish normalcy on the unstable continent.

This fragile reality framed Boulanger's efforts as a critic, performer, and lecturer as she worked aggressively to rebuild European artistic traditions. Upon her return, Boulanger gave numerous lectures, wrote criticism, and traveled regularly to places both familiar—such as London, England—and uncharted, such as Bryanston, England, and Solesmes, France. She threw her energy into lectures and performances of Stravinsky's works that were still

---

1. For recent scholarly discussions of early postwar Europe, see Lowe, *Savage Continent*, and Judt, *Postwar*.

unknown to many Europeans. She lectured extensively, imploring Europeans in general and Parisians in particular to engage with the high neoclassical output of her beloved composer. Her talks, mentioned in numerous letters, overflowed with personal anecdotes and stories collected during her frequent visits with the Stravinskys in California. Whenever possible, Boulanger, along with the help of Soulima and Jean Françaix, performed Stravinsky's wartime compositions in the form of two-piano transcriptions. One of the most fascinating of all her performance engagements involved her conducting the *Symphony of Psalms* in Brussels no less than seven times in four days (September 15, 1950). This series of concerts was the only time she conducted this symphony, and certainly is one of the rare occasions when Boulanger ever agreed to conduct a Stravinsky piece of such size, length, and complexity. Indeed, postwar Boulanger appeared open to new repertoire and new locations for performance. For example, on September 22, 1950, she suggested that Stravinsky commit to having his opera *The Rake's Progress* appear at the "Festival at Aix," the Aix-en-Provence summer festival that at that time had only just celebrated its first successful season. The Aix Festival would go on to be an impressive perennial event, running to this day.

Boulanger also often mentions her interest in—and intense disdain for—what she called the "dodecaphonic offensive" (November 25, 1950) that appears to have thrived on the continent in the early postwar climate. Referencing prior conversations, Boulanger admitted to Stravinsky that, were he there, he would admonish her that "only the weak submit" to such influences. This anti-dodecaphonic alliance Boulanger believed she shared with Stravinsky would soon dissolve, when Stravinsky began composing serial music in 1952. Directly after the war, however, the evidence suggests she assumed that Stravinsky shared her disdain for "systematic music" and "mystic-chromatic clouds" (June 15, 1946).

Stravinsky's letters show him sensitive to the distance between him and loved ones and greatly interested in news of his own family, whom Boulanger visited regularly. Dutifully shuttling information from 1260 Wetherly Drive to Soulima and Françoise Stravinsky, Boulanger also wrote back to Vera and Igor of their baby grandson, Jean, whom Boulanger adored, and of Soulima's own work ethic. The theme of family and the importance of loved ones is palpable in these letters, despite lapses when Stravinsky was traveling, on tour, or deeply immersed in composition.

Beyond that, Stravinsky appears the consummate businessman, aware of the yawning distance between himself and the reestablishment of his brand in postwar Europe. He writes regularly to Boulanger of new compositions (his Mass, *Orpheus*, revisions of the *Ave Maria* and *Pater Noster*, and *The Rake's Progress*). He also mentions his recordings often, reinforcing the importance of technology to the post-1945, transatlantic cultural dialogue. On September

16, 1950, Stravinsky wrote to Boulanger to say he sent her recordings of his Mass by way of George and Arthur Sachs, who were headed to Paris for a visit. Two months later, he wrote at length about differences in recording speeds (November 27, 1950), asking Boulanger to clarify for him what type of recording techniques the French were using. In this same vein, the letters make obvious the immensely important role radio played in the early postwar years, at times being the only means of enabling the international dissemination of works. There are moments in the correspondence when the poor quality of transmissions, the cutting of portions of works by radio producers, or the perplexing provenance of certain performances served as a point of tension or confusion for both Boulanger and Stravinsky. Overall, these letters reveal the fractured nature of transatlantic Euro–American exchange during early peacetime, a fraying that exacerbated a sense of lopsided cultural "advancement" on both sides following the war.

❧   ❧   ❧

Boulanger to Igor and Vera Stravinsky

36 rue Ballu, 9ème, Paris
Téléph: Trinité 90–17

Mr. and Mrs. I. Strawinsky
1260 N. Wetherly Drive
Hollywood 46
California
January 27, 1946

At last, the first letter, and it is only a small note! Dear Igor, Dear Vera, not a day goes by without speaking of you, but, at first it was so cold that I refused to write . . . and then [refused to do] anything. I don't know how to explain. Life is full of checking, looking, recognizing! Nevertheless, do I need to add that there isn't a day without speaking of you, without listening to you, without waiting for you (in a manner of speaking). Went to see Jean after disembarking, so as to instantly tell you my first impressions, and I truly believed I was going to write to you that evening, on January 20!! How shameful.

He is so beautiful, so strong and so imperious—no need to ask if he knows what he wants. But he is also so soft and gentle, happy—not a baby like any other, he is already himself, 100% Strawinsky. Sviétik and Françoise are beaming. Happy and so well adjusted! Sviétik works a lot, writing very clean, very clear, good music. Excellent spirits, finally, all is *well.* Their apartment is very nicely set up and would please you—the taste, the order, and the space.

By all respects, things seem to be sorting themselves out! Sviétik has sound friends, and Françoise is perfect.

I'd like to give you an idea of the situation here. I do not feel able to judge anything concerning politics. Everything is too fluid and complex. But the young people we talk to clearly fall into distinctive groups—spouting grand, vague, destructive theories. There is, as far as I can tell, a small number—[as opposed to the] majority, quite a clear majority—a sensible minority that sees things with a sense of order, loves what should be loved, fights for what is worth saving.[2]

Certain places haven't changed. The same habits, the same gossip, the same jokes. Only the outfits have changed a bit, and yet everything is still so difficult.

I saw Souvtchinsky,[3] and he looked well. Met Cingria,[4] how cultured, what finesse, and his manner of speaking, just striking. Missed *Mavra* the other evening . . . I didn't know . . . ! I console myself in saying the performances were poor. But I cannot be consoled.

You are well, as you ought to be, Dear Igor, the only one to whom the real youths attach themselves. But enough for today, you will be discouraged by these scribbles. Désormière will perform the symphony, what joy![5]

---

2. Boulanger's prose in the original is quite confusing and convoluted. I have smoothed out the translation as best I can.

3. Pierre Souvtchinsky (sometimes transliterated Suvchinsky) (1892–1985) was a close friend of Stravinsky's in the 1930s, though they had a tumultuous relationship after Stravinsky emigrated to the United States. Souvtchinsky was a Russian émigré musician and an independently wealthy scholar of Russian chant and Eurasianism. The role of Eumolpus in *Perséphone* was written for him. Toward the end of his life, Stravinsky asked Souvtchinsky to organize his archives, but this never came about. For a take on their dialogue, see Levitz, *Modernist Mysteries*, 128–30. For a discussion of Souvtchinsky's role in co-authoring written texts with Stravinsky, see Dufour, *Stravinski et ses exegetes*.

4. Charles-Albert Cingria (1883–1954), a close friend of Stravinsky's, was a Swiss writer and musician. See Levitz, *Modernist Mysteries*, 124. Boulanger kept in her archives a draft copy of the article Cingria co-wrote with Stravinsky on *Perséphone* in 1934: Stravinsky, "Article sur *Perséphone*," 1934, CINLB, Strawinsky: 95 A (A1-A2). The manifest for Boulanger's belongings from 1946 lists Cingria's *Stalactites* among the books she purchased in the United States. Boulanger, "Inventaire des caisses du retour des Etats-Unis," 1946, F-Pn, Box 11, Rés Vm. Dos. 129.

5. Roger Désormière (1898–1963) was a renowned French conductor. During the Second World War he belonged to the Front national des musiciens, supporting many composers persecuted by the Nazi government, including Jean Wiéner and Darius Milhaud. From 1945–46, Désormière was the associate director of the Paris Opera and served as a champion of contemporary music until a stroke ended his conducting activities in 1952. See Paul, "L'enfance mal connue de Roger Désormière"; Boulez, "'J'ai horreur du souvenir !'"; and Guillot, *Roger Désormière*.

With all my heart, I love you both madly,
NB

❧   ❧   ❧

Stravinsky to Boulanger

Hollywood
The house that you know by heart[6]
April 11, 1946

Nadia dear,

Let me tell you, even if only in a few words, my immense joy at finally reading a word from you. Not embarrassed at all by your telegraphic speed, for these last years, it has been our БЫТЪ [our habit]—our way of doing things, our method. Don't worry about it! I was of course eager to have your *statements*. Happily I read as much *in* as *between* the lines of your letter. Selfish conclusion: Inconsolable as I am to have lost you here, at least I have the satisfaction to think of and take pleasure in the crucial importance of your presence over there.

I am with you with all my heart,
I Str.

[P.S.] Good tour in all senses but ... tiring.[7] Have you finally heard the London broadcast of my new symphony which Nini and Milène heard a week after my broadcast from N.Y. (Jan. 27*)?[8] This possibility is miraculous, isn't it?

Tell Nini and Françoise that I wish to receive photos of my ВНУКЪ (grandson), I beg of them. He is superb, ravishing, and so daring. I want to write him a letter. It's so true!

The other day I produced some records with Columbia that go on sale toward the end of the year.[9]

---

6. By this he means 1260 North Wetherly Drive.

7. During March 1946, the Stravinskys traveled to Boston and Cambridge and thence to Miami, Havana, Cuba, New Orleans, Dallas, and San Francisco. Walsh, *Second Exile*, 189; Craft, *A Stravinsky Scrapbook*, 26; and Craft, *Dearest Bubushkin*, 136.

8. This is a reference to the broadcast of the premiere of his *Symphony in Three Movements*, which Stravinsky conducted at Carnegie Hall on January 24, 1946. Walsh, *Second Exile*, 186.

9. Stravinsky contradicts himself here, writing a verb in the past but a time in the future. Most likely he has confused "lendemain" (in the next little while) with "l'autre jour" (the other day). I have chosen the latter because of the dates of

At Winnifred's house in Boston, I took from your library *one* of the two photostats of my piano concerto.[10] One remains for you. Don't give me an earful over this, I really need it for next season because I plan on playing it again with Beveridge, this time with the C.B.S., i.e. the broadcast [orchestra].[11]

❧   ❧   ❧

Boulanger to Stravinsky

36 rue Ballu
Paris, IXème

[on stationery from]
Nadia Boulanger
Featherhill Ranch
Santa Barbara, California[12]

Mr Igor Strawinsky
1260 N. Wetherly Drive
Hollywood 46
California
April 27, 1946

What happiness to receive your letter, my dear, oh so dear, Igor. [I] suffer through death and passion because of you, but am such an angel that I thank

---

the recording, which fell before the letter was written. The recording session in question took place with the Philharmonic Symphony Orchestra on January 28, 1946.
10. Winnifred Johnstone was the administrative director for the Lili Boulanger Memorial Fund. The work in question is the *Concerto for Two Pianos* (1932–35) and the other soloist was to be American pianist Beveridge Webster (1908–99), also a former pupil of Isidor Philipp and Boulanger's. Boulanger's copy of this *Concerto* is rife with performance markings (both first and second piano), possibly from performances she shared with Jean Françaix and Soulima Stravinsky, F-LYc, UFNB M 11.02 STRAV.
11. Beveridge Webster played the *Concerto for Two Pianos* as part of a Town Hall Concert on February 26, 1949. Soulima, not Igor, Stravinsky performed the other piano part. Walsh, *Second Exile*, 240.
12. Supplies were difficult to come by in early postwar Europe, a fact to which Boulanger only fleetingly refers in her letters. For some time after her return to Europe, Boulanger used stationery acquired when in America and bearing old, out-of-date American addresses. In this instance, Boulanger has added a sticker with the Featherhill Ranch address on it. I suspect she was being nostalgic.

you for it nevertheless. Thinking of Tuesday, a lecture *on you*.[13] What humility it takes to know my inabilities and yet to throw myself into it. It's that, although I may not know how to say as intelligent, beautiful things regarding your work as trained, perceptive minds would be able to, at least I love, respect, and admire this work so much that it seems to me that my steadfast conviction will perhaps allow me to lead some young people to study your music. What can I say when I read, know, and love it—all of it?

Pasquier played the *Elegy*, and people were crazy about it.[14] He understood it, I believe, its spirit and *seriously trained* for it. Will hear it tomorrow.

Souzay is singing the *Histoires pour enfants*, and "Creon's Air" (outstanding, two-piano [transcription] by Sviétik).[15] Then we are playing the finale to *Dumbarton*, the second movement of the *Symphonie en ut*, marvelous transcription by Nini, Variations from the *Sonata for Two Pianos*, Nocturne, *Concerto for Two Pianos*, *Circus Polka*, [and] *Scherzo à la russe*.

There are so many examples I should share, but 1 hour and 15 minutes is short!! Managed to keep the melody. But it is hard to dare to speak of it. One feels so humbled, so very small, and so vain. Can't think too much of it before Tuesday.

I, who will never understand too well what is said or written about music. It only needs one thing: to be understood. All these commentaries . . . Would have wanted to buy some things to send to you, but . . . life is difficult, and the distress is so great. But what courage is hidden behind the black market's wares. You can't imagine the sacrifices allowed and accepted by people here. Even so, you can likely guess them.

---

13. The lecture is listed in Boulanger's diaries as falling on April 30, 1946. Boulanger, "Agendas" F-Pn, Rés. Vmb. Ms. 88. Soulima Stravinsky kept a copy of the program and it is now a part of his archives. The lecture took place at 9:00 p.m. and was held in the large amphitheater of the Sorbonne. Pierre Pasquier, Soulima Stravinsky, and Gérard Souzay all participated. The program also states that on the second and fourth Tuesday of the month from March until June, Boulanger gave a lecture at 8:30 p.m. in the Salle des Quatuors of the Maison Gaveau. See Soulima Stravinsky Papers, Music Division, US-NYp.

14. Pierre Pasquier (1902–86) was a renowned violist, who, along with his brothers Jean and Étienne, formed the Pasquier Trio in 1927. Pasquier became the professor of chamber music at the Conservatoire in 1943. The *Elegy* referenced here is the same *Elegy for Solo Viola* discussed in chapter 3.

15. Gérard Souzay (1918–2004) was a famous French baritone. He studied with Pierre Bernac and Claire Croiza, the latter a performer connected with the Boulanger sisters' works. Souzay was working primarily as a recitalist at the time of this concert. Steane, *The Grand Tradition*, 487–90; and Blyth, *Song on Record*. I have found no concert program for this particular event.

Jean is increasingly adorable. Will you not come see him . . . ? It would be worth the trouble, [he is] already *himself,* so defined, so gentle and strong.

And *everyone* is waiting for you. Mrs. Bouchonnet despairs over your silence.[16] They ask for you *everywhere.* What selfishness. But a well-deserved selfishness, because we need you furiously.

My love to both of you *with all my heart*

[P.S.] Thank you for the San Francisco article, touched you would think of me. But, can't read anything these days without feeling that: "no good deed goes unpunished." This time about Copland, Milhaud, and Prokofiev.[17] Did you read Souvtchinsky's article?[18] Tell me quickly, what did you think of it?

❧   ❧   ❧

Boulanger to Stravinsky

36 rue Ballu
Paris 9ème

Mr. Igor Strawinsky
1260 N. Wetherly Drive
Hollywood, 46
California
June 15, 1946

Dear Igor, Tuesday is your birthday . . . and the world [is] between us—what sorrow, sorrow every day. I miss you so much! For your birthday, I send

---

16. Probably a reference to Nadiajda Bouchonnet, a Russian expatriate artistic manager. She worked with Vladimir Horowitz and Nathan Milstein, among others; see Glotz, *La note bleue.* She is also listed as the general secretary for a production of Stravinsky's *L'oiseau de feu* mounted at Covent Garden July 20–27, 1937. See Wearing, *The London Stage,* 620.

17. Alfred Frankenstein, "Igor Stravinsky Introduces a Major Work to S.F." *The San Francisco Chronicle* March 23, 1946, p. 4H. This article reviews the San Francisco premiere of Stravinsky's *Symphony in Three Movements.* The reviewer comments on Copland's "timing of contrasts," comparing his creative instincts to those of Stravinsky, Milhaud, and Prokofiev. Frankenstein also wrote that "it is scarcely accidental that Copland is the most successful American composer of serious music." Boulanger likely misunderstood the English, interpreting this as an insult.

18. The article in question, to quote Tamara Levitz, "greatly pleased Stravinsky." For the article, see Souvtchinsky, "Igor Strawinsky," 19–31. For Levitz's discussion of the article and Stravinsky's reaction to it, see Levitz, *Modernist Mysteries,* 129.

my fondest wishes to Vera and you and pray that we will see one another
again soon.

If I were to begin to write in earnest, I would have so much to tell
you—a newspaper's-worth. Rest assured, a crazy work schedule [stops me].
Thursday is a concert of your works.[19] Sviétik has made *marvelous* transcriptions. Another the following week, Bach, then you again.[20] Pasquier
is replaying the *Elegy* that made *such* an impression at the Sorbonne. The
competitions, the students, my sick maid. Well, nothing can harm you.
Otherwise, this little note brings you so much fondness! You would be
touched, I believe, to see the reaction of the orchestra musicians at the
thought of seeing you again.

Music here, much of it bad as always, with the young university students
making a rather significant effort to listen, understand, and take part.

Missed a radio broadcast of *Mavra* and *Renard*. The reaction of the youth
who interest us was as it should be, the others [are] lost in the mystic-chromatic
clouds that bring the old-fashioned to tears.[21]

Remind Berman of me, and all your friends who still remember me, and
know that you are endlessly—and you do know it—a part of my life and my
heart and my spirit.[22]

---

19. Concert held on June 20, 1946. On the lengthy program were the *Four
    Norwegian Moods*; "Le moineau est assis," from *Quatre chants russes*, "Air de
    Paracha" from *Mavra*, *Trois histoires pour enfants*, *Scherzo à la russe*, *Sonata
    for Two Pianos*, *Circus Polka*, "Air de Créon" from *Oedipus Rex*, the Andante
    and Scherzo movements of the Symphony in C, and the finales of both the
    Dumbarton Oaks Concerto and *Perséphone*. Boulanger and Soulima Stravinsky
    played the piano with transcriptions completed by Soulima. The singers
    included Flore Wend, Gérard Souzay, and Hugues Cuénod (Eumolpe).
    Roger Cortet played flute, and the daughter of writer and journalist
    Edmonde Charles-Roux (listed only as "Mademoiselle") performed the
    part of Perséphone. Boulanger, "Concert Programmes," F-Pn, Rés. Vm. Dos
    195 (Folio 756) and Boulanger, "Agendas," June 20, 1946, F-Pn, Rés VmB
    Dos 88. Boulanger sent Stravinsky a copy of the program.
20. There is no reference to this concert in Boulanger's diaries, though a lecture
    on Stravinsky and Valéry is noted on June 24, 1946. Boulanger, "Agendas" June
    24, 1946, Rés, VmB. Dos 88.
21. "Mystico-chromatic" is a derogatory reference to the music of Olivier Messiaen
    (1908–92) whom Boulanger detested. For more on their relationship, see
    Simeone, "Messiaen, Boulanger, and Josée Bruyr," 17–22. Boulanger's com-
    ments further bolster Leslie Sprout's argument that Messiaen was more of a
    divisive figure for French musicians in the post-war era than Schoenberg was.
    Sprout, *Musical Legacy*, 154.
22. Painter and designer Eugene Berman; see chapter 3, n. 57.

To you both affectionately,
NB

❧   ❧   ❧

Boulanger to Igor and Vera Stravinsky

36 rue Ballu
Paris IX
Trinité 90–17

October 11, 1946

Dear Igor, Darling Vera,

It may seem that I don't love you anymore. You appear to have forgotten me, or at least that which concerns me . . . Well, the moments I could give to you, I give to Sviétik! He is making such progress, works hard, and he goes to so much trouble for it! I am sure you understand.

Jean is the most amazing baby that you could imagine. Ferocious energy, incredible charm, exquisite kindness. A "*Someone*" I believe, although to say that about a baby seems funny.

I received the symphony this morning.[23] *Thank you.* I know it, I am certain, by heart, but I love to look at it [anyway]. It speaks to the eyes as it speaks to the ears.

Is it true, is it really true that *you*, you will conduct it, Dear Igor? God willing!

A lot of silly things are said; theories, systems, ramblings mounting into a frenzied dance. But all the same, those who matter among the young know who projects the light.

I am trying to hide my grief. The truth is that I cannot be consoled over all that I have lost by leaving you. Those beautiful days . . . they are still with me. But I would really love a bit of reality added to the memories! All my deepest affection,

NB

❧   ❧   ❧

---

23. I suspect this is a reference to the published score of the *Symphony in Three Movements*, produced by Associated Music Publishers in 1946, or to the recording of the work, produced on January 28, 1946, with the Philharmonic-Symphony Orchestra of New York. See also the discussion of this work in chapter 3.

Soulima Stravinsky to Boulanger

La Clidelle
par Menet (Cantal)
Tel: 8 Menet
Gare Riom-Es-Montagne

October 15, 1946

Dear Nadia,

Helen, with whom I spoke on the telephone just a moment ago, will have told you that my father urgently requests his score for *Perséphone*.[24] I hope that she will have understood (we couldn't hear one another very well). To be safe, I'm quickly sending you this letter.

The American ambassador to Italy, Mr. James Clément Dunn, is in Paris these days and must return to America [after]. My father asked him to be so kind as to bring with him several scores (among them his manuscript for *Perséphone*) which he needs most urgently. All that needs to be done then is to drop them off at the embassy marked for Mr. I. Str., care of The Honorable James Clément Dunn.[25]

The manuscript can still be found at your place, in the safe. It could wait for my return, but that would probably be too late.

You are no doubt in London at the moment. We return on the 25th. I have finally gotten over a nasty flu picked up in Holland and am attempting to take advantage of a marvelous country and weather that seems made to order.

Annette sent me the enrollment brochure for your Wednesday course.[26] I am rather unsure I could attend regularly and so I dare not enroll. I'm terribly sorry about that. Would you allow me anyway, dear Nadia, to attend when it is possible for me to do so? Françoise is pulling her hair out at the idea that she is a civil servant and won't be free either.[27]

We both send you all our affection,

Your
S. Strawinsky

---

24. Likely Helen is a reference to a domestic worker at the rue Ballu at this time.
25. James Clément Dunn (1890–1979) was a diplomat and State Department employee. He retired in 1956.
26. Annette Dieudonné, see also chapter 3, n. 90.
27. Her exact job is not listed in the current secondary literature, though Walsh does state she was studying law when she and Soulima first met, *Second Exile*, 179. As for her work later in the United States, registers from the University of Illinois list Françoise Stravinsky as a student at the institution in 1958. In 1959, she is listed as a teacher. I have found no other records of her employment.

〜 〜 〜

Boulanger to the American Ambassador

36 rue Ballu
Paris IX

October 17, 1946

Mr. Ambassador,
Please excuse this package. Mr. Strawinsky has asked me to give the manuscript of *Perséphone* to you and to thank you for bringing it back to him.

May your Excellency find in this letter my highest consideration,
Nadia Boulanger

〜 〜 〜

Stravinsky to Boulanger

Hollywood

November 23, 1946

A[rthur] Sach[s] delivered your letter to us. What an honor! How to thank you. Today (Nov 23)—your telegram.[28] Thank you, thank you, thank you, thank you, impatient to know the details of the performance and the public's reception.[29]
No longer possible to write you letters—only phrases, and again without first names, if possible (like you [do]).
We are going on tour Dec. 3. Starting in Montreal. Returning Feb. 4.[30]
With all my heart,

Your
I Str.

---

28. Boulanger's telegram congratulated Stravinsky on the performance of his *Symphony in Three Movements*, November 23, 1946; CH-Bps.
29. Boulanger wrote to him of the Parisian premiere of his *Symphony in Three Movements*. On November 17, 1946, she attended a private lecture about the work given by Roger Désormière that she later discussed in her column for *Le Spectateur*: "Premières auditions musicales: La Symphonie d'Igor Strawinsky," November 26, 1946, 6. A copy of her column is in the Stravinsky archives, CH-Bps.
30. This tour took them from New York to Montreal to Cleveland to Philadelphia. Walsh, *Second Exile*, 196.

[P.S.] All our most loyal thoughts to the Abbott [*sic*].[31] For you my very dear Nadia, Love Kisses

❧   ❧   ❧

Boulanger to Stravinsky

36 rue Ballu
Paris, IXème

[N.D.]

Dear Friend,

How can I tell you what these rehearsals and concert were like. The *Symphonie en ut*, *Orpheus*, the *Chant du Rossignol*. A perfect performance: clean, honest, intelligent. Another rehearsal, and relaxation (*l'aisance*) would have given a *je ne sais quoi* that was lacking in places. But on the whole, good. All of us . . . we all rediscovered *Rossignol* (outstanding soloists), the *Symphonie*, and we all discovered *Orpheus*. How marvelous, what a sound. Everything was surprising, everything was obvious. You know better than I the extraordinary quality of this material, which determines the entire character of the work by its very nature. We are continually surprised at each interval, with each instrument, each connection seems new. And the sound, because never again [will it] be assembled just so, placed just so. Everything is found, everything is known, everything is discovered. One feels the joy you must have had, you must have known how to seize and organize [it]. You are extremely lucky. I don't have the time to try to impress you, without a doubt. I told you everything I heard note by note. And you'll see that I believe nothing has escaped me.

Only, every time I pick up the score it is the same, stunning delight. It will always be the first time, because this music preserves the freshness of its surprises and its evidence.

How I love this score, how beautiful, harmonious, alive, [and] unexpected it is. But enough—I feel ridiculous and I know that I am, [because] to speak to you about things that surpass me in all respects is inconceivable.

Orchestra was dazzled by the richness of *Rossignol*, [which] was dominated by simplicity, the melodies of *Orpheus*, of the Symphony, and the new shape it is clearly taking. The harpist understood, admirably, after being shocked

---

31. A priest from Montreal, Monsiegneur Elzéar Fortier or "Abbot Fortier" as Stravinsky referred to him in the 1940s, corresponded with Boulanger from 1943–78. F-Pn, N.L.a. 70 (273–323) and (330–44). See also chapter 2, n. 48. Stravinsky's letter suggests Fortier was visiting or studying with Boulanger at this time.

at seeing so few *glissandi* markings. But she played better than anyone, and understood everything and succeeded.

Ah, how I so want to say: here and there, this and that. I want to dazzle you but no, I want *to thank* you. What direction, what style, what a benefit from this music . . . It is difficult to leave you, but this letter is poorly written . . . and if I continue I will just be setting my confused and disorganized effusions next to the transparency and balance [of your music].

My affection, and my deep pride in loving you so much,

Your faithful
Nadia

P.S. My affection to Vera and to all. How I would like to see you!!!

🙠   🙠   🙠

Boulanger to Stravinsky

[on stationery from]
122 Bay State Road
Boston, Massachusetts[32]

November 25, 1946

Dear Igor,

Here again, such a painful date. I am thinking of you with much tenderness, with much faithfulness, of the child you lost, and of your granddaughter who has finally found a home where she can be cherished.[33] You are so present in my life. Each day, in thought, in my heart, through music, memories, hope, you are here, your memory always brings with it a great light.

I knew that it would be sad not to see you anymore. I did not know that it would be so sad. How lucky I was to be close to you, so often, so intimately. I could not tell you. Truly, I thank God *often* for this privilege, this happiness, this joy.

What a week we've just had, thanks to you. I arrived Sunday at the Champs-Élysées, so proud to know your symphony by heart, persuaded that I knew it *completely*. And from the first note until the last, I did nothing but discover and discover. What splendor! Everything was completely new, all as if it had

---

32. An example of Boulanger writing on American stationery after the war because of a lack of supplies in France.
33. Théodore and Denise Strawinsky began the process of adopting their niece after the war. The adoption was approved in April 1952. Walsh, *Second Exile*, 193 and 287. See also Craft, *Chronicle of a Friendship*, 75.

been inevitable. You cannot know what this reading was like. The orchestra was suddenly attentive, enthusiastic, and sightread in such a manner that, on the whole, the work was already faithfully there. Then, the intelligent, simple, precise work of Désormière. I know full well that, if you were to conduct this work, it would be different, but, apart from you, I do not know who would have done more exact and faithful work. He *truly understood* and made others understand. He lacked a certain abandon. He didn't dare indulge his pleasure at all, but the performance was marvelously clear, well-placed. And his remarks uncovered all of your organization. "Observe the nuance, it is caused by the tessitura (or the relationship, or the placement)" and the nuance took its obvious place, its necessary place. How I wish I could tell you [all this]. But, I feel ridiculous telling you what you already know better than I. I understood, I believe, and I know only after hearing it, that I see all the better what a masterpiece your symphony is.

I want to tell you everything that I heard, but . . . I will take pity [on you], my "quiet ones," but only a little. Certain people seemed quite grey in the lobby. They felt, in spite of themselves, that you *alone* were right, and they were not reassured! But the vast majority were extraordinarily impressed, sensing all too well that you *must* be followed, and following you we will breathe this pure air deeply. What a weak and foolish image. I am writing without thinking. But trust me, I disgust myself! Whatever the case, I am happy, and very proud, admire you so, and love you so!

To Vera, to you, with all my heart,
N

❧ ❧ ❧

Stravinsky to Boulanger

CLEVELAND, OHIO

NADIA BOULANGER
26 RUE BALLU
PARIS

HOPE NEW YEAR WILL BRING US TOGETHER WISHING YOU HEALTH AND HAPPINESS WITH LOVE=

IGOR AND VERA STRAVINSKY

1947

Stravinsky to Boulanger

Hollywood

Miss Nadia Boulanger
36 rue Ballu, 9th
Paris, France
April 19, 1947

Carissima Nadia,

Instead of Paris, here we are embarking for Washington, where Mrs. Bliss is waiting for me for my *Dumbarton Oaks Concerto* that I will conduct in Dumbarton Oaks itself. It's been nine years since you yourself conducted the premiere. Your shadow (or rather your light) will be evoked with dignity. We are passing through NY where I am rehearsing with the musicians. The concert at Dumbarton O. is April 25 and the next day the same program in public. The program:

Vivaldi	D Minor Concerto
Mozart	Divertimento in D Major (no. 11) with oboe and two horns
Stravinsky	*D.O. Concerto*
Falla	Harpsichord Concerto
Stravinsky	*D.O. Concerto* (second time)

The decision to postpone our trip to Europe was very beneficial for me even though I had to live through some rather difficult times before regaining my equilibrium and continuing my work. This work, as you probably know, is *Orpheus*. Balanchine is expecting it in the autumn.[34] Its premiere—probably the end of November. Two thirds (including orchestration) already done. I have great hopes that you will like this music.

What a joy to finally have Milène here and also to see her so happy. All three of them shine with happiness.[35]

---

34. George Balanchine (1904–83), a highly influential choreographer of the twentieth century, worked closely with Stravinsky on many of his ballets. *Orpheus* was a commission from Balanchine for the American Ballet School. For more on Stravinsky and Balanchine's working relationship, see Joseph, *Stravinsky and Balanchine*.

35. "All three" include Stravinsky's surviving daughter, Milène Marion, her husband André, and the family's *nyanya* Mina Svitalski (Madubo). This trio had emigrated to live with the Stravinskys in California. For more on their arrival, see Walsh, *Second Exile*, 193. For more on "Madubo" and her relationship with the family, see Théodore and Denise Strawinsky, *Au coeur du foyer*.

Attached are two little pages that require your signature, without which it's impossible to renew the *registration* on your car. Vera, who's packing the suitcases right now and who sends you her love, lent this car to a young man just back from the war who had not a cent to his name but who has a wife and two children. You will make this young man happy in returning these two little sheets filled in with your kind signature to us,* if possible by return post (and by air mail).

I will write to you after our return from Washington, i.e., after May 4, and in the meantime please find here, *carissima* Nadia, my affectionate love and many, many kisses from,

Always yours,
I Str

[P.S.] Have you received my *Ode*, that has finally been published?[36] This is not so that you thank me, but to know if it reached you.

*Before a *Witness* (and their address). Don't forget a legal signature complete with a "stamp."

❧   ❧   ❧

Stravinsky to Boulanger

Hollywood
May 5, 1947

My very dear Nadia, we are now back,
Very beautiful performance of the whole program before a room* filled with Mr. and Mrs. Bliss's invited guests—you can imagine their reaction and the nature of their applause. Imagine when they thanked me for their etti-quette. It's really all we should expect from people who don't know better.
Is it true that the U.S.A. will see you again this year? Say *yes*.

Your
I Str.[37]
*Two rooms (April 25 and 26)

---

36. Stravinsky wrote the *Ode* in memory of Natalie Koussevitzky (née Ushkova), who died in January 1942. Boulanger's copy of the *Ode* reads: "N.B. from I.S., April 1947" ("N.B. de I.S. avril 1947"). The score is otherwise untouched. F-LYc, UFNB MEp STR 400.

37. Six additional signatures were added to the letter, including those of Nicolas Nabokov, Mildred and Robert Bliss, Alexei Haïeff, R. P. Gabriel, and C. Daniels.

[P.S.] We impatiently await your response to my letter dated April 19 and your signature.

❧ ❧ ❧

Boulanger to Stravinsky

36 rue Ballu
Paris IX

Monsieur Igor Strawinsky
1260 N. Wetherly Drive
Hollywood, California
U.S.A.
May 5, 1947

Dear, Dear Friend, my silence weighs on me a million times more than it is worth. Thinking of you constantly and never telling you, what an aberration! It's true that you hold such a place in everyday life, that sometimes I seem to have written you everything that is said about you here!

Sorry for not having sent you the paperwork yet, but I have been to the embassy *three times* and waited *an hour*, and had to give up. I will try on Wednesday.[38] It has to be done in person, and there is [always] a crowd. It is not my fault.

Your decision was a deep disappointment—and an immense relief—to me. We would have killed you! But it's too bad. For you, it's something irrevocable. For the young people, it's catastrophic. All that they hear is done to make them stray from the right path. Nothing can guide them. And they awaited you so greedily.

Thank you for the *Ode*. I am so happy to reread this score, which I love so much—where everything is so right, so beautiful. I *beg of you*, on my knees, [to send] the *Kyrie*.[39] I only have the Gloria![40] Thank you. Jean Françaix and I played Bach and Strawinsky in Tours, and even in this tiny, old provincial village it's taking hold![41] On the 17th, we are doing it again in Roubaix and then at the Cité Universitaire for the students.

---

38. Boulanger resolved the issue in a letter dated May 9, 1947; CH-Bps.
39. Stravinsky sent Boulanger the Kyrie on May 15, 1947; CH-Bps. He declared the score's value as "none." It cost 20¢ to send the package.
40. Movements of Stravinsky's *Mass*.
41. Boulanger did not note these concerts in her agendas, and there are no extant concert programs. There is a concert devoted to Stravinsky listed in the programs as taking place on August 28, 1947. On the program was *Circus Polka*; the Variations (final) movement of the *Sonata for Two Pianos*; *Scherzo à la Russe*;

Sviétik has recently made stunning progress. His tour of Italy is a real success. The little one is adorable and already someone. You will be crazy about him.

So happy that Milène and André are finally near to you.

With her serious, peaceful and intense face, little Kitty is a child who does not resemble other children her own age. I could talk with you about her for hours. Her happiness at being with Théodore and Denise [is apparent].

Take Vera in your arms and kiss her for me. My God, how I miss the marvelous time when we looked at each other so seriously. I believe that you and I no longer love [word missing?] and that puts the world between us.[42]

Love to both of you,
NB

[P.S.] Thank you for the program from Washington. What memories!

ঝ   ঝ   ঝ

Boulanger to Stravinsky

Boston, MA

June 14, 1947

What festivities wouldn't we have prepared for the 18th, and you are, Dear Igor, on the other side of the world.[43] It's sad for us, despite all that we [could possibly] say to you. But it's better for you. So . . .

You know what wishes I send you, don't you? But can you know? No, don't try. Thank you for the *Kyrie*, not only for me, but for my boys.[44] I needed it. When will you finish the *Mass*? You can renew the tradition that has been lost

---

the Nocturne from the *Concerto pour deux pianos*; and the finales from both *Capriccio* and the *Dumbarton Oaks Concerto*. They also performed excerpts from the Bach cantatas 28, 54, 147, and 170. Boulanger "Programmes," F-Pn Rés Vm Dos. 195 (folio 769). The concert was part of a series organized by Monsieur l'Abbé. Boulanger advertised it as a lecture recital ("concert avec commentaires").

42. "Le monde entre nous"—arguably an awkward way of writing this.

43. Boulanger's being (awkwardly) sarcastic.

44. By "my boys," Boulanger means the boys at the Bryanston Summer School of Music where she served on the faculty. The program was connected to the private academy of the same name in Dorest, England. Bryanston did not become a co-ed institution until 1972, so Boulanger would have been teaching only boys. Along with Boulanger, Imogen Holst and Paul Hindemith were also featured guests of the summer school.

for ages. It has come to life in your hands, and we have such a need to find the proper direction again. The spirit, the technique of the *Kyrie* and Gloria are immeasurably important.

    If you could know what influences are being exerted, it's dreadful. You will tell me only the weak submit to them. No, they create a false ambiance that seduces young sensitivities, but . . . you are there, and you play a larger role every day. Slowly, they will come to you, and when they've understood you, they will have been saved. Preger wrote some beautiful, good, honest, authentic music.[45] Soulima is making immense progress. His last concert here had a serious impact. He *plays well.* We are overrun by the "prima donna" of the baton, of the keyboard, of the bow, and it's hard to swim against the tide. One can make the public cry with a crash of the bass drum and shameless sentimentality. Swimming upstream is not easy. When we succeed, it is a victory laden with results.

    Immense amount of work—empty head—so I'm sorry for this rather revealing letter. If you feel the tenderness, the attachment, and the longing that resides in it, would you think for a moment of your

Nadia B.

P.S. This also for Vera. And Milène, André, and Madubo.

1948

Boulanger to Stravinsky

February 14, 1948

Dear Igor,

    Official letter today. It has to do with assigning the Lili Boulanger award. If you agree, we could give $250 to Paul DesMarais and $350 to Claudio Santoro, a young Brazilian, a very talented, true musician, and great worker. In the event that you would be ready to agree to this project, the ballot is attached here. You only have to sign it and return it.

    I play *Orpheus* all day long. We are overwhelmed by this score where everything is in harmony and everything seems new, now and always. I seem rather stupid, but I assure you that I have heard and understood everything, and that I am very proud to love you so much, you whom I admire more than I know how to say. It seems that I destroy your secrets.

---

45. A reference to Léo Preger. For more, see chapter 3, n. 89.

And this orchestration, these relationships, these distances. This writing—the score sings in my ears and its order is in my spirit.

You cannot help me anymore. It is entirely my fault, but I suffer for it.

To Vera and to you, all my love,

N

❧   ❧   ❧

Boulanger to Stravinsky

36 rue Ballu

March 23, 1948

What can I say to you, my Friend, I understand. I rejoice for you, but I am sad, very sad. It was such a great and necessary happiness. We all needed you so much. The agreement (*l'accord*) that awaited you would have moved you. It cannot be so. It's sad for us—a cruel disappointment. But I'm convincing myself that it's better [this way], that you are right.[46]

Sorry for not being able to write you. I do nothing but produce variations on a single theme, [an] ostinato, and you would find me boredom personified. Therefore, having told you about my grief all the same, I thank you for this *Orpheus* that gives up a few more of its secrets to me every day [and] that has dazzled me with its beauty since the first reading.[47] What a marvelous *composition*. What beautiful music. What order and what invention. Every . . . but what ridicule I set myself up for. I see myself explaining your own score to you. How naïve. I know well enough that in front of you we must listen and keep quiet. I only want to speak so as to provoke and incite your reactions. How far away they are, and so present, the beautiful, dear days spent at your house. I think of them with joy, and find in them an ever-renewed spring that nourishes and drives me. Dear Igor, Dear Vera, I love you tenderly. I discover this with renewed feeling following your seemingly certain arrival.

And now Easter's here. I remember its promise and again want to believe in our reunion, God knows where and when.

---

46. The letter preceding this was not retained in Boulanger's archives. Her reaction here suggests the tour Stravinsky had decided to postpone on April 19, 1947, had instead been cancelled outright.

47. Boulanger owned two copies of this score. The first, likely the one referenced here, is a photostat of the original with analytical annotations and some corrections noted. F-Pn, Vma. 4008. The second is the published version of the score (including two copies of its errata sheet). Boulanger inserted the corrections into her copy of the published version. F-LYc, UFNB ME STR 400.

With fondness, I am your
NB

P.S. *Tell me what I owe you for the score.* I am so happy to have it. I liked Haïeff's article a lot![48]

❧ ❧ ❧

Boulanger to Stravinsky

PARIS

IGOR STRAWINSKY
AMBASSADOR HOTEL
PARK AVENUE, NY
APRIL 22, 1948

RADIO WISHES PERFORM *ORPHEUS*[49] JUNE 10th ARE SCORE AND PARTS AVAILABLE PLEASE CABLE LOVE =

NADIA[50]

❧ ❧ ❧

---

48. A reference to Aaron Copland's article: "The New 'School' of American Composers: Young Men Now Maturing, Says . . . ," *New York Times* March 14, 1948, SM 18. In addition to Haïeff, Copland discusses Leonard Bernstein, Harold Shapero, Robert Palmer, John Cage, and Lukas Foss.

49. Boulanger's students sent Stravinsky a card congratulating him on the first performance of *Orphée* in Paris, July 8, 1948, CH-Bps. Included among the card's many signatures are those of both Paul and François Valéry, Mario di Bonaventura, and Igor Markevitch.

50. I do not know if Boulanger means the BBC or Radio Française or some other radio ensemble. That said, Boulanger's 1948 diaries are rife with references to rehearsals with Soulima and to *Orpheus*. Indeed, on May 31, she wrote in her diary, "Strawinsky radio," an annotation that was then crossed out. Boulanger, "Agendas," F-Pn, Rés VmB. Ms. 88.

Stravinsky to Boulanger

NADIA BOULANGER
36 RUE BALLU
PARIS, FRANCE
April 23, 1948

REGARDING *ORPHEUS* PERFORMANCE PLEASE CONTACT ROTH
BOOSEY HAWKES LONDON. LOVE

STRAVINSKY

❧ ❧ ❧

Boulanger to Stravinsky

36 rue Ballu

June 5, 1948

You cannot know, Dear Igor, the joy the package you sent brings me. Everything is such a source of astonishment, joy, and amazement in this *Orpheus*. The more I understand you, the less I dare say it to you. How [can I] judge myself worthy of speaking about something you dominate so much.

Yet, from the first to the last notes I believe I heard everything. We play *Orpheus* from morning until night, and without a doubt in a few days you will have put more than one young musician back on the right path. You don't know how they wait for you. They immerse themselves in your music with a sort of greed. They come from far away and begin to understand the influences they have escaped.

I would like to proceed measure by measure and tell you all of my little notes: such an arrangement, such harmony, such connection—and to not seem ridiculous to you, show you for yourself all of the beauty, all of what touches us in your score, every time . . . [but] enough, it must bore you to death. I embrace you, thank you, and am crazy with joy at the thought of seeing you again.

You know that I once again see all of the pleasant and anxious hours with you and you never leave my thoughts. How I await your arrival. It is an *indescribable* impatience. To Vera, Milène, to André, and to you wholeheartedly,

Nadia

P.S. Would you please tell me what I owe you for the score? I would be too embarrassed if I didn't pay for it. Thank you again.

❧ ❧ ❧

Boulanger to Stravinsky

July 11, 1948

Dear Igor,

What a terrible shock for your poor Sokoloff, for you.[51] What an arrival for Soulima. I imagine the confusion, the distress of these days when such a great joy coincides with sadness.

Can you [imagine], have I ever let you know that everything that touches you is so close to me that I believe I participate in it too? I never write to you [because] my letters are always so hurried, of so little interest. But I never leave you, and I am much closer to you today than ever!!

I imagine you must be crazy about Zizi, and I hope that Françoise's presence and kindness, and that seeing her again with your son, are such a happiness for you, that they help you to bear the sadness that befalls your friend and takes away from you such a close friend.

I'm writing you again these days to thank you for the armoire. I am so happy to have it—and to speak to you about *Orpheus*. The orchestra sounds so *unimaginably* beautiful. The music is . . . Well, this is why I don't write you. I feel unworthy of speaking when I know only too well how to keep quiet. Nevertheless, I know that not a note escapes me, and that I *hear* you! How I love you, Dear Igor, and I am so happy to love you . . . as much as I admire you. Your dear Nadia is very weak, but she is close to your heart and spirit, in a word.

Nadia

      ❧   ❧   ❧

Boulanger to Stravinsky

36 rue Ballu, Paris IX
Trinité 90–17

August 29, 1948

So . . . you don't love me anymore! I, who love you more all the time. Dear, Dear Igor. It is true that there are obvious reasons for this crescendo and this fading. But . . . I don't like to admit to them. It's also true that I hardly write you. It's because I don't see how my letters could amuse you, let alone please

---

51. Lisa Sokoloff (sometimes transliterated as Sokolov) was Vera Stravinsky's business partner and close friend. Sokoloff died of a sudden heart attack on June 22, 1948. Days later, Soulima, Françoise, and Jean Stravinsky all arrived in California after emigrating to the United States. Walsh, *Second Exile*, 228. Boulanger wrote to Vera on July 8, 1948, to personally console her; CH-Bps.

you. I content myself therefore with playing your music constantly and conversing with you, no, hearing you. What endless joy this renewal. What complete satisfaction the score to *Orpheus* is. I am sending you the program from Bryanston.[52] You cannot imagine what took place there. These people, coming from all parts of society, have arrived, the nicest of them believing themselves incapable of understanding you. And day after day, I have seen their faces light up. They knew that they could not penetrate everything, but they loved your music—and were so happy. These young men—criticism terrified them, but you conquered them. I believe that you would have felt such joy in seeing their attention and their discovery.

Thank you for the armoire. Can you understand the childish yet contemplative pleasure I take in organizing your music in it. You will never know.

I have found only one copy of the Couperin which, I'm sorry, I could not acquire for the requested price. But I will find it, and you will have it.[53]

How sad it is to no longer have Nini, Françoise, and the little one here. It was so nice, but I do understand that Nini wasn't able to allow himself to be far from you any longer, as he had been!

"And you," you would say? "All these beautiful lines and you let me down?" I know, and I tally all that I lose. But I have my work here, and obligations, and then . . . but no lyricism. I would give I don't know what to see Vera and you, to live close to your future music as well as with your music that sheds light both on the present and the past. Because, thanks to you, I understand better. We all understand better, the sound and real meaning of music.

I've just finished Fontainebleau, am *dead*, literally dead, but still have a small glimmer of consciousness to tell you how much I love you.

---

52. Boulanger sent Stravinsky the entire program for the summer school at Bryanston that year. All of Boulanger's students and fellow lecturers signed the program. Imogen Holst lectured that summer on "How to Listen" and "Dance in Music." Boulanger gave four lectures on Stravinsky and performed his music in five concerts. Erich Gruneberg performed the Elegy for Solo Viola, and he and Boulanger together performed the *Duo concertant.* Boulanger also performed the Sonata for Two Pianos and *Scherzo à la Russe* with William Glock. As her final performance, Boulanger, René Soames, and the Brompton Oratory Choir performed the *Ave Maria* and the final chorus from *Perséphone.* See Boulanger to Stravinsky, July–August 1948, CH-Bps. She also sent him the signed 1949 Summer School program, September 4, 1949, CH-Bps.

53. In 1952, Stravinsky wrote to Hughes Cuénod, asking him where he could find the sheet music to François Couperin's *Leçons de Ténèbres* after hearing Cuénod's recording of the piece. Walsh, *Second Exile,* 281; and White, *The Composer and His Works,* 471. This letter from Boulanger suggests Stravinsky had begun looking for the music of Couperin earlier even than 1952.

To you all with all my heart,
NB

[P.S.] Thank you to Françoise and Nini for their letter.

❧ ❧ ❧

Stravinsky to Boulanger

Hollywood

September 5, 1948

How to thank you for your nice letter and for the program (Bryant [*sic*] Summer School) with this impressive collection of signatures. I am very touched by them.

I would so like to write to you (volumes!)—but when? All my time (three months already) has been devoted to composing the opera *The Rake's Progress*— three Acts, eight tableaux.[54] And I am still [working on] the end of the first tableau (it is true, it's the longest). Soprano, alto, tenor, and two basses as characters and a small orch. (same as in *The Marriage of Figaro*), small choir, recit.— harpsichord or piano.

Forgive me* and accept, very dear Nadia, a very affectionate kiss from

Your
I Str., who loves you

*for not having written you a longer letter.

---

54. On May 2, 1947, Stravinsky attended an exhibition of William Hogarth's paintings at the Art Institute of Chicago. During this visit, he saw and was inspired by the eight-panel work entitled *The Rake's Progress*. By September 30, 1947, Stravinsky began working with W. H. Auden on an opera on the same subject. Paul Griffiths, *Igor Stravinsky: The Rake's Progress* (Cambridge: Cambridge University Press, 1982).

1949

Stravinsky to Boulanger

1260 N. Wetherly Drive
Hollywood, California

March 18, 1949

Dearest Nadia,

Just a note accompanies this Latin version of my a cappella chorale works with which you are familiar—"Pater Noster" and "Ave Maria."[55] I have just arranged this version for use in the Catholic Church, of course, but it would certainly be desirable for Protestant churches to take advantage of them as well.

Did you hear my *Mass* by Ansermet in London (BBC) not long ago? The BBC also performed *Orpheus*.* I've just recorded both of them (*Mass* and *Orpheus*) in New York (Victor).[56] *Orpheus* will come out in September and the *Mass* at Christmas. I did the latter with children (not with women, like Ansermet) who were unfortunately not quite of the highest level. Unlike in Europe, here they don't have the tradition of training discanti and alti. However, I had to settle on the children, because the presence of women's voices, however perfect they might be, would be a much more serious error in the music of my *Mass* (for the sense and the spirit of this music) than the imperfection of a children's choir.

Love,
I Str.

*I tremble at the idea of what the music of my *poor Orpheus* must have been in the hands of Mr. Lichine and the Ballet des Champs Elysees![57]

---

55. The "Otche nash'" (1926), revised as "Pater Noster" in 1949, and "Bogoroditse devo" (1934), revised as "Ave Maria" in 1949, are short choral settings of prayers. The original text of the works was Russian, but the revised versions of the prayers use Latin instead. These pieces, particularly the "Ave Maria," were favorites of Boulanger's to program on concerts. See Francis, *Teaching Stravinsky*, 78–79.

56. Igor Stravinsky, *Mass*, with the Choir of the Church of the Blessed Sacrament and Victor Wind Ensemble, recorded April 1949, RCA Victor WDM-1349, 45 Box; and Igor Stravinsky, *Orpheus*, recorded with the RCA Victor Symphony Orchestra, February 1949, VSM FALP 181.

57. David Lichine (1910–72) was a Russian-American ballet dancer and choreographer. He and Aurel Milloss of the Festival of Contemporary Music in Venice were the first to develop choreography for *Orpheus* after the work's premiere on April 28, 1948. See White, *Stravinsky, The Composer and His Works*, 406.

✌   ✌   ✌

Boulanger to Stravinsky

March 18, 1949

Dear Igor,

This note is not what I need to write to you, but it is what I must write to you. It has to do with the Lili Boulanger Memorial Fund. For reasons I believe you will judge to be unnecessary to expose you to, I hope this year that the prize can be shared between Preger, whom you like and appreciate as I do, and a little, immensely talented Czech student, Karel Husa, who must at all costs be helped right now. I would rather have sent you one of his manuscripts, but he isn't able to photograph them. He has had many manuscripts lost and I don't dare to ask him to send the sole examples that he possesses. I therefore ask you to trust me. I am certain that you would agree.

Thank you for the telegram that touched me so much. I have a million things to tell you, but this cold has done me a nasty turn. I am, once again, very tired and can't even do what is required of me each day. I think of you ceaselessly and am more than sad not to see you anymore. It is such a great sorrow.

I send you both my love, and know that I am your,
Nadia

[P.S.] I cannot speak to you about the *Mass* this way. It is of an incalculable importance, and an unlimited significance. I love it more than I know how to say. It is ridiculous to try to express such things. But you know them . . .

✌   ✌   ✌

Boulanger to Stravinsky

La Moubra, Montana
(I'll be here April 1; [return to] Paris around May 1)

Dear Friend,

You can imagine with what joy I received your letter and the prayer settings with the Latin verses. This translation will be a big help as it was too bad that the Russian pronunciation created a sort of anxiety among the singers.

I missed the *Mass* in London by *one* day. But it seemed that it was very well done by Ansermet and very well sung by the BBC choirs. Certainly the children's voices have to be omitted, but the vocal production of the English must have made it less noticeable than elsewhere. We await your recordings with such impatience! You *alone* can establish a tradition that corresponds completely to your music. And in the middle of so many horrors, created by the awful notion of "performers." What will they not deform to distinguish themselves from one another? Who will be their Molière, because they deserve the satire with which you have already assassinated them.

I came here to try and get rid of a flu that left me in a wretched state. I also wanted to see my dear Dinu Lipatti, who is very ill.[58] How you would like his playing, his spirit, his thought. Alas . . . he will never do it again. Every word that you said when you came to his classes is present, and you are mixed in with his life. He is sleeping right now . . . and the future is dark for him. He asked me to assure you of his respect and to thank you. When he speaks your name, a beautiful joy illuminates his poor face.

You will never know how sad I am not to see you, but it is too late to divide up my life. Already so difficult to do something properly while concentrating on something else.

I received the proposals for the Oja [*sic*] festival.[59] I will respond to them soon. They are certainly making quite the effort in paying all the travel costs, but I would have to give up everything that I earn here, and I don't believe I'm able to take such a heavy financial loss. And then, am I capable of conducting *L'histoire du soldat?* I will keep you up to date.

My warmest thoughts for Vera, Soulima, Françoise. Tell me how you and the little one [grandson] are getting along, and know with what warmth and deep attachment I am with you all,

Nadia

❧   ❧   ❧

Soulima Stravinsky to Boulanger

8624 Hollywood Dr.

---

58. Dinu Lipatti (1917–50) was a Romanian pianist and composer. He died of Hodgkin's disease at the age of thirty-three. Boulanger and he recorded together the Johannes Brahms waltzes for piano four hands in February 1937. EMI released the recording in 1989 (*Great Recordings of the Century* series). For more on Lipatti, see Dragos Tanasecu and Grigore Bargauanu, *Lipatti.*

59. The Ojai Festival was founded in 1947 in Ojai, California, by John Bauer and conductor Thor Johnson. In its original conception, the festival featured a blend of classical and contemporary repertoire. In 1954, Lawrence Morton assumed the position of director for the festival, shifting its focus to modern music. Robert Craft first served as music director in 1954. From 1955–56, he and Stravinsky codirected the festival. See "About-History" *Ojai Music Festival,* http://www.ojaifestival.org/about/. It would appear Boulanger was invited to participate in the annual event from its inception.

Hollywood 46 Cal.

May 4, 1949

Very dear Nadia,

I was so touched that you thought to write to me after receiving my sonata and so happy that it continues to please you. I fear disappointing you a great deal in telling you that it has not been possible until now to write anything. I was finally able to apply myself a few weeks ago. If the result of my efforts is presentable, you know with what impatience I would await your opinion. Up until now, I have had to devote myself to my piano, constantly polishing and re-polishing some of Scarlatti's sonatas, Mozart concertos, some Bach, some Debussy, and I have the very sober realization that I will never play them well enough.

The news you gave of Dinu Lipati[*sic*] upset me greatly. I think of him and his inimitable playing often.

And yourself, Nadia, you have gone to Switzerland to rest. I worry and rejoice all at the same time. Knowing how seldom you suffer from fatigue, I was afraid you wouldn't improve this time, and I was happy to know you were in Montana, far from classes and concerts.[60] Are you certain you've stayed there long enough?

Since I know you carry the entire responsibility of Fontainebleau, I no longer harbor great hopes of seeing you here soon.[61] And I would give so much to see you. Not a day goes by that we don't speak of you. In Boston, where all of your students are, it's as if you were [still] there.

In our families, all goes well, thank God. Father is in excellent form, racks up pages day after day that will once again provide a great lesson.

Jean has had his first week of school and he likes it a lot, although he is not yet familiar with the English language.

We are spending the summer in Santa Barbara where I have a piano class at the Music Academy of the West. We are so happy to see the Sachses.

Françoise joins with me in sending fond wishes from both our hearts.

Your
S[oulima] St[ravinsky]

❧   ❧   ❧

---

60. Crans-Montana, Switzerland.
61. Boulanger had not yet been named director of Fontainebleau. That happened in 1953. See Rosenstiel, 349; and Leonard, *The Conservatoire Américain*, 87–108.

Boulanger to Stravinsky

*annotations Stravinsky's

36 rue Ballu
Paris, IXème

Mr Igor Strawinsky
1260 N. Wetherly Drive
Hollywood, California U.S.A.
October 30, [1949?]

Dear Friend,

One of my most treasured dreams has finally been realized. I conducted *Apollon, Dumbarton Oaks* and the *Mass* in London.[62] I had missed all the performances of them. It was therefore, for me, my first real, living contact with [the work]. I cannot tell you what the rehearsals were like—not only was I myself going through discovery after discovery, better understanding the value of each note, but [also] the musicians [were] *dazzled* because you permitted them to do such things with notes that at first seemed so simple—they understood, and played with an ever-growing joy. They went to the trouble of really doing what you asked of them: breaths, phrases, silences, ratios (*rapports de quantité*), and at the end of the performance, they all came to tell me of the extraordinary feeling they had about the result you allowed them to achieve. The choirs were good, with women, unfortunately, but the English sound production was not shocking. The soprano and the contralto solos were well done, the tenor and bass less so. In the Gloria, I had to hurry the tempo after the opening, because it was bad, the voices were unstable. Everything became shaky. I therefore deliberately inserted a mistake in order to obtain something close to correct, *glossing over, in a manner of speaking and with decency, a few measures before the Hosanna.*

[Stravinsky's annotation: *What does this mean?*]

Since then, I've wanted to write to you, but, what could I say? I believe truly that I understood everything, that the concert was as good as possible without you. Now, speaking of the Mass seems presumptuous and impossible. Silence suits it better. I send my love, I thank you, and I know that once again, you have *succeeded.* You have renewed the old, betrayed, misunderstood, and forgotten tradition. But not by looking behind you, by moving forward. What admirable music, what *spirit.* But, I stray and in my own turn betray. What you have given this Mass is of an

---

62. These were concerts with the British Broadcasting Corporation. The full dialogue surrounding programming and rehearsals can be consulted at the BBC Archives in Caversham, England (GB-CaBBC). Mention of these concerts can also be found in Boulanger, "Agendas," F-Pn, Rés VmB Ms. 88 (1949).

immeasurable significance. Now, no one has the right to ignore it, and [will see in it] what they ought not to do, and what they ought to. The path is newly opened. *Everyone* seems to have understood—how happy I am.

We've performed *Apollon* again in Birmingham three times in two weeks.[63] It is also thanks to you that the Brandenburg [Concertos] have been played with their [proper] rhythms, because I could show what I wanted, what is required in Bach, thanks to what you accomplished in *Dumbarton*. It's always the present that clarifies the past and vice versa, the real meaning of the tradition.

I admire you, love you, and thank you a little more each day because you always open new paths for me.

Your
Nadia

[P.S.] My love to Vera

1950—Meeting in Venice: *The Rake's Progress*

Soulima Stravinsky to Boulanger

Hotel Hargrave
112 West 72 St.
New York City

January 13, 1950

My dear Nadia,

Let me tell you first and foremost that we will have the extreme joy of seeing you again in the month of May. The Ile de France will drop us off on May 10 and will collect us at the end of June. I have to teach again this summer at the Academy of the West in Santa Barbara, starting in July, which will cut our stay in France very short.[64] But short as it is, we will be thoroughly delighted to spend it with you.

---

63. These events are all listed in Boulanger's diaries, with various labels such as "Strawinsky," "Strawinsky, Bach, Bryanston," and "Dumbarton Oaks." Rés VmB Dos 88 (1949). For more on Boulanger's juxtaposition of historical and contemporary repertoire, see Brooks, *Musical Work*.

64. Among the founding patrons and artists of the Music Academy of the West were soprano Lotte Lehmann and conductor Otto Klemperer. The Academy was established in 1947 and held at Cate School in Carpinteria. Arnold Schoenberg, Reginald Stewart, and Darius Milhaud were all involved with the institution in the beginning. For more on the Academy's history, see "Mission, Values and History," *Music Academy of the West*, http://www.musicacademy.

We have left Los Angeles for good. There was no work for me there, and something depressing about the climate. I'm happy to be in N.Y. for a few months with the prospect of more work here in the winter than I've had in eighteen months in California.

A marvelous project is taking shape. I was asked to teach piano in a permanent capacity at the University of Illinois where the Music Director, Mr. John Kuypers, whom you no doubt know, at least by reputation, is a first-class musician.[65] The business is settled in principle, with only formalities to carry out. Among these are my letters of reference. I don't believe I could do better than to ask you for this favor—all while [not] wishing to bother you about it. Two words from you to Mr. Kuypers—University of Illinois, Urbana, Ill.—would lend enormous weight to this application, which they are putting the greatest effort into, so as to [have it] approved. As always in these cases, the interested persons have to present the thing to committees that are less competent but upon which the final decision rests, and they wish to ensure the highest and the best recommendations possible. Thank you in advance a thousand, thousand times.

My father is coming soon to N.Y. to conduct *L'Oiseau de feu* and *Orphée* with Balanchine.[66] Meanwhile *Rake's Progress*, and it is so beautiful that there are no words . . .

Françoise asks me to send you her tender wishes. (Zizi) Jean is becoming a strong, disobedient, but very kind boy. You would no longer recognize him. Personally, I have you so often in my thoughts, you guide me from afar through all of my musical hesitations . . . With fondest wishes, I am always your,

Soulima

❧   ❧   ❧

org/about-us/mission-history. Soulima's appointment came when tensions between Igor and Soulima Stravinsky were reaching a boiling point. For more, see Walsh, *Second Exile*, 244.

65. John Marinus Kuypers (1946–71) was a professor of music at the University of Illinois from 1947 to 1961 and served as the School's director from 1947 to 1950. His papers can be found at the University of Illinois Archives. For more about Soulima and his appointment to the University of Illinois, see Walsh, *Second Exile*, 257.

66. The concert took place on February 21 at the City Center with the New York City Ballet. Robert Craft drove the Stravinskys from California to New York, see Walsh, *Second Exile*, 254–5; and Craft, *Dearest Bubushkin*, 147.

Boulanger to Stravinsky

PARIS

1260 NORTH WETHERLY DRIVE,
HOLLYWOOD, CALIFORNIA
January 27, 1950, 3:00 A.M.

WOULD YOU ALLOW US TO COPY SCHERZO A LA RUSSE
PERFORMANCE AT MONTECARLO DURING PRIVATE CELEBRATIONS
FOR CORONATION OF YOUNG PRINCE.[67] OR CAN YOU SEND IT
URGENTLY STOP WHAT ROYALTY MUST WE EXPECT TO PAY PLEASE
CABLE SO DESIRE SCHERZO IN PROGRAMME FAITHFULLY=

NADIA

❧ ❧ ❧

Stravinsky to Boulanger

IGOR STRAWINSKY
1260 N. WETHERLY DR.
HOLLYWOOD, CALIFORNIA

NADIA BOULANGER
36 RUE BALLU, PARIS

SO SORRY NOT ABLE TO GIVE [unintelligible] AUTHORIZATION
    TRY TO ARRANGE IT WITH ESCHIG WHICH PROBABLY REPRESENTS
AMERICAN PUBLISHER[68]
AFFECTION
STRAVINSKY

❧ ❧ ❧

---

67. Boulanger was named Maître de chapelle for Monaco in September 1947. Spycket, *Nadia Boulanger*, 120; Rosenstiel, *Nadia Boulanger*, 347. As such, she oversaw the music for Prince Rainier's coronation on November 19, 1949, a day still celebrated as "Prince Rainier Day."
68. Éditions Max Eschig was a publishing company founded in 1907 in Paris. The press was and continues to be devoted to modern music. The word "Preille" in the French original might be a reference to Pierre of Monaco, though it is otherwise difficult to discern what the origins for this typo were.

Boulanger to Stravinsky

Ecoles d'art américaines
Fondation reconnue d'utilité publique
Conservatoire de musique—Ecole des beaux-arts
Palais de Fontainebleau

September 1, 1950

Dear Friend,

Why do I never write you? I have too many things to tell you, no time, and lack the means to tell you what a place you hold in all our lives, in mine, in such an absolute fashion. And yet, I speak so much of you, *with you*, through your works, that it saves me the struggle of *trying* to tell you what I would like to.

But today: Gunsbourg, oh yes, Gunsbourg, can mount your opera in Monte-Carlo.[69] Because he is certain [*ne doute rien*], he says (he is ninety-two years old) "if not in 1951, then in 1952." Didn't speak of business, but said: "Of course I could only give this opera in French. The English title, translated, is: *La Carrière d'un roué*, not the best for advertising an opera. So, [we'll use] the name of the principal character 'Thomas Rakewell.'" If this interests you, will you tell me if this title and the idea of the opera in French seem acceptable to you, and what amount you would request to reserve the premiere for Monte-Carlo?

From the 10th to 16th of September at Accademia Chigiana, Sienna, Italy. Then, after a few days, Paris.

You know, don't you, that I don't spend a day far from you, but I have nevertheless refused Koussevitzky's very friendly offer for Tanglewood next year. It is impossible to abandon the school here. It has its thirtieth anniversary next year and then, given the state of things, a departure can be planned, but can a return on a fixed date be [guaranteed]?

I have so many things to tell you. Let's move along, it's hopeless. Yet I must ask one thing: May I, is there any way I might read the opera? All those who know it are making me frightfully jealous. It's not good for my mental health . . . nor my physical state.

My love to you and Vera and Milène and Soulima and Françoise and Jean and André and Madubo. But . . . Don't just say that I send my love to everybody.

Your
Nadia B
[P.S.] My thoughts to Berman, Dahl, and Gnau and, my love once again![70]

---

69. Raoul Gunsbourg (1860–1955) was a Russian-born impresario who served as the longest-standing director of the Opéra Monte-Carlo. See Scott, "Raoul Gunsbourg and the Monte Carlo Opera," 70–78.

70. Ingolf Dahl (1912–70) was a composer, performer, and conductor. Dahl fled Germany during the Nazi occupation, and after emigrating to the United

❧ ❧ ❧

Soulima Stravinsky to Boulanger

1802 Carle Drive
Urbana Illinois

September 14, 1950

My dear Nadia,

You letter moved me, touched me. I understand your reactions against the madness carrying the world away. We cannot stop thinking about it, without arriving at a single solution (who would have enough strength to oppose all this evil?). Day by day we make a point of solving the little problems we need to in order to keep going, and so far, we are more or less succeeding.

As for myself, I'm writing to send you best wishes for your birthday; may all sorts of blessings come to you . . . You know the place you occupy in our hearts, in our life. And shall I tell you that in my teaching, which seems to be taking the form of a vocation, I strive to make clear to others what you have made so evident to me?

I hope at last to find here the calm necessary for composing. I probably also need to learn to write with less reserve. [The need to] control every moment, every combination, stops each of my steps and forbids me from advancing. And I haven't forgotten that one must *do* first and then *discuss* afterward. I am striving to find this balance.

What a joy to have seen George and Art Sachs again—and Marthe Nalet who brought to these distant environs something of the rue Ballu.[71]

My very dear Nadia, Françoise, Jean and I are yours with all our hearts—

Always,
Soulima Stravinsky

❧ ❧ ❧

States studied with Boulanger. Dahl became associated with the "Evenings on the Roof," a concert series founded in 1939 by Peter Yates and Frances Mullen in Silverlake. Stravinsky attended his first "Evenings on the Roof" concert on March 6, 1944. See Crawford, *Evenings On and Off the Roof.* Dahl would go on to conduct a number of Stravinsky works.

71. Marthe Nalet was a student of Boulanger's. Only one letter written by her remains extant in the Boulanger archives, and it dates from 1941. See Letter, Marthe Nalet to Nadia Boulanger, F-Pn, N.L.a. 51 (207). Nalet was also present in 1952 when Boulanger took her students to Stravinsky's Paris rehearsals, May 23, 1952, CH-Bps.

Boulanger to Vera Stravinsky

Ecoles d'art américaines
Palais de Fontainebleau
Fondation reconnue d'utilité publique
Conservatoire de musique
Le Directeur[72]
(Le Moubra, Montana, Suisse)

Mrs. Igor Strawinsky
1260 N. Wetherly Drive
Hollywood 46
California
U.S.A
September 14, 1950

Dear Vera, soon it will be your birthday! Where is Santa Barbara? "Where are the snows of yesteryear?"[73] I miss you so, both of you who occupy my thoughts day after day. And only silence between us, because I live life too quickly, because . . . And time passes, and ultimately, though we *love each other*, we live like strangers.

Well, here at least are some wishes so that one day per year you *see* I am with you. I remember everything, and I can't accept the idea we won't see each other anymore. It is too absurd. Why is the world so big and Hollywood so far from Paris? Koussevitzky had asked me to come to Tanglewood next year. I think I wrote about this to Igor, but *everything* makes this trip impossible, and I declined, after weeks of indecision.[74] Certainly, if I thought I would have seen you, something inside me would have rebelled. But I would have had to arrive for the opening of classes by plane and leave the following day. So, California was out of the question. And, honestly, I cannot hope that you'll come to Europe, a Europe that everything threatens. What savages, what fools we are who, no matter what, want to find nothing more than perfect ways to destroy everything. But . . . all I need is to think of Igor, working

---

72. This letter is the first time Boulanger wrote to Stravinsky on stationery from "Le Directeur" at Fontainebleau (despite being in Montana, Switzerland, at the time).

73. The original French reads: "Mais où sont les neiges d'antan?," a line from the medieval ballad "Ballade des dames du temps jadis" by François Villon (1431–63) from his collection of poetry, *The Testament*. Dante Gabriel Rossetti (1828–82) coined the term "yesteryear" in his translation of Villon's poem into English in 1869.

74. Tanglewood is the summer home of the Boston Symphony Orchestra. See chapter 2, n. 24.

at his opera, to prepare the *Symphonie de psaumes* that I am conducting seven times in four days in Brussels (imagine my joy, and my terror, after everything the symphony *is*—and I risk nothing, I alone am in danger, and that gives me courage, one feels so small. I hear Igor's pulse, I know all too well how far away, and it can be no other way, but I am so happy to have this project), and, when confronted with the only values that matter, we fight, each in his own way.[75] Has Igor read Gisele Brelet's book, *Le temps musical?*[76] I would like to know what he thinks of it, but doubt that he has been able to immerse himself in these two dense volumes.

Like a child, I tell myself stories. I dream that I am arranging my cushions at your place so I can sleep on the couch. I watch Igor's hand, his fingers, moving a marble in Chinese Checkers. I see his table again, the frame he rebuilt so patiently for George, the telegram from Dolin,[77] the *Sonate* at Milhaud's.[78] Altogether, these small details make me believe, once I really start to imagine, that we are together and the conversation will begin again.

Why is this only a dream?

I forgot to tell you, in July I saw Théodore, Denise, and little, *adorable* Kitty. She's very fragile, but so well looked after. And so happy to be with "a dad and a mum."

Dear Vera, I send my love to you and Igor and have the pretension, foolish perhaps, to believe quite certainly there is no one who loves you more

than your,

Nadia

75. For the program and program notes, see September 14, 1950, CH-Bps.

76. The book was a staggering 804 pages long. Stravinsky owned many of Brelet's works in his own library and corresponded with Brelet (1919–73) on several occasions. A list of relevant materials can be found in Craft, "Selected Source Material," in *Confronting Stravinsky*, 354.

77. Reference to a telegram from Anton Dolin, a dancer for the Broadway revue *The Seven Lively Arts*, for which Stravinsky composed his *Scènes de ballet*. The work was conceived by the Broadway impresario Billy Rose. On November 30, 1944, the pre-Broadway run began rehearsals at the Forrest Theatre in Philadelphia and Dolin wrote a telegram to Stravinsky requesting certain cuts and reorchestrations of the score. This, understandably, infuriated Stravinsky. See Walsh, *Second Exile*, 162–64. For more on *The Seven Lively Arts*, see Schuster-Craid, "Stravinsky's *Scènes de ballet*," in *Music in the Theater*, 285–89.

78. A reference to the performance of the *Sonata for Two Pianos* at Mills College on October 27, 1944. For more on this concert, see Rosenstiel, *Nadia Boulanger*, 328; Spycket, *Nadia Boulanger*, 114; Walsh, *Second Exile*, 162; and "Mills Students Hear Strawinsky Recital," October 26, 1944, *Mills College Today & Tomorrow*, 14, Mills College, Department of Music Archives, Oakland, California.

❧ ❧ ❧

Stravinsky to Boulanger

1260 North Wetherly Drive
Hollywood 46, California

Mademoiselle Nadia Boulanger
36 rue Ballu
PARIS—9th (France)
September 16, 1950

My very dear Nadia,

Believe me that I am experiencing the same feelings and the same difficulties as you; I, too, would like to be able to write to you at length just as I would like to be able to speak with you; but I am so taken by my work that I must limit myself to matters of urgency like what you provided me with in your letter of September 1, for which I thank you with all my heart.

Certainly long-shot projects are risky at this time but I am very favorable to the idea of seeing Monte Carlo stage my Opera, because the theater lends itself particularly well to it, owing to its limited dimensions which match the chamber character of my work: instrumentation resembles *Cosi fan tutte* or *Marriage of Figaro* (double winds, two horns, two trumpets, timpani and strings).

My enthusiasm for this Monte Carlo project is unfortunately not unadulterated. First of all, there are the almost insurmountable difficulties of translating my work into French without mutilating the vocal parts. All my work and its musical prosody are conceived of as a whole to highlight the truly magnificent English text by Wystan Auden. You know as well as I do the impossible difficulties of translating into French with regard to both Auden's brilliant poetry and my music, which will inevitably undergo unforeseen changes to its structure.

As for my material interests, they go hand in hand with those of my editors at Boosey & Hawkes, and it's up to them to negotiate and make the decisions. Ralph Hawkes had these matters directly within his control. Unfortunately, he just died unexpectedly eight days ago in New York, and I am currently unaware of how the publishing house will be reorganized and who will look after my affairs.[79]

---

79. Boosey & Hawkes was formed by Leslie Boosey and Ralph Hawkes in 1930 by the merging of Hawkes & Son and Boosey & Company. During the war, this publishing house also purchased Éditions Russes. Ralph Hawkes died on September 8, 1950. His brother, Geoffrey Hawkes, took over in his place. For the history of Boosey & Hawkes, see Wallace, *Boosey & Hawkes*.

So that's the situation.

I won't talk to you about the French title because it has to be translated, like the names of the characters, in keeping with the principal idea inherent to each character (their role in the work). And for that, I doubt we can succeed without collaborating directly with Auden himself. (His address is: Mr. Wystan Auden, 7 Cornelia Street, New York 14, N.Y.)

If I had on hand an available copy of the two acts of the opera already composed (350 pages), I would send them to you right away. But all my copies are tied up because of the negotiations I have ongoing here. The simplest [solution] would be to drop by Boosey & Hawkes (295 Regent Street, London W.I.) during your next trip to London, where you can ask on my part for Mr. Erwin Stein*) so you might acquaint yourself with the first two acts.

I am working ceaselessly in the hopes of finishing before the spring, but I don't know if I will manage to do it.

Vera and I are doing well physically but morally are worried about the present and the future; Hollywood. furthermore, is devoid of interest and California has changed a lot since you left (**). The Sachses, who have just decided to return to France, will be able tell you what they think of it.

As for Soulima [and his family], whom we have had little chance to see during his academic stay in Santa Barbara where they were very busy, they are in the process of settling in Urbana (Department of Music, University of Illinois, Urbana, Illinois).

The only consolation that remains for us here is that Milène and André are close by, as well as the staunch Madubo.

Tomorrow and next week I have to welcome your two students.

I will ask the Sachses, whom I will see again in three days, to take you the recordings of my Mass, because I suppose you still don't have them. I made this recording with the men's chorus (children and adults) of a Catholic church in New York at the end of the first American concert in New York. I am not saying that these children had ideal training but even so, I prefer their timbre to that of women's voices, which are always too impassioned for liturgical song.

Don't forget me; even short letters from you always give me great pleasure.

Vera and I think of you very affectionately.

Your
I. Str.

*The editor
**even the climate

꙳ ꙳ ꙳

Boulanger to Stravinsky

La Moubra, Montana, Valais
(In Paris on October 3, 36 rue Ballu, IX)

Monsieur Igor Stravinsky
1260 North Wetherly Drive
Hollywood, California
U.S.A.
September 22, 1950

Dear, very dear friend, what happiness your letter caused. It seemed to me as if I was going to climb the steps to the garden, to throw myself into your arms. What a great joy that would be!

I wrote as soon as possible to Raoul Gunsbourg, summarizing your letter and advising him to write to B&H, to write to Auden, and, if questions remain to which only you can respond, to let me know. In the meantime, another idea came to me: The Festival at Aix where *Don Juan* and *Cosi fan tutte* were staged in extraordinarily good conditions—superb set, by Cassandre and Balthus.[80] The orchestra, under the direction of Rosbaud, was *perfect*.[81] But the deficit being such as it was last year, and the economic outlook being obviously difficult, what is Mr. Bigonnet going to do? It's possible he doesn't even know himself. This state of uncertainty, the fear of catastrophic events, give all undertakings such an unstable character that no one dares commit to the future. This nervousness is perhaps the most serious problem. Because, if everything remains in suspense, it is by its very nature deeply demoralizing. And this demoralization is maintained carefully, patiently, by the merry propaganda that is sometimes a little too insistent. It must be weakened, by making plans, by admitting, certainly, that the worst could happen, *without knowing*. Thus, I wrote to Cassandre. I answered R. Gunsbourg, and will see Pierre de Monaco upon my return. That is, at the beginning of October.

---

80. Adolphe Jean-Marie Mouron (Cassandre) (1901–68) was a Ukrainian French artist and typeface designer; see Mouron, *A. M. Cassandre*. Balthasar Klossowski de Rola (1908–2001) was a Polish French artist who denounced connecting biography with an artist's work. For more on Balthus, see Weber, *Balthus*; Neret, *Balthus*; and Clair and Monnier, *Balthus*.

81. The Festival in Aix-en-Provence was founded in 1948 by the Countess Lily Pastré. It was designed to mount relatively unknown works of Mozart. An Algerian impresario, Gabrel Dussurget, directed, along with Roger Bigonnet, and stage design was overseen by George Wakhévitch. The Austrian conductor, Hans Rosbaud (1895–1962), also participated. The former archbishop's palace served as the locale, and viewers sat on garden chairs while the artists sang from a wooden stage. For more, see Poray, "Letter from Aix-en-Provence," 18–19.

Your letter, a marvel of clarity, order, care, did not give a reason for the unexpected arrival of the Sachses, which delighted me, as you can imagine, but is it George's mother's health that made them come back? I hope not! Thank you for all the news. You don't know how much I miss you. *You alone* have such an influence. But you work there, and your influence exerts itself from afar. It is necessary given current machinations, like these "systems" that fail to hide their shortcomings, which would not be a crime in and of itself, but their lies, etc. those are a much more serious matter. Happily, they affect only those poor miserable souls whose lack of power is no excuse for not opposing [this influence]. Kiss Vera for me and know that not a day passes when I don't think of you.

With all of my heart,

Your
Nadia B.

❧ ❧ ❧

Boulanger to Stravinsky

36 rue Ballu
Paris IX

Mr. Igor Strawinsky
1260 N. Wetherly Drive
Hollywood 46
California
U.S.A.
November 25, 1950

My thoughts are always close to you, Dear Igor, but with such particular emotion when November 30 approaches. I know, dates are nothing and change nothing. But they bring us close: some in the happiness of being reunited, and others in the certainty that nothing separates those who love one another.

Saw Théodore recently, *so well*; spoke of little Kitty, so happy around him and Denise. To see her—serious, deep, gentle—one imagines how much like her mother she is, and it is a great joy to know she is in these new surroundings, among family.

I did not speak to you about a recent performance of *Orphée*—rather unpleasant, with cuts that would merit violent objections if the intelligence of the work had not been drawn out with the greatest reluctance. Otherwise, it was not as bad as I seem to insinuate, but [it was] far from what this marvelous score deserves. But . . . It is always the blindness of the disciples at Emmaüs.[82] They don't want to see, and always see too late. Their blind, undiscerning infatuation, suddenly, with Bartok is all the more shocking given their long indifference toward him.[83] Let's not shock you. It is the eternal story—but let's remain exasperated. The door is opened, everyone enters, and the result is catastrophic. Time passes and gently things take their place again. And despite all the misunderstandings, Bach is doing very well (*se porte fort bien*), and so are you.

Your Mass conquered all spirits at Solesmes.[84] They, well, they understood, and this made up for the rest. What's more, when one sees the excitement around the revival of *Siegfried* and its sequel, one understands the confusion of the poor public, which could pretend to be a little better guided.[85] It's Wagner,

---

82. This is a biblical reference to the story of two disciples who, accompanied by a stranger, walk to Emmaus during the first evening of the Easter season. The two disciples debate the veracity of the story of Jesus' resurrection. When night falls, the disciples ask the stranger to stay with them and share a meal. At the moment they break bread, they recognize the stranger to be the risen Jesus. Luke 24:13.

83. Boulanger championed Bartók's music—more so, it seems, after the Second World War. In her "Lectures on Modern Music" from 1926, Boulanger spoke at length about Bartok's compositions and his engagement with folk influences. See Boulanger, "La musique moderne" *Le Monde Musical*, 37 année, nos. 2, 5 and 6 (February, May, and June 1926). On July 23, 1941, Boulanger purchased Bartók's *Hungarian Folk Music* while visiting the Santa Clara Convent in Madison, Wisconsin. Later, in 1948, she included lectures on Bartók as part of the Bryanston summer camps and programmed his music in her Wednesday Afternoon Classes in 1958 (Violin Concerto, no. 2); 1959 (*Music for Strings, Percussion and Celesta*); and 1961 (*Bluebeard's Castle* and Suite, op. 14). A thoroughly annotated score of Bartók's Violin Concerto (1938) can be found in Boulanger's Lyon archives, F-LYc, UFNB M 161 BAR.

84. Solesmes Abbey in Solesmes, France was a stronghold for Gregorian chant in the Catholic liturgy. In October 1950, Boulanger gave an extensive presentation there on Stravinsky's *Mass*, arguing for the work's appropriateness for inclusion in the Catholic liturgy despite requiring wind instruments, which were at that time banned from use in the church. For Boulanger's lecture notes, see CNLB "Stravinsky Documents" I1-I5, ca. 1950. For Boulanger's analysis of the Mass as well as the text for a subsequent lecture given in Zurich in 1972, see CNLB AD N1-N32 "Analyse Messe et Conférence 1972."

85. July 29, 1951, marked the reopening of the Bayreuth Festival under the baton of Hans Knappertsbusch (1888–1965) (conductor). The following month, on August 10, 1951, the Palais Garnier mounted *Lohengrin*, featuring Régine Crespin, a recent graduate of the Conservatoire de Paris. See "Journal de l'opéra," F-Pn, Bibliothèque-Musée de l'opéra, August 1951.

Strauss, the Schoenberg school, that are presented as trends across the world, and the world is not finding them particularly enjoyable. They take it in rather poorly.

Happily, among the young people who pay attention, the trend is good. There is a heavy dodecaphonic offensive, but it will not hold its position for long.

Have you ever heard Wozzek [*sic*]?[86]

We've just *carefully* worked on *Renard*—what a pity to not have the orchestration for it.[87] It is a famous score, which is difficult at first but becomes so natural. But there, too, the judgement is distorted. At the heart of it, people do not know the music. There's a lot of literature, a pseudo-philosophy, but it's impossible to perform any of the rhythms without upsetting these old mechanical habits a little.

I wasn't able to accept Koussevitzky's offer nor that of Juilliard and can't console myself when I tell myself that it was the way to see you. But really, we aren't leaving [one another] right now. And that which *ought* to be done cannot be abandoned.

Give Vera my love, and know how deeply I am always with you, Dear Igor. I love you so.

Nadia

[P.S.] How terrible! I did not thank you for your records, and yet, what a joy it was to hear the Mass. I'll enlighten you: every bit of the work is essential. *Thank You.*

❧   ❧   ❧

---

86. Of all the members of the Second Viennese School, Alban Berg (1885–1935) was the composer whom Boulanger seems to have respected the most. She owned the piano/vocal score for *Wozzeck*. Taped to its inside cover is her copy of the program for the Paris premiere, which took place on November 9, 1950, at the Théâtre des Champs-Élysées. Jascha Horenstein directed the performance, which starred Lucien Lovano (Wozzeck), Lucienne Marée (Marie), and Joseph Peyron (the Captain). F-LYc, UFNB M 541 BER W. Boulanger also owned pocket scores (all at the F-LYc) for the Violin Concerto (Vienna, Zurich, London: Universal Edition, 1936); String Quartet, op. 3 (Berlin: Schlesinger, 1920); and *Lyric Suite* (Vienna, Zurich, London: Universal Edition, 1927). These scores have not been annotated.

87. The "we" here is unclear, though I suspect she is referencing her students at the École normale, given the date of the letter and that I cannot find a concert program that shows she ever performed or programmed *Renard* on a concert.

Stravinsky to Boulanger

1260 North Wetherly Drive
Hollywood, 46, California

Mademoiselle Nadia Boulanger
36 rue Ballu
Paris—9th (France)
November 27, 1950

My very dear Nadia:

Just a few lines. I knew the Sachses arrived safely in Paris but I worry about the records I entrusted them with for you. Be kind and reassure me, or, if they forgot to give them to you, please remind them.

Equally, I don't want these records to be misplaced as they are the "standard" (78 rpm), now endangered, type around here, but are still current until the appearance of the "long-playing" (33 1/3 rpm with a running time of up to around 30 minutes) and the 45 rpms that are made exclusively by RCA-Victor.

On this topic, could you tell me if the French are now using the "long–playing" (33 1/3) or if you are still limited to the older models (78 rpm). I'm interested because I'd like to know if I can send "long-playing" records when asked for the technical information about the performance of my works.

I never found the time to read *Le temps musical* by Gisele Brelet. I am familiar with her previous work, or articles, which seemed to me to have merit though, in my opinion, were limited to the domain of pure philosophical speculation.

Nothing new for the moment, immersed as I am in my work.

Give me news about you and tell me if your concerts in Brussels took place. If yes, how did they go?

In a letter I just received from Boosey & Hawkes, they've entered into contracts with two French theaters for *The Rake's Progress*. I wonder if they're talking about the Paris Opera and Monte Carlo, because London has not provided details.

I am very far from being reassured as far as the French and Italian translations are concerned, which are in the process of being done under Boosey & Hawkes's responsibility; I have neither the time nor the means to take care of this and I can imagine the difficulties that will arise when bringing the French and Italian into alignment with my music, composed for an eighteenth-century English text and in verse on top of that . . .

I impatiently await word from you.

Vera and I send along our affectionate wishes.

Yours,
I Str.

1951

Boulanger to Stravisnky

36 rue Ballu
Paris IX

March 22, 1951

Dear Friend,

This is not the letter I would like to write you during this month which brings us together with such sad memories.

But today I'm only going to talk about the Lili Boulanger Memorial Fund. This year we would like to give the prize to a young boy who deserves it—and who greatly needs us to support him: Jean Michel [Dufay]—a true musician, a cultivated and well-guided spirit heading in the right direction. I am sure you would agree with the quality of his work—his taste and his technique—and his intuition. He is eighteen years old and is *good in every respect*. Moreover, he has a difficult situation—he lost his mother and little brother at eleven.

Thank you, and if you are in agreement, the attached ballot is to be sent signed to Winifred Johnstone, 122 Bay State Road, Boston, Mass. Have you read Leonardo's writings? I believe his interest in the subject, his care for doing things the right way, his realism—no, his sense of a subject's reality and its possibilities and limits—will please you.

Each day I think of you and understand better what we all [owe] you.[88] But that's for another day. All my love to Vera and you.

Nadia B.

❧   ❧   ❧

---

88. Boulanger forgot a verb in this sentence.

Boulanger to Stravinsky

Cap d'Antibes, Alpes
36 rue Ballu, Paris

Mr. Igor Strawinsky
1260 N. Wetherly Drive
Hollywood 46
California
U.S.A.
April 11, 1951

Dear Friend,

Where to begin? First with questions, one above all the others: Your opera, will it take place in Venice? When?

Please, let me know, because I would like to change all my plans in order to hear it.

I've just given two lectures on you.[89] Not good, not complete, they need more work. But I have reread all your music in one go . . . and . . . but what can any of that do for you. Yet, in the end, among all those who know this work the best, where everything is different and everything has come at the same time, I feel myself very unworthy of so great an honor. The *audience was excellent,* an outstanding reaction. In Cannes!! In Nice!!

I write to you like I write to all the others, but, God knows how much I love you, and I feel myself close to you. But I cannot for a single moment forget my reverence, my gratitude [to you]. And there you are all alone, so high above, separated from us forever and ever. What a sad story, because in the grand scheme of things, you are *also* a man like us and need us to surround you, to fawn over you, to joke with you. I cannot.

Well, my beautiful letter finishes abruptly. I look around me, I say to myself: I will tell him, and . . . nothing seems to me worthy of taking up your time. How peaceful you would be if everyone were stricken by the same paralysis.

One day, I'll speak to you of some young people who merit your attention, of some books that are worth your reading. But as for the artistic and musical life, I will have the courage, no, might I say the charity, to tell you nothing.

Did you know about the *marvelous* performances they tell me Markevitch has given of *Le Sacre, Perséphone, Orpheus?*[90] I can believe it without any difficulty, because he worked [hard] and understood.

---

89. Not mentioned in Boulanger's diaries.

90. Igor Markevitch (1912–83) was a Ukrainian-born conductor and composer. He studied with Boulanger in the early 1930s alongside Soulima Stravinsky. Markevitch was an adored pupil of Boulanger's, and they kept in close contact after he ceased studying with her. This is the "Igor" of Boulanger's diaries,

How I miss you, and how sad it is not to see you anymore. The sofa is waiting for me, I remember every minute. Why is the world so troubled, California so far, and trips so complicated?

Know that I forget *nothing*, it's the same as telling myself: You, and all that you are, are part of my own life.

My affection, my tenderness, and my fondness to both you and Vera

Nadia B.

[P.S.] *Thank you—thank you* for the card. It was ravishing.

🙣 🙣 🙣

Stravinsky to Boulanger

1260 North Wetherly Drive
Hollywood 46 California

Mademoiselle Nadia Boulanger
36 rue Ballu
Paris—9th (France)
April 27, 1951

My dear Nadia,
A thousand thanks for your very kind letter of April 11 (Cap d'Antibes).

I signed a contract with the Biennale to conduct the premiere of *The Rake's Progress* at the Venice Festival on September 10. But it seems that my editor [at] Boosey & Hawkes was more or less further along with things at la Scala and, to avoid trouble, (which, personally, shouldn't concern me) he is looking to find a compromise of a nature that satisfies the Biennale as much as la Scala and myself. [A compromise] of the sort that would allow for la Scala to participate in the Festival, because as far as I'm concerned I do not want to modify the time of my arrival in Italy, which must be in Venice, rather than Milan.[91]

I have indeed heard murmurs of Markevitch's success with *Le Sacre* but I did not know that he had done *Mavra* and *Perséphone*. I knew that he had

---

whereas Stravinsky is always listed as "Strawinsky," "Straw," or "IS." Boulanger often taught Markevitch's music in her classes and advocated for it in her criticism. For the Markevitch–Boulanger correspondence, see F-Pn, N.L.a. 83 (169–407).

91. Confirmation of the premiere taking place at La Fenice came on June 20. Letter, Ernest Roth to Igor Stravinsky, June 20, 1950, CH-Bps, cited in Walsh, *Second Exile*, 263.

conducted *Orphée* at the Venice Biennial in 1949, but I did not know that he had given concert performances of it.

The opera is finished except for the short Prelude that I am in the process of composing; there will not be an overture. I still have lots of work because Boosey & Hawkes are printing the piano/vocal score, and I am constantly receiving proofs from Germany to correct.

I am really counting on us seeing one another in Venice . . . But what madness awaits us there!!! Théodore's family will come from Switzerland with Kitty, and Milène and André (who will be in Nice this summer) will also pop by.

Write me always dear Nadia, telling me a bit more about yourself. All my love, unfortunately, as always, with great haste.

Your
I Str.

[P.S.] Where and when did you give the lectures (on my music) that you speak of? And what has become of Gunsbourg's beautiful project in Monte-Carlo? There's been no word.

❧ ❧ ❧

Boulanger to Stravinsky

36 rue Ballu
Paris IX

Mr Igor Stravinsky
1260 N. Wetherly Drive
Hollywood 46
California
U.S.A.
June 6, 1951

Such memories go with S. K.[92] I imagine, Dear Igor, your sadness, and am so close to you. Useless, isn't it, to say what we think when the heart and mind are in agreement. He reached so deep within himself and gave so much. What sadness to survive [. . .]

---

92. S. K. is Sergey Koussevitzky, who died on June 4, 1951. Koussevitzky was a Russian-born conductor and longtime director of the Boston Symphony Orchestra (1924–49). Along with his first wife, Natalie Ushkova, he established the publishing house Éditions russes de musique. For more on Boulanger's relationship with Koussevitzky as concerned Stravinsky, see Francis, *Teaching Stravinsky*, 122–23.

Could it be true that you are not coming and that your work will not be given on September 9? I beg of you, send a card—everything is hanging on this project.

Impossible to imagine such a disappointment!

With such tenderness for Vera and you,

Your
Nadia

❧   ❧   ❧

Stravinsky to Boulanger

1260 North Wetherly Drive
Hollywood 46, California

Mademoiselle Nadia Boulanger
36 rue Ballu
Paris, 9th (FRANCE)
June 13, 1951

My dear Nadia,

Your letter touched me greatly; we were all affected as well by the swift and almost unexpected death of Koussevitzky. At the request of *Time* magazine, I wrote these few lines included below:

"That Serge Koussevitzky was a great celebrity, everybody knows; but that many careers were created by his generosity, very few know.

When a man passes away those wishing to pay tribute to his memory recollect his good deeds, the things he did most ostensibly.

Let us dwell today on those things that Serge Koussevitzky did for others without telling anyone about it. And for these secret things let him be rewarded manifestly."[93]

I think my homage, limited to what is true, is in this way more sincere than many of the others that are being published right now.

What is this pessimistic news that you're only partially sharing with me? You seem to know more in France about the Italian premiere of *The Rake* than I do here. As for myself, I have a solid contract in my pocket with the Biennale and I will be in Italy on the scheduled dates (mid-August) to perform it. A couple of days ago I learned officially that La Scala has agreed with the Biennale to mount the Venetian production. But I have no other details; these Italians don't seem to like to write. Therefore, I would like to know more about this

---

93. Stravinsky's article was never actually published by *Time Magazine*. See Craft, *Stravinsky in Pictures and Documents*, 282.

from you if—as your letter left me to assume—you are collecting information from various sources. Who is saying what??? In Italy or elsewhere about my *Rake*?? . . . Don't leave me in the dark.

Vera and I send you our great affection,
I Str.

❧ ❧ ❧

Boulanger to Stravinsky

36 rue Ballu
Paris IX

June 14, 1951

Dear, Dear Igor, will I be with you on the 18th? I am so afraid I left it too late. I give you a kiss on both cheeks. I say a big thank you to you who, every day, gives us such joy. And I say to you Happy Birthday, Happy New Year and . . . see you soon! Because you are coming, aren't you? The news is all frighteningly contradictory, but I don't want to doubt it. because that would be a terrible disappointment.

Fondly and with all of my affection,
Nadia B.

❧ ❧ ❧

Boulanger to Stravinsky

36 rue Ballu
Paris IX

Monsieur Igor Strawinsky
1260 N. Wetherly Drive
Hollywood 46
California
U.S.A.
June 18, 1951

What Happiness, Dear Friend—*thank you* for having responded so quickly. The rumors that run through Rome and Paris are so varied and contradictory that one must give up trying to understand. One day "the premiere will take place in Milan" the other "in Venice" then, "nothing is decided, everything is to be struck and will be remounted in Paris in the spring," then, "the 9th in Venice,"

"monstrous attempt by the Scala [to go after] the Biennale." "American performers have been hired." "What, it is the Italians who are doing everything."
"Stage design by Balthus." "No, by Berman." This back and forth only tormented me at first and now seems to me to be exaggerated, so I want to try not
to hear anything about it, and will wait.

How can I say what happiness it will be to see you again and to hear your
opera.

Forgive me, but between competitions, lessons, [and] concerts, I've lost my
head. But I've found it again to tell you of my joy [and] my tenderness.

To Vera, to you,
NB

[P.S.] Admirable, your message.
[P.P.S.] Ah, it's the 18th—happy birthday!!

❧ ❧ ❧

Boulanger to Stravinsky

Ecoles d'art américaines
Fondation reconnue d'utilité publique
Palais de Fontainebleau (S.&M.)

Conservatoire de musique
Le Directeur du Conservatoire

Personal address: 36, rue Ballu,
Paris-IX

July 21, 1951

Dear Igor,

Will this letter still reach you? I certainly hope so, because I must tell you
with what wild impatience I await the moment when I will see you and Vera
again. Are you still arriving in Naples on August 15? When will you be in
Venice? *Until when?*

A line to settle things would do me a great service, because I would like to
arrange all my plans in accordance with yours, if possible.

So:

Date of arrival in Naples?
Name of the boat
Date of arrival in Venice
Date of departure from Venice

Destination
Date of departure for the United States
Just think what it means [to me] to hear *The Rake's Progress*—and to see you—you can't imagine!!

To both of you with all my heart,
Nadia B.

❧　❧　❧

Stravinsky to Boulanger

Mademoiselle Nadia Boulanger
36 rue Ballu
Paris 9eme, France

July 27, 1951

Dear Nadia,

Just a letter in response to the questions you sent me in your letter from Fontainebleau on July 21, received just now.

I leave here July 30 and will be in New York (Hotel Lombardy, 111 East 56th Street, New York 22, N.Y.) from August 2 to August 7, on which date I embark on the SS Constitution (American Export Lines) to arrive in Naples on August 15.

I will be in Milan until September 3 (c/o Scala or Hotel Duomo).

Following that, Venice (c/o Biennale or Hotel Bauer-Grunwald).

The premiere I'm conducting is on September 8; afterward two other performances, the 10th and the 12th, under an unknown director, probably someone from [La] Scala (I have recommended Markevitch, but it appears that will not work out).

After the shows I will probably make recordings of [*The*] *Rake*, but where?. . .(Venice or Milan) . . . and when exactly? . . . I have no idea.

Afterward I have a pair of concerts in Milan at the Scala on the 27th and 28th of September.

Then October 8: Cologne (*Oedipus Rex*);

October 14: Baden-Baden;

October 21: Munich (the new *Oedipus Rex* with Cocteau).

I must reboard the SS Constitution in Genoa or Naples the 29th or 30th of October to come back to New York for November 7.

See you soon.

In all haste, I am very affectionately,

Your
Igor Stravinsky

❧   ❧   ❧

Stravinsky to Boulanger

Excelsior Napoli

August 22, 1951

Dearest Nadia,

I received your telegraph upon my arrival.

Thank you! Unfortunately, the "air conditioning" on the SS Constitution wished me a case of *pneumonia*, Yes! A very good local doctor took agressive measures = penicillin (strong doses) and at the end of this week (August 26) I am going to Milan (Hotel Duomo) to start to work.

Théodore's family is here close by.

Very, very affectionately,
I Str

P.S. Vera has had horrible, unending bronchitis this whole time!!

❧   ❧   ❧

Boulanger to Igor and Vera Stravinsky

Hotel Bauer Grünwald
Venice

Monsieur Igor Strawinsky
Hôtel Excelsior, Napoli
September 11, 1951
Premiere of *The Rake*

Will meet you at the door to the Theater, my very dear ones. Oh what emotion to spend this time with you. I've just reread the third act.

Thank you.

Hugs,
N

Chapter Five

A Friendship Unravels

1951–1956

There are fewer letters after *The Rake's Progress* reunion, the result of Stravinsky and Boulanger's immensely busy schedules in the 1950s. In this decade, both musicians rose to new levels of professional prestige. Though Boulanger turned down the majority of North American invitations she received, she otherwise commonly references tours returned from or those for which preparations were under way. For both musicians, brevity and concision became essential, which may explain some of the changes in rhetoric that creep in, including Stravinsky sometimes writing to Boulanger in English or sending dictated letters entirely missing diacritical marks.

In 1953, Boulanger was appointed Director of the Écoles d'art américaines at Fontainebleau, and she threw herself into the role with vigor. She believed fervently, as she wrote to Stravinsky on September 21, 1953, that she wanted "the École de Fontainebleau to have a real purpose, or else [they] should let it go." This new directorship drove her. For Stravinsky, the years directly following 1951 were ones of significant metamorphosis. His experience touring Europe after the premiere of *The Rake's Progress* exposed him to a musical world vastly different from that of the United States. He deeply feared he had fallen by the wayside and would be omitted from the music-historical narrative. I suspect Boulanger, too, remained sensitive to Stravinsky's insecurities, given the frequency with which she reassured the composer that he continued to hold sway on the continent.

One of the greatest factors affecting the rapport between Boulanger and Stravinsky rested in the latter's decision to explore serial composition. In 1952, Stravinsky began to experiment with these precompositional procedures, a decision no doubt made easier following the death of Arnold Schoenberg on July 13, 1951. Stravinsky was also encouraged in this pursuit by his new assistant, Robert Craft (1923–2015), a young conductor who had studied at Juilliard and was a passionate champion of modern music. This is the "Bob" mentioned by Boulanger in letters beginning on September 20, 1952. Craft's own dialogue with Stravinsky began soon after the war, and by December 1948 Craft had moved into the Stravinskys' home to serve as the composer's amanuensis and assist with his professional endeavors. According to Craft, Stravinsky was depressed upon returning from his 1951 tour of Europe, deeply distressed about his place in the postwar musical climate. Craft stoked Stravinsky's interest in serial music, especially the compositions of Anton Webern. Following this encouragement, Stravinsky began to place a renewed premium on rebranding himself as a post-tonal composer.

Stravinsky never articulated his decision to compose serial music to Boulanger, but her letter of November 7, 1954, contains his rather confrontational underlining where he annotated Boulangers prose thus: "one quickly gets the impression that *these types of* complications *are only a* crutch." Boulanger's inability to welcome Stravinsky's switch to serial composition creates around this time a barrier between the two. Indeed, the reader encounters two different Stravinskys and two different Boulangers in this portion of the letters. There is both the hasty Stravinsky who dictates a cold, officious message to Boulanger, and the Stravinsky who signs that same gruff letter with the words, "Love, kisses" (for example, June 15, 1954). As for Boulanger, she is both the author who criticizes serialism and the one who praises Stravinsky's serial work—such as the *Canticum Sacrum*—for possessing all the right notes, knowing full well it had been composed with twelve-tone techniques (as her analytical markings indicate). Perhaps Stravinsky's shift in musical language did not distress Boulanger as deeply as many assume. And yet it is difficult not to wince as Boulanger's words of love and devotion become repetitive, recycled, and arguably insincere. There is a disconnect between the Boulanger devoted to the *idea* of an academic, constructed, neoclassical Stravinsky and the one who enthusiastically praises works such as the *Cantata* (January 22, 1953) and *In Memoriam Dylan Thomas* (November 7, 1954) in her letters to him.

The tension between the loving friendship Stravinsky and Boulanger had established—and which I believe to have been genuine during and immediately following the war years—and the new, conflicting professional ambitions that developed after 1951 inevitably led to difficulties. The letters make it clear that Boulanger became cumbersome to Stravinsky. Her demands for perfection—such as her insistence that the French translation for *The Rake's Progress* be corrected (first mentioned on February 5, 1952)—and her requests concerning commissions and visits with students proved incompatible with Stravinsky's pursuits. Though she wrote repeatedly with criticisms of performances, personnel, and suggestions about performance venues, her letters were now annotated when received, suggesting a more exploitative cataloguing of her references alongside or perhaps in lieu of any interest in her commentary. Someone—likely Craft—now fact-checked her claims about radio transmissions and stagings of *The Rake's Progress*, and when her information was incorrect, Stravinsky followed up quickly and abruptly.

This section of the correspondence, therefore, resonates with tension—tension between the respectful friendship that Boulanger and Stravinsky never truly abandoned and their need to disentangle, or at least significantly alter, their professional connection; tension between the written and the unwritten. This conflict reached a head on October 15, 1956, when Stravinsky suffered a stroke in the middle of conducting a concert in Berlin.

Soulima Stravinsky to Boulanger

1802 Carle Drive,
Urbana, Illinois

September 30, 1951

Dear Nadia,

May these lines convey to you my very faithful thoughts which go out to you so often, and particularly today on your birthday.

We have experienced from afar the creation of *The Rake's Progress*. Knowing that among all of the indifferent or neutral ears there were your own is reassuring. The articles in all of tomorrow's newspapers and magazines have even given us an idea of what kind of event it was, what the work [means] to Music and to History. I am sure that you and I think the same thing about this. Times will change and prove it to those reluctant ones. But maybe they won't be so numerous this time around, or am I mistaken?[1]

And now, here, a second university winter semester starts. We've taken root in this place. (Don't smile, things take root quickly in fertile soil). We love this life. I love my students and find myself in the best working conditions there are. Lots of concerts as well this year, like last year. Françoise thinks I accept too many of them.

Could we come spend a few weeks in France next spring? It is our greatest desire, but we still can't decide on anything.

---

1. Soulima Stravinsky kept over thirty article clippings on the premiere of *The Rake's Progress* in Venice through to the American premiere in 1953. These include a review in *Time* magazine (September 24, 1951), and reviews by Virgil Thomson (1896–1989), Miles Kastendieck (1906–2001), Ernest Newman (1868–1959), and Richard Capell (1885–1954). See US-NYp, Soulima Stravinsky Papers, newspaper clippings.

Jean has started school (first grade) and is distinguishing himself there by his natural abilities (proud father speaking) as well as by his passionate temperament.

One of my former students, Patricia Hepner, is going to be in Paris this winter.[2] She does not know anybody there and I thought your guidance could be invaluable to her. Would you be so kind as to welcome her when she telephones you? I'm also recommending her to Jacques Février, who I hope will be able to follow her training for the competition in Brussels where she hopes to perform this spring.[3] Thank you in advance for what you might be able to do for her.

Françoise asks me to pass along her affectionate thoughts. I add to them Jean's and, of course, my own.

Always, your
Soulima.

🙟 🙟 🙟

Boulanger to Stravinsky

26 rue Ballu
Paris IX
November 30, 1951

The Bibliothèque nationale would like to have, if not a manuscript, at least a photo of one of them—would you allow them to reproduce at their expense

---

2. There is no mention of Patricia Hepner in Boulanger's correspondence list nor in her archives.

3. Jacques Février (1900–79) was a pianist who specialized in the performance of twentieth-century French music. He premiered Francis Poulenc's *Concerto for Two Pianos* along with Poulenc in 1932. His recording of Ravel's piano works won him the Grand Prix du Disque in 1963. See Marie Duchêne-Thégarid and Diane Fanjul, "Apprendre à interpréter la musique pour piano de Debussy au Conservatoire de Paris entre 1920 et 1960," in *Regards sur Debussy*, 79–99 (Paris, France: Fayard, 2013). There are three extant letters between Février and Boulanger; see F-Pn, N.L.a. 69 (403–5). The "Brussels Competition" is a reference to the prestigious Queen Elisabeth Competition, first opened to pianists in 1938. It is named for Queen Elisabeth of Belgium and was founded by Eugène Ysaÿe (1858–1931), a Belgian concert violinist and, interestingly enough, an early collaborator of Raoul Pugno. For more on the competition, see "All Competitions," *Queen Elisabeth Competition*, http://www.cmireb.be/cgi?lg=en&pag=1677

the score of *Rake's* that Nabakoff [*sic*] has? Or the orchestral score of *Oedipus*? Or the manuscript of the *Sacre* finale?

I'm sorry for boring you, but it is so important for the B.N.

We would have been at the church together today![4] I send my love—I'm so sad not to have seen you [both] at Orly—and am always, much more than you know, with you,
Nadia B.

[P.S.] I've managed to obtain the orchestral score of *Rake's*. What a victory and how important.
[P.P.S.] Thank you for everything.

❧   ❧   ❧

Stravinsky to Boulanger

Gladstone
114–122 East 52nd Street at Park Avenue
New York City 22
Plaza 3–4300

Cable address
"Gladsto"

December 8, 1951

My very dear Nadia,

Thank you for your affectionate letter of November 30.

Nov. 30, 1938! What a long-ago date and yet so ruthlessly present "every day" of my life.

What do you mean by the phrase *"Have managed to obtain a copy of the orchestral score for the Rake. What a victory and how important."* Which orchestra or orchestral score does this concern? The one at Boosey & Hawkes? It is definitely not published yet—there are still corrections to complete.

Would the Bibiliothèque nationale you spoke to me about in your last letter like to acquire my manuscript? I have *two* in Hollywood—one set of *summary sketches* and another, the *large orchestral score*—both written in a beautiful hand on transparent paper (for copying). I would be very happy to sell them—but unfortunately they would be very, very expensive.

---

4. Anniversary of Mika's death.

We are staying here until the New Year, kept back by different minor things besides one very important one: *The Rake* at the Metropolitan in February 1953.[5]

Write, my very dear Nadia,

Hugs and kisses,
I Str.

[P.S.] In Cologne I recorded *Oedipus* and the *Symphonies of Wind Instruments* for Columbia, which will be released in a year.[6]

[P.P.S.] London let me know that as of today there are seven theaters in Germany playing *The Rake*.

🙚 🙚 🙚

Boulanger to Stravinsky

* Stravinsky's annotations

36 rue Ballu
Paris IX

Such sadness to think that you are here, so close, that you represent so much for me, and that my obligations—that seem to me of such little importance when compared to the joy of seeing and hearing you—keep me here.[7] It's an issue of money as well! How can I express—my real grief!

---

5. Negotiations with Rudolf Bing to mount *The Rake's Progress* with the Metropolitan Opera began in December 1951. By December 8, 1951, Stravinsky felt confident enough to write to Boulanger that the Met had committed to performing the work in 1953. See Walsh, *Second Exile*, 279.

6. The recording took place on October 8, 1951, at the Nordwestdeutscher Rundfunk in Cologne. Werner Hessenland was the narrator for *Oedipus Rex*, but Columbia overdubbed Jean Cocteau's speeches from a performance eight months later. Also involved in the original recording were Martha Mödl, Peter Pears, Helmut Krebs, Heinz Rehfuss, and Otto von Rohr. The recording is now available as part of the Columbia Legendary Performances—The Composer as Performer series. Stravinsky, Igor. *Oedipus Rex*. Cologne Radio Symphony Orchestra and Chorus. Igor Stravinsky. Columbia Odyssey, Y33789, 1951, vinyl.

7. I am confused by this portion of Boulanger's letter. The Zurich production of *The Rake's Progress* took place in December 1951, therefore the document above must date from after that time. Yet Stravinsky returned to the United States in mid-November 1951, making him not even remotely "close" when Boulanger wrote this letter. For Stravinsky's return to the United States, see Walsh, *Second Exile*, 278.

It seems that the <u>Rake's in Zurich</u> was received with extraordinary enthusiasm.[8] It was a performance without celebrities, leaving only the work itself the task of producing its effect and achieving it completely. Pierre of Monaco went to Zurich to hear it and told me of the public's immediate, constant, striking reaction. We have dived into the score, all the young people are deeply affected by everything it brings them.

I send you both hugs and kisses, love you both madly, and am astonished at my not flying to meet you. Something must truly be preventing me!

Your
Nadia B.

❧   ❧   ❧

Boulanger to Stravinsky

36 rue Ballu
Paris, IX
[December 25, 1951]

Will this arrive on the intended day so that my wishes might convey to you my constant thoughts? What prayers wouldn't I say so that you would conduct *The Rake*, Dear Igor, but I don't dare believe it yet!

Recently heard an incredibly striking rehearsal for *Noces*—amateur choir, disoriented at first, soon took the score on, and ultimately were overtaken by a not impeccable enthusiasm, but modestly did their best. Good soloists, a conductor who knew his role, [but a] foolish public. It's running for only one repeat performance.[9]

Excuse this second letter—about the theme—I doubt you have accepted, but understand that Gavoty insisted I countersign his letter.[10]

---

8. A Zurich, Switzerland production of *The Rake's Progress* was mounted in December 1951. For one attendee's reactions, see Walton, *Othmar Schoeck*. In addition to underlining the information in this sentence, Stravinsky also inserted the date of 3.11.51.

9. There is no mention in the diaries of a performance of *Les Noces* in 1951. Rosenstiel mentions that Boulanger requested that Noël Lee substitute for her in a performance of *Les Noces* that dates from roughly around this time. Rosenstiel, *Nadia Boulanger*, 363.

10. Bernard Gavoty (1908–81) was a renowned organist and also a music critic for *Le Figaro*, where he wrote under the pseudonym "Clarendon." Gavoty requested of Stravinsky a chorale theme for a gala concert of improvised music to be held at the Université des Annales and performed by Marcel Dupré (1886–1971). Gavoty intended the theme to be projected on to the Salle Gaveau screen for

Try to pull yourself away from the delights of Capone and come quickly—we need you here! And everywhere. How I miss my couch and those days in Hollywood! But telling you how much I miss you, I wonder if you know, and think sometimes of me? Lie [if you must], but just tell me that you do.

Dear Vera, dear Igor, with hugs and kisses, I love you deeply.

Your
Nadia B.

[P.S.] *MERRY CHRISTMAS*
[P.P.S.] Finally have "my" orchestral score for *The Rake's*—what joy!

1952

Stravinsky to Boulanger

1260 North Wetherly Drive
Hollywood 46, California

Mademoiselle Nadia Boulanger
36 rue Ballu
Paris, IX
January 8, 1952

Dear Nadia,

I just received your charming letter with Gavoty's request.

Here is a little chorale theme that I would ask you to give to him.

I'm delighted that you have the orchestral score for *The Rake* . . . But I am curious to know how you were able to obtain it since it is neither commercially available nor published yet.

You will receive three volumes—probably from Milan—that are photocopies of my summary sketches of *The Rake* containing my numerous (but never sufficient) corrections.[11]

---

the audience to see while Dupré improvised. The letter from Gavoty is still retained in the Stravinsky archives as part of the Boulanger–Stravinsky correspondence. See Boulanger to Stravinsky, December 22, 1951, CH-Bps. The project is touched upon in Walsh, *Second Exile*, 280; and Craft, *Stravinsky: Selected Correspondence*, 251.

11. The question of these summary sketches arises on numerous occasions in this section of the correspondence. Following Boulanger's death, the three volumes of summary sketches were donated to the Bibliothèque nationale de

I leave it up to you whether to keep them for yourself or to hand them over to the Library as you had written to me.

I am waiting for Nabokov's response to know if they (Nabokov and his Congress) accept my conditions to conduct *The Rake* myself.[12]

Always eager for news from you,

Fond wishes,
I. Stravinsky.

[Here is] a chorale theme for Marcel Dupré that I offer for his use in improvisation with the sole regret of not being present to hear it.

❧   ❧   ❧

Boulanger to Stravinsky

Ecoles d'art américaines
Fondation reconnue d'utilité publique
Palais de Fontainebleau (S.&.M.)

Conservatoire de musique
Le Directeur du Conservatoire

Monsieur Igor Strawinsky
1260 N. Wetherly Drive
Hollywood 46
California

France. See Stravinsky, "Summary Sketches for *The Rake's Progress*," F-Pn, Rés Vma 329 (1–3).

12. In 1951, Nicolas Nabokov became the Secretary General of the Congress for Cultural Freedom, a body formed in 1950 and bankrolled by the Central Intelligence Agency of the United States government. Its purpose was to advocate for democracy through the promotion of certain artists. See Wellens, *Music on the Frontline*, and Ansari, *The Sound of a Superpower*.

U.S.A.
First Class
Air Mail
January 17, 1952

How kind and generous of you—and this theme is so beautiful. But . . . who deserves to work with it? You can imagine the joy of those who begged you for it! Have I been horribly indiscreet, Dear Igor, in keeping one of the two copies? But, you will be completely indulgent, won't you?

Yes, after having pleaded my case, having sworn that I would not rent the score to *Rake's* to anyone, that I would copy it neither in whole nor in part, that I would not open a theater to perform it and [having] signed a mass of paperwork . . . The three volumes arrived. We have not ceased to read it—all my boys—and girls!—are mad about it. What a marvel.

Everyone here awaits you with such impatience that you can hardly imagine it, and I more than anyone.

I don't dare believe the package from Milan, it is too beautiful to be true. In any case, your intentions touched me deeply.

The radios everywhere play you ceaselessly, some performances are quite good. Here this Sunday it was the *Octet*—excellent, clean, well placed.

I hope that Vera had my telegram for her birthday.

Nothing of what I could tell you would be of interest. I work crazily and am well and truly shut away with these young people who tread the right path thanks to you and you alone.

With fondest wishes, I am always with you, with great affection,

Your
Nadia B

❧   ❧   ❧

Stravinsky to Boulanger

1260 North Wetherly Drive
Hollywood 46, California

Mademoiselle Nadia Boulanger
36 rue Ballu
Paris, IX (FRANCE)
January 22, 1952

My dear Nadia,
    Thank you for your affectionate letter (of January 17).

You did well in keeping a copy of the little chorale for yourself, because one of the two was in fact intended for you, the other for you to give to Gavoty at *Le Figaro*, which you have surely done.

I am happy and reassured to know you have finally received the three volumes of *The Rake* (photocopy of my summary sketches).

Do you know a professor (I do not know of what) by the name of Leon Oleggini?[13] I recently received a letter from the editors Maurice and Pierre Foetisch, of Lausanne, telling me that they had bought the manuscript of a book written about me by this gentleman. They asked me to supply them with photos to illustrate the book that they propose to publish with a catalogue of my works!!! I calmed them down, knowing neither the author nor the book and not having the time to dedicate to them. But on the other hand, I am in the process of making, on my own, and little by little, a complete (and, for the first time, *exact*) catalogue of my complete works.[14]

Nabokov tells me that they, in principle, agree I may conduct *The Rake* at the opera, but that Lehmann cannot decide anything for three weeks.[15] On the other hand, Dr. Roth writes me from London that Bondeville is managing the opera.[16] Ultimately, I do not understand who is in charge of whom or what. Nabokov pointed out to me new singers that I of course do not know: Janine Michaud (Anne), Roger Bourdin (Shadow).[17] Do you know them?

Have you seen the French translation? If so, what do you think of it?

Be an angel and respond to me as quickly as possible, it would be a pleasure to hear from you.

Love,
I Str.

❧ ❧ ❧

13. This book was eventually published. See Oleggini, *Conaissance de Strawinsky*.
14. This catalogue was never finished.
15. Maurice Lehmann was the head of the Opéra; see Giroud, *Nicolas Nabokov*, 256.
16. Emmanuel Bondeville (1898–1987) was a French composer, and at the time of this letter Director of the Opéra de Paris. Boulanger would have also known Bondeville from her work with Radio Paris, which he directed after 1935, along with Radio Tour Eiffel, and Radiodiffusion française. See Chamfray, "Additions aux biographies de compositeurs," 20.
17. Janine Michaud (1914–76) was one of the leading lyric sopranos of the time. Roger Bourdin (1900–73) was a French baritone especially known as a performer of French contemporary repertoire. Both are mentioned in Rosenthal et al., *Guide de l'opéra*. For more on Bourdin, see Pâris, *Dictionnaire des interprètes*.

Boulanger to Stravinsky

Ecoles d'art américaines
Fondation reconnue d'utilité publique
Palais de Fontainebleau (S.&.M.)
Conservatoire de musique
Le Directeur du Conservatoire

February 5, 1952

Dear Igor,
    Upon receiving your letter, I telephoned rue d'Anjou to obtain the translation. Some passages are good, but others are *impossible*. All of your rhythms are changed. Where the syncopation is *everything*, equal values render it unacceptably monotonous. Some expressions also, such as: "The deuce," whose resonance is so striking and whose meaning is supposed to convey at once so many things through the force and complexity of words as [Kraus] performed it, for which the tone—which is too clear—and the silences (*le vide*) are terrible at this incredibly important point.[18]
    What do you want to do?
    1) Write to the translator yourself to indicate to him the parts you don't like.
    2) Find someone here (I know someone) to try to set to rights what *must* be changed.
    I'll await your instructions. This work must be done quickly, even if the Opéra's date remains uncertain, because learning a text that is then changed would be just maddening for the artists.
    Concerning the performers: Bourdin will be *perfect*. Michaud is slightly lacking in her lower [register], maybe in lyricism, but she will not accept, I believe, if she doesn't feel she can do a good job.
    You ought to, at all costs, get Cuénod for Sellem and Simoneau for Tom. For the latter, they are thinking of Lucca [*sic*] who is not as good as Simoneau.[19]

---

18. Otakar Kraus (1909–80) was the original Nick Shadow; see Griffiths, *The Rake's Progress*, ii.
19. Hugues Cuénod (1902–2010) was a Swiss tenor who had worked a great deal with Boulanger. He is a featured soloist on her Monteverdi Madrigals recording: Victor Red Seal Record (USA), set M 496, 1937, 6 discs. For their correspondence, see F-Pn, N.L.a. 64 (55–245). For more on Boulanger's singing group, see Brooks, "Salon of the Princesse de Polignac," 415–68; and Kahan, "'Quelque chose de très raffiné," in *Témoignages et études*, 85–98. Léopold Simoneau (1916–2006) was a French Canadian lyric tenor known for his performances of Mozart. Libero de Luca (1913–98) was also a Swiss tenor. He began his career in Zurich, but in 1949 established himself in Paris at both the Opéra comique and the Palais Garnier. Both Simoneau and Luca can be found in Rosenthal et al., *Guide de l'opéra*.

I leave Thursday for Monaco. Lecture on *The Rake*.[20] I am terrified because ... I am incapable of properly saying what these people nonetheless must know. They are led constantly down the wrong path!

If you need to reach me between the 8th and the 18th: Monaco Palace, Principality of Monaco

Hugs and kisses to both of you. I am your,
Nadia B

[P.S.] Received first and second acts from Milan. A telegram announcing a letter to come. This never arrived, nor did the third act, and the copy I received doesn't contain your written corrections, nor anyone else's!

❧ ❧ ❧

Stravinsky to Boosey & Hawkes

(original in English)
Dr. E. Roth
Director
Boosey & Hawkes Ltd.
295 Regent Street
London W. I. (England)
February 8, 1952

Dear Dr. Roth,

I have just received a letter from Nadia Boulanger whom I had asked to give me her opinion about the French translation of the *Rake's*.

Her answer is not too cheerful.

I understand that the French translation by this Mr. de Badet (by the way I have never understood who commissioned him: you or the Grand Opéra?) in many instances is completely off and, still worse, has led to some musical changes which completely erase the original rhythmical sense.[21]

---

20. A recording of Boulanger giving a lecture on *The Rake's Progress* in Monaco exists at the Bibliothèque nationale de musique and is the earliest known recording of one of her talks. Boulanger, "Conférence sur *Rake's Progress*," F-Pn, SDCR-7154. The talk is dated as 1954, though I am inclined to think it was instead recorded in 1952. Jeanice Brooks discusses the content of this lecture in *Musical Work*, 182–84.

21. André de Badet (Jean Charles André Giot de Badet) (1891–1977) was commissioned to create the French translation. He eventually completed the work, receiving full credit in additional publications. Désormière is not mentioned

I know that some alterations are unavoidable but the result must not be complete nonsense, as the case seems to be.

Please contact Miss Boulanger and ask her to handle the problem of straightening out the mistakes herself. I cannot do it from here; time is running short and moreover Miss Boulanger is at hand and perfectly aware of the situation. Till Monday, February 18th, she will be lecturing on the *Rake's* at the Monaco Palace, Principality of Monaco. Thereafter she will go back to her regular address, 36 rue Ballu, Paris 9ème.

Sincerely,
IS

❧   ❧   ❧

Stravinsky to Boulanger

> 1260 North Wetherly Drive
> Hollywood 46, California

Mademoiselle Nadia Boulanger
Monaco Palace
Principality of Monaco
February 8, 1952

My dear Nadia,

I was quite disappointed to learn the results of your investigation at rue d'Anjou concerning the French version of *The Rake*. I would like to believe that it is not a complete catastrophe but limited to a few places.

I just wrote to Dr. Roth to ask him to get in touch with you immediately to place you in charge of putting all this in order. Otherwise, I do not know who to contact and you are in a position to choose someone competent in the matter. As for myself, I am too far away and don't have the time.

Keep me up to date about what comes of this.

Tell me as well for which audience you gave your lectures about *The Rake* to in Monaco.

Still no decision from the Paris Opera. But the programs that have already arrived here announce a heap of Strauss operas and *The Rake* isn't mentioned in them . . .[22]

---

as having been involved. See Griffiths, *The Rake's Progress*, 104 and White, *Stravinsky*, 451.

22. Stravinsky is exaggerating here. Strauss's *Salomé* was programmed twice (May 23 and 26, 1952) by the Palais Garnier that season. *The Rake's Progress* premiered at the Opéra-Comique on June 18, 1952, with André Cluytens conducting, but

Fond wishes,
I Str.

❧   ❧   ❧

Stravinsky to Boulanger

(*starts with copy of a letter to Antonio Ghinghelli, Italy*)
Dr. Antonio Ghiringhelli
Superintendent
Teatro alla Scala
Milan (Italy)
February 13, 1952

Dear friend,

Thank you for your letter of February 7 which cleared up the confusion surrounding the question of the volumes of *The Rake's Progress* for me.

No matter what the origin of one or the other, the reality is that the two volumes that Mademoiselle Boulanger has already received from you are not those I had intended for her. In this case, I ask you to please send Mademoiselle Boulanger, 36 rue Ballu, Paris, 9e, the three volumes that you still have at my disposal in your archives.

Thank you in advance and excuse the inconvenience.

❧   ❧   ❧

Dear Nadia,

Having received word from Ghiringhelli, I was finally able to sort out the story of the *Rake's*. In fact, they didn't send you my own copies (complete opera in three volumes) but two volumes (Acts 1 and 2) which were all that Boosey & Hawkes had, and which they had made available to La Scala.

According to the preceding letter you see that you are going to receive the three volumes. Decide for yourself what you want to do with the other two, or, to be safe, ask Boosey & Hawkes what they would like to do about them.

Love,
I Str.

❧   ❧   ❧

---

the Palais Garnier did not produce the opera within Stravinsky's lifetime. See "Journal de régie, deuxième série," 1951–53, F-Pn, département Bibliothèque-musée de l'opéra, RE-369.

Boulanger to Stravinsky

Ecoles d'art américaines
Fondation reconnue d'utilité publique
Palais de Fontainebleau (S.&.M.)
Conservatoire de musique
Le Directeur du Conservatoire

Dear Igor,

1) Translation: François Valéry is in the process of seeing what he can do.[23] As it is, it's *impossible*—too many rhythms are completely destroyed and some syllables are impossible for the voice. What's more, the text is without character, weak. I know, it is easy to criticize, yet I truly believe that it is possible to do better. It must be done.

2) It would appear that Ghiringhelli hasn't found the intended score, but the search continues between Boosey, N.Y., and Milan.

3) Would you be opposed to the performance of fragments from *Rake's*? I believe it would do the work as a whole a lot of good to have the melodies become individually familiar. The public has such a great need to hear them before they can recognize them. It would do for the music what photos do for details in paintings.

Don't kill me, but I can even envision some instrumental transcriptions of these excerpts framed by interludes. The music is of such quality it can support even these betrayals. Forgive me, if you think I'm talking nonsense.

Would you come one day in May (between the 7th and the 8th?) to play your *Sonata for Two Pianos* and *Scherzo à la russe*, after the 19th, and maybe a fragment from *Mavra* at the new Cercle Interallié.[24] I don't believe they could pay more than 40,000 fr.[25] There are no possible proceeds [to be given]. Do I even have the right to ask this of you?

---

23. François Valéry (1916–2002) was the son of Paul Valéry. His letters to Boulanger can be found at F-Pn, N.L.a. 113 (55–202).

24. Boulanger was serving as the music director for the Cercle [de l'Union] Interallié at the time. The Cercle had been founded in 1917 as a support mechanism for Allied soldiers. It was housed in the posh Hôtel Henri de Rothschild in the 8th arrondissement (33 rue du Faubourg-Saint Honoré). In program notes to a late February performance at the Illini Theatre Guild, Stravinsky complained that *Mavra* had been performed only rarely. For the Illini performance in particular, Soulima Stravinsky compiled a two-piano transcription of the orchestral score. See Levitz, "Who Owns *Mavra?*," 55, n. 31. Perhaps Boulanger's urging to have *Mavra* performed—a work that she rarely treats elsewhere—in Paris reflects her knowledge of Stravinsky's frustration with the piece's legacy at the time.

25. The American dollar cost approximately 350 French francs in 1952, which means Boulanger offered Stravinsky $114 for this request. Adjusted for

It would be an immense joy.

You do not know how much we long for you. You do not need anyone, but such a sentiment is nonetheless touching.

From the bottom of my heart, all my love to you and Vera,
Nadia

❧ ❧ ❧

Stravinsky to Boulanger

1260 North Wetherly Drive
Hollywood 46, California

Mademoiselle Nadia Boulanger
36 rue Ballu
Paris, IX (France)
March 3, 1952

Dear Nadia,

Very touched by your two letters which I'm responding to quickly.

TRANSLATION: Dr. Roth wrote me that the translator is collaborating with Désormière to straighten out things that aren't working. Since you can't take care of this yourself, which I doubted, I prefer to let Dr. Roth manage and take care of all that. If I get mixed up in this it would require completely committing myself, and I don't have the time.

SCORE FOR *The Rake:* My three volumes of Summary Sketches for *The Rake*, on the word of Ghiringhelli himself, were in la Scala's possession. I have written to him to send them to you and if something unexpected had come up he would have certainly notified me about it.

FRAGMENTS OF *The Rake* IN CONCERT: I was ferociously opposed to this and in this I am in agreement with Dr. Roth. I have recently written to him again regarding Schwarzkopf who, it appears, was supposed to sing some fragments in London.[26]

Of course, after all opera houses have performed *The Rake*, this will be different.

YOUR INVITATION: Don't hold this against me, but it is impossible because I already have too much to do in Paris where my stay will be very limited and

---

inflation, that would equal approximately $1,000 today.

26. Dame Olga Maria Elisabeth Schwarzkopf (1915–2006) was an internationally acclaimed soprano. She premiered the role of Anne Truelove in *The Rake's Progress*; see Liese, *Elisabeth Schwarzkopf.*

furthermore I do not have the opportunity to exercise my fingers enough. I beg you, dear Nadia, do not insist.

I leave you today by saying, in any case, "see you soon" and in sending fond wishes.

I Str.

❧   ❧   ❧

Boulanger to Stravinsky

36 rue Ballu

March 28, 1952

Dear Igor,

Pardon me, but Dr. Roth has taken the score back and made arrangements for Badet and Désormière to do the translations.[27] God willing they will succeed. Some passages are good, but there are so many things to redo. After having studied the question quite closely and assessing the difficulties, François V. had arrived at the conclusion that a good result was possible.

Fond wishes,
N.B.

[P.S.] *Demand* to review it before a decision is made.

❧   ❧   ❧

---

27. Roger Désormière. See also chapter 3, n. 3.

Boulanger to Stravinsky

Gerry's Landing
Cambridge
Massachusetts
Trowbridge 7339

1260 North Wetherly Drive
Hollywood 46, California
Studio
197 Coolidge Hill
April 9, 195[2]

Dear Igor,

Forgive me for writing again!

1) I've received the score from Milan, *Thank you* with all my heart

2) Would you please tell me your exact flight (number, time, day) because I'd like to meet you at Orly. I cannot enter without this information.

3) I'd like you to agree to see some young musicians, then I'll organize a small reception at the end of *Oedipus* or of the concert on the 22nd.[28]

I am very conceited!! Because I will bring a *crowd* to your three concerts.

Not a word more, I take pity on you. I send you both my fond wishes and deepest affection.

Nadia B.

❧ ❧ ❧

Stravinsky to Boulanger

Mademoiselle Nadia Boulanger
36 rue Ballu
Paris 9th (France)
April 14, 1952

My dear Nadia,

A final note to respond to your letter of April 9.

We are leaving New York on Monday April 28 at 5:00 p.m. with TWA Flight 922. We have a short stop at the Paris-Orly airfield on Tuesday, April 29 around

---

28. Boulanger attended the performances, along with some students. It was on May 25, on the last evening of the tour, that Boulanger, the Stravinskys, and Robert Craft attended a concert of *Musique concrète* at the Salle de l'ancien conservatoire and then proceeded to a reception at Boulanger's home. See Walsh, *Second Exile*, 289; and Craft, *Chronicle of A Friendship*, 83.

1:25 p.m. and continue on the same airplane to Geneva, to attend performances of *The Rake* in French on May 2 and 4.[29] We will then return to Paris
on May 8.

As for the small reception after *Oedipus Rex*, I cannot answer from here. We
will need to talk about this again in Paris and see how everything looks then.

Regarding *The Rake*, I do not know if, in the end, we will put it on in Paris
in May. After what happened to poor Désormière, it seems doubtful.[30] But you
must have known about this sooner than I.

Fond wishes. "See you soon,"
I Str.

❧   ❧   ❧

Boulanger to Stravinsky

Ecoles d'art américaines
Fondation reconnue d'utilité publique
Palais de Fontainebleau (S.&.M.)
St Jean de Luz
Maitagarria
B.P.

Mr. Igor Stravinsky
1260 N Wetherly Drive
Hollywood, California
U.S.A.
September 20, 1952

One year ago in Venice, *The Rake*, you, all of us. How far away it is, and [yet]
so close. I have not written to you, my Friend, because I hardly dare to take
your time. What could I tell you that you don't already know and that would be
worth keeping your attention.

All the same, it is so good to think of those wonderful days, it is so marvelous to love you this much, and one day of gushing is allowed, after all.

---

29. On May 3, the Stravinskys and Craft attended the Parisian premiere of Berg's
opera *Wozzeck*. Craft and the Stravinskys did not make it to the Geneva performances of *The Rake's Progress*, for which Théodore Strawinsky had designed the
sets. Walsh, *Second Exile*, 287–88. See also chapter 3, n. 87.
30. Désormière had just suffered his career-ending stroke. See also chapter 3, n. 3.

Sometimes it seems that I never left you, because even in silence, or better yet in solitude, your music is a part of my life, as is my memory of you. Perhaps it's too sentimental, but so true.

You do not know how important your visit to Paris has been. Certainly, you had spoken before appearing, and those who could understand must have understood. The fact is that you took them by the hand, and pulled many out of a rut.

But, no more long epistles. I wait for you. When will you come back, where? I beg of you, when you manage to think of me, would you send me a copy of your Cantata?[31]

Dear Igor, excuse me, we are completely boring you, but that's the way it is, it is your fault. Will you be in Europe during the summer, in France? Insidious question, full of treachery and hope.

Tell Vera that we all found her as beautiful as ever, tell Bob that I would like to get to know him better, so intelligent, lively, and calm, and that I love you all so deeply and tenderly,[32]

Your
Nadia B.

❧   ❧   ❧

---

31. Stravinsky's Cantata is regarded as one of his first proto-serial works (along with the Septet). The sets old English texts in a similar vein to that of *The Rake's Progress*. Stravinsky's setting of "To-morrow Shall be My Dancing Day" has received attention from Richard Taruskin for its arguably anti-Semitic content. See Taruskin, "Stravinsky and Us," in *The Danger of Music*, 420–46. Boulanger owned four versions of the score, all of which are located in Lyon, F-LYc: UFNB ME STR 530 (full score); UFNB MEp STR 530 (short score); UFNB M 531 STR (piano/vocal reduction); UFNB 525 STR (seven large vocal scores and ten piano/vocal reductions parts). All choral parts were mounted on cardboard for the purposes of performance.

32. This letter marks Boulanger's first reference to "Robert Craft." They would have initially met at the premiere of *The Rake's Progress* and then again during this second tour of Europe.

Stravinsky to Boulanger

1260 North Wetherly Drive
Hollywood 46, California

Mademoiselle Nadia Boulanger
36 rue Ballu
Paris, 9th
October 11, 1952

My dear Nadia

A few days ago I received your letter of September 20, which touched me greatly.

As always, I respond in haste.

The quickest way for you to obtain my Cantata is for you to contact Dr. E. Roth directly.

London has already made the engraving, I corrected all the proofs, and I myself am expecting the full and vocal scores any day now.

Thank you also for having sent me the many signatures of your students and their (your) kind thoughts.[33]

Very affectionately,
I. Str

❧   ❧   ❧

Soulima Stravinsky to Boulanger

1802 Carle Drive
Urbana, Illinois

October 13, 1952
(Starting Nov. 1, our address will be: 910 West Oregon, Urbana, Ill.)

My dear Nadia,

Oh, how your letter gave me such pleasure and I am so touched that you remembered my birthday. I am filled with remorse after having let your birthday pass last year without sending you my wishes—will you still accept them?

---

33. Boulanger's entire class signed the accompanying letter, thanking Stravinsky for allowing them to attend rehearsals of his Parisian concerts. I suspect this was sent in part as an olive branch, given that Stravinsky had explicitly requested of Boulanger that such a deluge of her students not occur. Included in the class that year were Mario di Bonaventura, Thea Musgrave, Noël Lee, and Idel Biret. The class signed on May 23, 1952. Boulanger sent the letter four months later, September 23, 1952; CH-Bps.

You are right. Without a doubt I need to write. I tell myself this often. Not so long ago I wrote lots, and nothing came of it. If one could write in the moments lost or gained during a schedule crammed full of teaching and concerts, that would be the trick. I still haven't developed the necessary concentration. Maybe one day? I'm not giving up on this.

From the end of September, we'll be coming to spend next summer in Europe. We have you to thank for all the emotions this stirs up in us. We are counting the days.

We are looking forward to *The Rake* in New York, it will be a grand event for us. Until now we have only heard but a little snippet on the radio. Two songs sung by Schwarzkopf at a festival in Holland, conducted by Markevitch.[34] We have waited too long.

Jean is well. If it is true that it is better to have a difficult character than to have no character at all, he has great things ahead of him.

Françoise joins me in sending you all of our affection,
Soulima

1953

Boulanger to Stravinsky

Villars sur Ollon

Igor Strawinsky
Hotel Grandstone
114E 52nd Str
New York City, NY
U.S.A.
January 4, 1953

Thank you, my Dear, Dear Friend, for this card that I adore. I see you, recognize the hand, back, neck, movements, expression. It is like the canvases of great painters who in only a few lines on the pages of a notebook manage to convey all the necessary details.

I'm here at the Markevitches for a few days. Your ears must be burning. It is true that many people in the world are doing the same thing, but score after score, everything is known precisely, instrument by instrument.

I've not yet received the Cantata and am furious. Hope to find it upon my return.

---

34. Stravinsky did not authorize this performance, or one similar to it in London. See letter of March 3, 1952.

I couldn't go to Strasbourg—exams, etc. But all those who were there told me that Bour, the conductor, was perfect.[35] Lalande and the conducting were very good, performers *good, fifteen curtain calls* and in Colmar, yes in *Colmar,* a little sleepy village, fifteen encores as well.[36]

How I regret not being in New York on February 14![37] You are a professional above all else, but what about us! The performances last year, lunches in our little restaurant, and . . . but I won't wax on. You are always here, and you are also such a dear friend. My love to Vera. Pass along a million thoughts to Bob Craft. Fondly, with all my deepest affection.

Nadia

ʐ◐ ʐ◐ ʐ◐

Boulanger to Stravinsky

January 22, 1953

Dear Friend,

How do you find the time to think of us still in the midst of your incessant work? We are so far away, so little, and things are difficult over there. The fact is that we take a foolish pleasure in it! How this warmed the heart. And I thank you for it greatly.

Now I have the Cantata for piano and orchestra. We sing, read, and study—in your absence, my eloquence is superb, but what can I say to you? Even my emotion seems indiscreet—and vain. You yourself know what the Cantata is, and I think you know that I hear, I see, I understand, and I love this music with my ears, my eyes, my hands, and my mind. Everything sounds [so beautifully], everything is a surprise, nothing could be any other way.

---

35. Ernest Bour (1913–2001) was a conductor of international renown. At the time of this letter, he had been the conductor of the Strasbourg Philharmonic Orchestra for three years. Bour's archives are currently held by the Paul Sacher Stiftung in Basel, Switzerland. For more on Bour, see Häusler, *Im Zeichen von Ernest Bour,* Ligeti, "Hommage à Ernest Bour," 511–12; and Varga, "Ernest Bour," in *From Boulanger to Stockhausen,* 67–75.

36. Roger Lalande (1893–19. .) was the artistic director for the Théâtre municipal de Strasbourg from 1848 to 1953. He directed this production and died sometime after 1953, the year he ceased to work at the Théâtre.

37. Boulanger noted the event in her diary; Boulanger "Agendas," F-Pn, Rés Vmf. Ms. 107 (1) February 14, 1953, "Cable Str. Igor, *Rake* à NY." Boulanger sent Stravinsky a telegram the day of the premiere to congratulate him; CH-Bps.

A well-made object is a source of unending joy, and henceforth it travels very far, but . . . enough. No unpalatable pedantry! Every day the *Cantate* brings me new satisfaction, satisfaction that doesn't lie, and goes far ahead.

You are always, each time, *different*, but always, you. The story is somewhat the same with those few who have changed the face of the earth. But, possibly never to the extent that you have had to—the invincible need to move forward, to always open one's eyes as if for the first time.

Incorrigible babbling. You well know that it is better to just be silent!

I send my love, I thank you, I lament at being so far from you and I am yours and Vera's *with all my heart.*

Nadia B

[P.S.] Could you please give this small card to Bob—thank you!

꽃   꽃   꽃

Boulanger to Stravinsky

May 31, 1953

Judging by the letters received from Boston, I suppose you were very happy, Dear Igor, with the performance. I am working a lot here, but I don't know where I am with it. Will the Cantata go well this evening? I will write to you . . .

The more I read and play this work, the more I love it. No, I loved it immediately, but the more I see, the more I hear everything. When we see the excess of notes that the . . . well, alright, the "musicians" give in to, we understand all too well the sad reason for their apparent richness.

As Mozart was before, there you are with a few notes—but they are the right ones.

There is a great commotion everywhere. "Much ado about nothing" most of the time, but from time to time, a surprise. But I don't wish to speak to you about aesthetics. I miss you, I'm sad, your presence is so necessary. But we remain so attached to this wish and, after all, try so humbly to lead ourselves toward the right path. Perhaps it is not so bad for those who are capable of so little!

My love to Vera and you and I am, always,

Your
Nadia B.

[P.S.] Best wishes to Bob Craft

Stravinsky to Boulanger

1260 North Wetherly Drive
Hollywood 46, California

Mademoiselle Nadia Boulanger
36 rue Ballu
Paris 9th, France
June 17, 1953

My very dear Nadia,
    Received your kind note upon my return from Cuba/Venezuela/Boston.[38]
    I spent three very tiring weeks in the last city, performing *The Rake* with students from Boston University.
    It was an immense success, even in the malicious Boston press. The two performances each had different artists, which made them all the more difficult and trying. The first group was very good, the second much less so.
    I was quite ill afterward with a bad case of colitis and was forced to withdraw from a concert, though not a particularly interesting one, in Chicago, and return here where I resumed my customary activities.
    You and others mentioned to me the performance of the Cantata in Paris, but without telling me where or by whom . . . I suppose on the radio? . . . and who were the singers? . . . what was the reaction? . . .
    You also haven't mentioned how you yourself are doing?
    Try to respond to me quickly.

Fond wishes,
I Str.

⅔   ⅔   ⅔

Boulanger to Stravinsky

June 24, 1953

Dear Friend,
    To have not yet written to you is shameful. But life during the Concours is relentless.[39]

---

38. Stravinsky had been travelling since March 31 to the locations mentioned. While in Boston, he met and began negotiating a collaboration with the poet Dylan Thomas (1914–53). Walsh, *Second Exile*, 301–4.
39. The Concours is the Belgian Queen Élisabeth Competition, the same one mentioned by Soulima Stravinsky in his letter of September 30, 1951, in this chapter. Boulanger was a judge for the competition in 1953.

The Opéra Comique had asked me to help with rehearsals, but I was in Brussels for the Queen Élisabeth competition, and therefore arrived too late to be of any help whatsoever. Certainly, you were greatly missed, but, [it must be said] you alone give some focus to the rhythm of life that makes it seem as if life itself were music. I found Cluytens *good*, understanding, satisfying.[40] The musicians were enthusiastic, happy to perform a score where each felt the importance of their role and understood it. Some of the soloists were remarkable, and the sound of the ensemble was truly excellent.

The staging was *very successful*, particularly the scene at Mother Goose's house and at the House of Fools. Set design and costumes were beautiful; a lively production.

Michaud (Anne) lacked the mid-range, but sang *very* well, the berceuse admirably.

Simoneau was excellent vocally, a bit neglect[ful] in his acting but infinitely superior to our poor Venitian sort. Nick Shadow, [sung by] Depraz, was *remarkable*.[41] Each syllable distinct, intelligent, good. Herrand didn't for an instant allow one to forget Cuénod, but he wasn't bad.[42] Couderc[43] was *very good* as Baba after: ♪ . She was too soft at the beginning of her aria. Trulove, good. The choruses *very good* at the House of Fools, good enough at Mother Goose's.[44] One serious error, the pause in staging. It would be better to sacrifice the scenery than to cut the scenes. It was already better at the premiere than it was at the dress rehearsal. I couldn't go Saturday, but I will go tonight.

I forgot the pianist—good enough, but a little indecisive, and it was almost always the same question of approximate values of ♪ instead of ♪ or

---

40. André Cluytens (1905–67) was born in Belgium but became a French citizen. He was the conductor for the Opéra comique's production of *The Rake's Progress*. For more on Cluytens, see Baeck, *André Cluytens*. A discography of Cluytens's works has been published, as well; see Hunt, *The Post-war German Tradition*.

41. Xavier Depraz (1926–94) was a French baritone who trained at the Conservatoire. In 1952, a watershed year for him, he performed the roles of Basile in Giacchino Rossini's *Barber of Seville* and Palémon in Massenet's *Thaïs*. "Depraz (Xavier), Basse Française (Paris, 1926)" *Dictionnaire de la musique* (Paris: Larousse, 2005), 292.

42. René Herent (1897–1966) was a French tenor, primarily associated with the Opéra comique. He performed Sellem in the 1952 production of *The Rake's Progress*, Wolff, *Un demi-siècle d'Opéra-Comique*, 106.

43. Simone Couderc (1911–2005) was a French mezzo-soprano. For more, see Wolff, *Un demi-siècle d'Opéra-Comique*, 106.

44. Marguerite Legouhy performed Mother Goose, Wolff, *Un demi-siècle d'Opéra-Comique*, 106.

a mechanical stiffness. I believe the entire problem arose out of a confusion between the measure and the rhythm. But, to return to the pianist, acceptable.

As far as *The Rake* is concerned, each time I hear it, its marvels become more noticeable. I can see you, impatient with my useless assessments, but I nonetheless believe I know *each* note, and just as I adore rereading a score by Mozart, rediscovering it over and over, I discover *The Rake*—and everything *new* and eternal it brings me.

Enough, I cannot speak to you about your music, I feel ridiculous. But I love it, and I love you.

To Vera, to you, all my love,
Nadia

[P.S.] The audience was *very taken*; Reviews . . . (I haven't seen them yet . . . and it doesn't really matter.).
[P.P.S.] Have you read the article by Boulez in *Musique russe*? They tell me you were thrilled with it??[45]

❧ ❧ ❧

Stravinsky to Boulanger

1260 North Wetherly Drive
Hollywood 46, California

Mademoiselle Nadia Boulanger
36 rue Ballu
Paris, 9th (France)
June 27, 1953

Dear Nadia,

I was happy to have your letter giving me your comments on the performance of [*The*] *Rake* at the Opera Comique.

---

45. Boulez, "Strawinsky demeure," in *Musique Russe*, vol. 1, 221–22. Walsh provides a translation in "Stravinsky Remains," *Stocktakings from an Apprenticeship*, 108. See also his discussion of this exchange in Walsh, *Second Exile*, 349–50. In this article, Boulez analyzes *The Rite of Spring* but then disparages Stravinsky's neo-classical output as a "sclerosis of every element . . . a painful atrophy"; cited in Walsh, *Second Exile*, 349. To make matters worse, Pierre Souvtchinsky edited the volume in which Boulez's essay appeared. Boulez's title is a play on his previous essay: "Schoenberg Is Dead" ("Schoenberg est mort," *Score* (1952)), in which he criticized what he viewed as the unfulfilled legacy of serialist techniques.

I received word from Françoise yesterday, and I notice that your impressions were similar. All the better. At the heart of it, it must be a good performance, but I, like you, deplore that there were changes [that caused problems] with continuity between scenes. It is precisely what I feared everywhere, and I had finally managed to avoid in the Boston performance.

I have asked Swarzensky, from rue d'Anjou, to send me the press clippings, and I hope he will do it.

Those who told you I was thrilled with the Boulez article are in all cases quite adept at invention. In any case, I only became aware of it eight days ago, and consequently no one has had the time to hear about my reactions since, in any case, it would suffice to read the middle of page 221 to be sure I am not at risk of being more charmed by Boulez than he pretends to be by me.

If you have the time, I suggest you also see Souvtchinsky's article:[46]

Page 21: ". . . the young, contemporary music's aspirations which are no longer *with* Stravinsky . . ."

Also page 22, note I: "Above all, it is evidently a question of Stravinsky's great works like *Le Sacre du printemps, Les Noces, Le Rossignol.*"

The Salon's careerism continues!!! . . .

Did you receive my letter? You haven't told me about the Cantata . . . I would like, however, to know how they sang and played it and how it was received?

Do not be "lazy"; answer me soon.

While waiting, I send fond wishes,
I. Str.

❧ ❧ ❧

Boulanger to Stravinsky

36 rue Ballu 9th
September 21, 1953

Very Dear Friend,

It's been impossible to write to you during this overwhelming summer. Certainly, what I am doing is not important, but it is all I can do, and so I put all my energy into it.

The Opéra Comique performs the *Rake* often enough (in a manner of speaking, unfortunately), and the number of people who attend *each* performance is comforting. The faults of the performances remain the same. I had

---

46. A reference to Souvtchinsky's introduction to the issue, *Musique Russe*, vol. 1, 21–22.

written on this subject to Beydts, who listened, [but] he just died.[47] But the time will come soon, I believe, when the necessity of staging this work in [the correct] conditions will be imposed. Because, judging by the mail I myself receive regarding it, I understand the extent to which people want this to happen. Sooner or later, it must be retranslated, and the continuity imposed once again. No matter what the design errors of the different performances are, it has been proven that the work has won people over. I will endeavor to send you, one day, excerpts from these letters. It would be worth the trouble.

Students performed *The Rake* at Tours this summer. It was during a general strike. I could not leave the School, but the GD students I sent to listen to it found the whole thing good—excellent orchestra, and an acceptable staging. As for Edinburgh, I understand the production was remarkable. All things considered, the Opéra Comique was not so awful. Little by little, they will all understand. One must give them a lot of time!

But the critics are such an impoverished type—pretentious, because they are too aware of their own weakness; or, out of fear of being wrong, they stay quiet; or out of bravado, they rip [the work] apart with relish. Which is to say the only thing left for them is ridicule. The majority among them have never understood anything about anything, and neither the *Rake* nor the Cantata is an exception. Sometimes I so want to fight with them, but more often, I ignore them.

But, I have a request—a request that I imagine must be refused—but nothing ventured, nothing gained. So, here it is. For multiple reasons, I want the École de Fontainebleau to have a real purpose, or else we should let it go. So I choose to fight—and for a well-defined cause. Would you offer the help that will make it even more so?

For the piano competition, to which I would like to attract good musicians, I wish (one can hope for the impossible) that you—yes, I said *you*—would write a concert study around 5–6 minutes long, that you would dedicate to whoever wins first place and who would have the privilege of the premiere. "And . . . ," I understand that on this point, you must think me completely crazy. I'm not sure I believe it myself, but the crisis hasn't reached its peak—I have to tell you everything, with as much slight of hand and juggling as it takes . . . but I won't lie . . . and forgive my audacity—but, I have, despite an enormous effort, [scraped together] only 100,000 fr.[48] It's ridiculous, shameful. But think, next

47. Louis Beydts (1896–1953) was a composer and served as the director of the Opéra Comique from 1952 to 1953. See Combarieu and Dumesnil: *Histoire illustré de la musique*, 152–55; and Landormy, *La musique française après Debussy*, 302–5.

48. She was offering him approximately $250 to do this; adjusted for inflation, that would be approximately $2,240 today.

year will be my fiftieth anniversary as a professor. If I succeed with such an ambitious project, I will feel myself as proud as Artaban.

Ah! Don Quixote, how I need you! Reply in any case, insult me if you must, but consider this for a little while, to find in your heart a little indulgence, and who knows, perhaps an unbelievably charitable impulse.

I send fond wishes and say again how much I love you,
Your
Nadia.

❧ ❧ ❧

Stravinsky to Boulanger

1260 North Wetherly Drive
Hollywood 46, California

Mademoiselle Nadia Boulanger
36 rue Ballu
Paris, 9th (France)
September 28, 1953

Dear Nadia,

We are happy to finally have news from you. Thank you for giving me your comments on *The Rake* and the Opéra Comique. I didn't know that Beydts had died. Who will take over from him?

I had always thought the French version would be the most difficult to stage and, most certainly, the present translation did not help to overcome these difficulties, but did quite the reverse.

Let's hope that one day, as you imagine, we will succeed in doing better.

Soulima, back from Urbana, told me that Swarsenski (from Boosey & Hawkes, rue d'Anjou) had organized a group to present *The Rake* in the provinces. Is this what you are speaking of in mentioning Tours?

Great success in Edinburgh—I have received quite a bit of feedback from there.

As for your "request," as nice as it seems to me, I can only—unfortunately!—respond to you in the negative, because I am absolutely overrun with work and a surplus of commitments. After having lost about two months this summer to an operation[49] and getting myself back on my feet, I have just agreed to write a ballet for Kirstein-Balanchine (New York City Center).[50] I am in the middle

---

49. On July 23, 1953, Stravinsky underwent a planned prostatectomy. Walsh, *Second Exile*, 305–6.

50. On August 26, 1953, Stravinsky accepted a commission from Kirstein and Balanchine for a new ballet. The work would become *Agon*. Walsh, *Second Exile*,

of another project, I have a two-month American tour followed by a two-and-a-half-month European tour (Rome at Easter, Turin, Switzerland, Germany, England, Lisbon). After that, I will just have to try to catch up on the work that will have piled up.

So, my dear Nadia, please forgive me and understand.

With an affectionate kiss,
I Str.[51]

🕊　🕊　🕊

Soulima Stravinsky to Boulanger

910 W. Oregon
Urbana, Ill.

Mlle Nadia Boulanger
36 rue Ballu
Paris, 9th
France
September 28, 1953

Dear Nadia,

Here are my wishes for your birthday, your health and for your priceless work. May you continue to create around you that unity of thought which is more necessary today than ever.

And it was so comforting to see you, even for such a short amount of time. So many things weren't said . . . At least I know that we always speak the same language, that the same values are dear to us both.

These days I receive excellent news from my father, including the score for his Sextet (Clar., Horn, Bassoon, Piano, Viol, Vla, Cello).[52] I read it and reread it, but that isn't enough for me. There are always great surprises for the ear with his music. Is it not that which is so often missing from all other music? I send you fondest wishes, my dear Nadia, with all my affection. Françoise and Jean join me in my wishes.

Your
Soulima, Str.

308; Joseph, *Stravinsky and Balanchine*, 211–27.

51. A brief postscript from Vera thanking Boulanger for thinking of her on Saint Vera's Day appears at the end of this letter.

52. Soulima means the Septet.

1954

Boulanger to Stravinsky

36 rue Ballu
Paris IX

Monsieur I. Strawinsky
1260 N. Wetherly Drive
Hollywood 46
California
U.S.A.
February 27, 1954

So many things to tell you, My Dear—but have no fear, time will not allow me.

For the 3rd—I want, I need to tell you that I remember.[53]

For Rome, I need to tell you that I'm sorry—I'm afraid that for complicated reasons, this trip will be impossible.[54] It's sad, but . . . what can be done?

I've plunged into the Septet. I do not possess the presumptuousness to speak to you about it, how could I dare.[55] But I marvel before this masterwork that is all it could be.

What am I doing, these vain sentences are becoming threatening. No more.

Won't you come to Paris[?]. If Bob Craft were an angel—why say *if*—he would send me your dates, places, because . . . how can I accept not seeing you at all.

You are tremendously entwined in life here, in our daily thoughts, it seems you know everything I do not say. And yet—what would it mean to you? You don't need anyone, but we cannot do without you.

While you make decisive gestures and write down notes as you want them, so many [others'] unfortunate attempts lack power. And it isn't a question of "what" but a question of "who." What a lesson.

My love to both of you and know, Dear Igor, my deep and faithful attachment. I love you so, you whom I admire more than I know how to say.

---

53. Boulanger lists the wrong date. This should be March 2. Stravinsky corrects her in his reply.

54. Nicolas Nabokov was planning another Paris Festival to take place in Rome, part of a conference entitled "The Situation of Music in the Twentieth Century." Stravinsky was intended to serve as head of the advisory board, but refused and would only participate if paid. Walsh, *Second Exile*, 316.

55. One of Boulanger's most technical extant lectures involves an analysis of Stravinsky's Septet. The lecture, written for the British Broadcasting Corporation, was prepared in advance of the London premiere of the Septet on June 27, 1954. See Nadia Boulanger, "Conférence sur le Septet," *CNLB*, D 1–21(22).

To you, to Vera, and best wishes to Bob, to Milène, to André,

Your
Nadia

ﾖ   ﾖ   ﾖ

Stravinsky to Boulanger

Hotel Olympic Seattle, Washington
March 7, 1954

My very dear Nadia—
    Thank you for your letter, for having remembered March 2 (not the 3rd)
and for the past fifteen years!
    Happy that you are reading my Septet. I conducted its premiere at
Dumbarton Oaks. Bob is conducting it tomorrow in Los Angeles—as for me, I
have also conducted a symphonic concert here. Ask Boosey & Hawkes to send
you my new *Three Shakespeare Songs*, which Bob is also conducting tomorrow.[56]
    I need to be in Rome April 4 and stay there until the 18th, then Turin
(*Perséphone* and the Violin Concerto), then Lugano*) (radio Monte Carlo) the
27th, then staying with Théodore, then Cologne and Baden-Baden in May,
then London (Royal Philharmonic) May 27, then Lisbon at the beginning of
June, then returning by plane to the U.S.
    Is it really possible we will not see one another this time?

Love, kisses,
I Str.

*Septet and chamber music

ﾖ   ﾖ   ﾖ

56. Stravinsky's *Three Songs from William Shakespeare* (London: Boosey & Hawkes,
    1953) is set for mezzo-soprano, flute, clarinet, and viola. Grace-Lynn Martin
    originally performed the mezzo-soprano role, Walsh, *Second Exile*, 314.
    Boulanger owned two versions of the score, though both are without anno-
    tation. F-LYc, UFNB MEp STR 511.2 (pocket score); and F-LYc, UFNB M
    511.112 STR (full score).

Soulima Stravinsky to Boulanger

University of Illinois

March 23, 1954

My dear Nadia,

Your words, your thoughts have touched me infinitely. I would like to tell you that we were also very close to you, we are always, but most especially this month. And soon [we will have] the joy of seeing you. But will you be in Paris at the end of June? I hope this with all my heart. We arrive in Paris on June 12 and will stay there until the end of the month. Then we're going to spend two months in southern France and will leave again around September 1.

May this letter find you in good health. Wholehearted and fond wishes,
Soulima

❧   ❧   ❧

Boulanger to Stravinsky

* annotations Stravinsky's

36 rue Ballu
Paris, IX

June 10, 1954

[This is] to say that I will not be near you, my dear friend, on the 18th. I would like to come and bring you all the most beautiful surprises, you who give me so much, all the time.

What joy these days in London have been.[57] But . . . I will control myself, because my effusions know no limit. In one instant, in one gesture, you render everything clear, inevitable, evident: what a lesson! But . . . I am not going to explain to you what you know better than I. What I can tell you is that these performances, this concert have highlighted and put things in order. I will make fewer mistakes when trying to guide all my students toward your work.

I couldn't listen to your records of the Septet without hearing what life you have given to the rhythm. We remain ignorant of its essential character.

On Sunday (June 6) I heard your concert <u>from Lugano (??)</u> which was broadcast everywhere. <u>Have you definitively deleted the canon from the</u>

---

57. This is a reference to a talk on the Septet that Boulanger gave for the British Broadcasting Corporation. All negotiations and the full program for her "Illustrated Talk" are now at the BBC Archives in Caversham, England (GB-CaBBC).

<u>Scherzo à la Russe (???)</u>. I like it so much and regretted [not hearing it]. I haven't seen the edition and hope [the omission of the canon] was . . . just something that happened during the broadcast.

I still have so many things to tell you, but want these wishes to leave tonight. Fond wishes to you, and to Vera and yourself my deepest attachment.

Thinking of Bob and my affection to Milène,

Your

N

[P.S.] Do not forget the Webern[58]
[P.P.S.] Thank you again for London[59]

❧   ❧   ❧

Stravinsky to Boulanger

1260 North Wetherly Drive
Hollywood California

June 15, 1954

Nadia dear,

Thank you for your kind letter (June 10). We just arrived (with Milène and André) from Lisbon; what a flight! As fast as it was calm. I won't forget the Webern arrangement of the Bach Ricercare: as soon as I find it, I will have it copied for you.

I understand nothing of what you wrote to me about the *Scherzo à la Russe* and Lugano, where I conducted a program of *chamber* music. You must have heard the broadcast from Rome where I actually played it in my *symphonic* concert on April 15, and without cuts of course. The idiotic cut of the First Trio (the canon with the piano and harp) was made, I suppose, by the broadcasting station for reasons that I can only guess at; either they were short on time (the cut of this canon would gain them 1 minute), or they didn't care for the music

---

58. Boulanger's request for a copy of Webern's orchestration of the six-part Ricercare from Johann Sebastian Bach's *Musical Offering*.

59. Stravinsky appeared in London to conduct a concert at Royal Festival Hall and to accept the Gold Medal of the Royal Philharmonic Society one day after Boulanger completed her BBC talk. She had lunch with Stravinsky on May 26 and with Théodore the following day. Boulanger, "Agendas," F-Pn, Rés Vmf Ms. 108 (2); The BBC was well aware of the proximity of the events and hoped to capitalize on Stravinsky's presence in London as part of promoting Boulanger's own talk, *GB-CaBBC*.

of the canon, or, perhaps, the two reasons together. In any case, I had nothing to do with it.

It was good to see you in London. How did your performance of the Septet go?

Love, kisses,
I Str.

❧ ❧ ❧

Boulanger to Stravinsky

*annotations Stravinsky's

Ecoles d'art américaines
Fondation reconnue d'utilité publique
Conservatoire de musique—Ecole des beaux-arts
Palais de Fontainebleau
36 rue Ballu
Paris IX

Monsieur Igor Strawinsky
1260 N. Wetherly Drive
Hollywood, California
U.S.A.
November 7, 1954

Dear, dear friend,

What a long time has passed without news from you. I dare not ask you to write to me, but . . . I hope that you have an irresistible desire to do so. The In Memoriam—what music, everything is there.[60] I would like to speak to you about every note, but . . . you know these truths better than me. What we have in our hands is real, concrete, and thus we acquire what I will not have the poor taste to express.

---

60. *In memoriam Dylan Thomas* is a work for tenor and string quartet, with intervening dirge canons performed by strings and five trombones. The work uses a strict five-note row and sets the text "Do not go gentle into that good night." Joseph Strauss, *Stravinsky's Late Music* (Cambridge: Cambridge University Press, 2001), 191–93. Stravinsky wrote the piece after the unexpected death of Dylan Thomas, with whom he was in the early stages of discussing a collaboration. Boulanger purchased a copy of the work's full score in 1954, F-LYc, UFNB ME STR 511.2. This score was published with three copies of an errata sheet, corrections Boulanger penciled into her own copy. A year later, Boosey & Hawkes sent her the pocket score, F-LYc, UFNB MEp STR 511.2.

When are you coming to Europe? Where, if you are coming? We all need you furiously, but, despite my selfishness, I will choose to leave you to your work. Why are the distances so great and the expenses so high? I would come to see you, but . . . it is only a dream.

We've recently had a festival[61]—lots of notes, "impressions," "emotions," and little music. Many systems, without any real technique, and one quickly perceives that *these types of* complications *are only a* crutch.

But, no matter what language they choose . . . the result would be in vain, because they produce nothing more than the banal and the odd. Desire is what is missing from their music.

Wasn't able to hear *Noces* yesterday. Scherchen conducted.[62] It was likely good but dogmatic.

Nothing else to tell you that is worth being said. I send my love, *thank* you and I believe I benefit completely from everything you have given us.

With all my heart, your faithful
Nadia B

❧ ❧ ❧

Stravinsky to Boulanger

Hollywood
November 14, 1954

Carissima Nadia,
Your kind letter gave me great pleasure. Indeed, we've been without news from you for a long time, but, as you say nothing to me about yourself, being full of discretion, I will not ask you questions and will try to convince myself that everything is following its normal course. It depends on one question: am I right? Please respond.

We are going to Europe once again this spring, at the end of March this time, because Vera will have (at the start of April) her first art show (Galleria Obelisco in Rome). Exciting news, isn't it? To make this journey work I have

---

61. A reference to Nabokov's Rome Festival, Giroud, *Nicolas Nabokov*, 283–85. Among the works included on the program were those by Stravinsky, Hans Werner Henze (1926–2012), Luigi Nono (1924–90), Goffredo Petrassi (1904–2003), Luigi Dallapiccola (1904–75), Bruno Maderna (1920–73), and Samuel Barber (1910–81), as well as works by Boulanger alumni Aaron Copland (1900–90), Virgil Thomson (1896–89), and Elliott Carter (1908–2012).

62. Hermann Scherchen (1891–1966) was a German conductor who championed contemporary music; see Pauli, *Hermann Scherchen.*

arranged a few concerts. So, we fly from NY to Lisbon to conduct my first concert in Madrid (March 25), from there to Rome (April 6), then Baden-Baden (April 22), then Lugano (April 28) and Stuttgart (May 3) from where we go to Copenhagen to take this new SAS Danish airplane from there that as of today flies to Los Angeles (22 hours through the Arctic). Will we see one another somewhere in Europe? Please respond.[63]

Happy to have your kind remarks about my *In Memoriam.* I have already recorded it (Columbia), yes, just a few days before its premiere in concert (conducted by Bob Craft) in Dylan Thomas's memory, this piece was played beside unforgettable works by Purcell, Gabrieli, Schütz, and Bach.[64] Aldous Huxley also very graciously took part in this, paying homage to the great poet. I will conduct *In Memoriam* in Rome (probably Cuénod) with my Cantata (probably Laszlo and Cuénod); the second half of the program will be *Oedipus Rex* (probably Laszlo and Peter Pears). It would be too good so see you at this concert![65]

Love,
I Str.[66]

❧ ❧ ❧

Boulanger to Stravinsky

Ecoles d'art américaines
Fondation reconnue d'utilité publique
Conservatoire de musique—Ecole des beaux-arts
Palais de Fontainebleau
November 18, 1954

---

63. On the inside cover of her April 1955 diary, Boulanger wrote out this itinerary, perhaps trying to work out when she might be able to see the Stravinskys during their tour. Boulanger, "Agendas," F-Pn, Rés VmB Ms. 88 (1955).

64. The recording took place on September 13, 1954, in Hollywood. The premiere was on September 20, 1954, as part of the Monday Evening Concerts. It was the first Stravinsky premiere conducted by Robert Craft. Richard Robinson sang the tenor part in both the recording and the live concert. Walsh, *Second Exile*, 323.

65. Magda Laszlo (1919–2002) was a Hungarian soprano known for performances of contemporary literature. See Harold Rosenthal, "László, Magda," *The New Grove Dictionary of Opera. Grove Music Online. Oxford Music Online.* Oxford University Press, accessed May 28, 2016, http://www.oxfordmusiconline.com.

66. Vera added a brief postscript to this letter, writing that she hoped to see Boulanger in Europe and that she was very excited about the upcoming art show.

Dear Friend,

What a letter . . . and what good news!!

And it's given me a bunch of ideas.

I'm going to do the impossible to be in Rome on the 6th, but, again . . . don't protest before having finished the paragraph:

The Olympic Games have opened a competition for the composition of a hymn intended for the 1955 Games.[67] Three minutes of music, a prize of $1000. The jury will meet in Monaco on April 18 (until April 21), invited by the Prince to the Palace, travel included, for example Rome–Monaco–Baden-Baden. We could begin the 17th (or the 17th to the 20th) (or even 18th to the 19th) (or 16th, 17th, 18th). It is *impossible* to tell you how happy I'd be if you agreed to be a part of this jury. I beg of you ~~to try to~~ to remain open-minded. If the date must be pushed forward a bit, it will be done.

I will be watching for the mail with utmost impatience!! Tuesday I will conduct a concert that the radio kindly offered to celebrate my fifty years as a professor.[68] I wouldn't dare play music in front of you, but . . . I would love for you to be there, you, who plays such a role in my life.

What success for Vera. I am so happy for her. Truly count on my being there on the 6th. What hotel are you staying at?

With fond, wholehearted wishes,
Nadia B.

❧   ❧   ❧

Stravinsky to Boulanger

1260 North Wetherly Drive
Hollywood 46, California

Mademoiselle Nadia Boulanger
36 rue Ballu
Paris 9th, France
November 22, 1954

My dear Nadia,

Received your charming letter . . .

---

67. For more on this competition, see Jérôme Spycket, *Nadia Boulanger*, 132. A dossier of archival documents concerning the competition remains extant. See Boulanger, "Documentation sur une partie de l'activité de Nadia Boulanger en 1955," F-Pn, Rés. Vm. Dos. 159.

68. There are no documents to support this being a concert with the BBC. Perhaps the concert was with a French radio station.

I am sorry not to be able to respond to you favorably, but this jury business in Monaco is completely impossible for me.

I want to stay in Rome for a few days to rest before going directly to Baden-Baden, where I will have more work than normal because of Rosbaud's absence at the moment.[69]

On the other hand, I look forward to seeing you in Rome, where I will stay as usual at the Hassler. We will arrive there on March 31.

All my congratulations on fifty years of teaching ... What an important number!

I, who am older than you, cannot say the same, because my career as a composer started in 1907 with my first Symphony and my Suite for Voice and Orchestra, *Le Faune et la Bergère*, for which Rimsky arranged a performance in the Imperial Court.

See you soon,

Fond and affectionate wishes,

Love,

I. Str.

❧   ❧   ❧

Boulanger to Stravinsky

Écoles d'art américaines
Fondation reconnue d'utilité publique
Conservatoire de musique—École des beaux-arts
Palais de Fontainebleau

December 7, 1954

It's me again, my very Dear Friend!! After you so kindly complained of my silence, you're going to regret it!

But I'll quickly support Passerone's request, he has much talent, he is serious, so "informed" and so modest.[70]

---

69. Hans Rosbaud (1895–1962), was an Austrian conductor who, in 1954, served as primary conductor for the Southwest German Radio Orchestra. See also chapter 3, n. 76. For more on Rosbaud, see Evans, "Hans Rosbaud and New Music," 117–29; and Evans, *Hans Rosbaud: Bio-Bibliography*.

70. Felix Passerone first approached Stravinsky to request permission to publish excerpts from his "Danse Sacrale" in his textbook *TEST: Exercices d'épreuve de technique pour 4 timbales.* Passerone also inquired whether or not he needed to contact Boosey & Hawkes. He sent this correspondence through Boulanger.

How the Rome plan tempts me. It is so sad to see you so rarely. I think of Santa Barbara, of those hours with you. Nothing seems more important to me, and yet, I sacrifice them.

The so-called "modern" works triumphed, [there was] a violent reaction to Varèse.[71] [The critics] are so old-fashioned and pretentious. Bah! Water rushes, washes them away, and . . . nothing remains.

I send my love to you both and am with all my heart,

Your
NB

[P.S.] Don't take the trouble to write to Passerone, just tell me if you are in agreement . . . or not.

❧　❧　❧

Stravinsky to Boulanger

1260 North Wetherly Drive
Hollywood 46, California

December 13, 1954

My dear, dear Nadia,

Here is a response to your letter of December 7.

1) Tell Felix Passerone that it is not a question of my permission (I give it to him with pleasure) but that of Boosey & Hawkes's (Dr. E. Roth in London) which causes me to advise him against keeping the anonymity of the source (because he writes to me: . . . "these 'rhythms' are taken from the repertoire *without indication of the source*"). It would be more prudent to guarantee an OK from B&H themselves.

2) Despite your hesitations, I hope all the same to see you in Rome or elsewhere in Europe.

Love,
I. Str.

Passerone's letter at the Sacher (CH-Bps) has been filed along with Boulanger's letters according to the date on which it was written, November 26, 1954.

71. A concert conducted by Scherchen on December 2, 1954. Boulanger made a note of the event in her diary: Boulanger, "Agenda," F-Pn, Rés Vmb. Ms. 88 (1955).

1955

Stravinsky to Boulanger

Hollywood 46, California

February 5, 1955

My very dear Nadia,

Thank you for your letters of January 27 which I found upon returning home from a concert tour here . . . besides that, I am now starting my preparations for our trip to Europe next month (leaving from here March 4).

Regarding projects with Venice, I believe Nabokov is a bit too wrapped up in his own enthusiasm.[72] The fact is that ten months ago the Venice Biennale submitted a project to me to compose a religious work for them (they wanted [it for] 1956) that would be performed for the first time under my direction at St Mark's Cathedral. Personally, I am very interested in this, but nothing will get done or even get started so long as I have not received and signed the contract with the Biennale.[73]

The misfortune is precisely that this contract is dragging and is making me wait indefinitely.

I proposed a short "Passion according to Saint Mark" which pleased them greatly.

But as for me, as the Unions here say: "No contract, no work" . . .

We hope to see you somewhere during our European stay.

Love,
I. Str.

❧   ❧   ❧

---

72. In her letter of January 27, 1955, Boulanger passed along that "Nabokoff told me about your new project: the Patriarche de Venise, the Mass. Only you could answer such a request as that, what news!" ("Nabokoff m'a dit votre nouvelle entreprise : La Patriarche de Venise, la Messe. Vous êtes le seule qui pouviez répondre à une telle demande, quelle nouvelle!!") Boulanger to Stravinsky, January 27, 1955, CH-Bps.

73. This commission would eventually become the *Canticum Sacrum*. For a discussion of Boulanger's thorough knowledge of the piece as well as the lecture she gave on it for the BBC, see Francis, *Teaching Stravinsky*, 224–32.

Stravinsky to Boulanger

Hotel Hassler-Roma
Trinita Dei Monti

Miss Nadia Boulanger
36 rue Ballu
Paris 9th
France
March 29, 1955

Dearest Nadia,

Here we are in Rome, with *me* in bed with a bad cold.

Would you be an angel and call for a bottle of *Balsamorhinol*,* which we can't find here?

Thank you for your telegram.

I will be waiting for you on the 2nd

Love,
Str.

*French nose drops

❧   ❧   ❧

Stravinsky to Boulanger

ROME

NADIA BOULANGER
36 RUE BALLY [*sic*], PARIS
MARCH 30, 1955

WEVE RESERVED TWO ROOMS FOR YOU EDEN HOTEL HAPPY TO SEE YOU AGAIN

STRAVINSKY

❧   ❧   ❧

Boulanger to Stravinsky

June 11, 1955

Dear Igor,

Your birthday is soon. I don't know what it means because . . . do you have an age . . . or are you always the same, or better yet, always new? This is only meant to bring you wishes full of affection, fondness, and gratitude. I still don't know—never know. But with you it's worse, because everything seems so small and useless. And yet I cannot stop myself from sending you this note that is absolutely filled with my affection.

We've spoken at length with Nabokov this morning about *The Rake*. We have been dreaming of a truly homogeneous performance. For so long, the people have needed some perspective to help them see, and curiously, despite your recordings and all the directions you have given them, they continue to "interpret" rather than "to transmit."

But why rebel? It's always been the same, and despite everything the great works survive.

How I miss those beautiful days in Rome, to see you again was such a great happiness, you bring so much to those whom you meet, and as for me . . . I love you so much, Dear Igor, as much as I admire you.

And now, enough declarations from such a young and beautiful woman . . . what a lack of restraint!

Give Vera my best. I regret that her exhibit left before I was able to prove to her I had looked at it carefully.

Best wishes to Bob, my tenderness to Milène, and my constant thoughts to you both.

Fond wishes,
Nadia B.

[P.S.] Could you tell me if Alan Hovhaness has any talent, do you know him?[74]

---

74. Alan Hovhaness (né Alan Hovhaness Chakmakjian) (1911–2000) was a prolific American composer. Hovhaness and Boulanger do not appear to have exchanged correspondence. For more on Hovhaness, see Cotter, "Alan Hovhaness," in *Music of the Twentieth-Century Avant Garde*, 211–16.

1956

Boulanger to Stravinsky

36 rue Ballu, 9th
Telephone: Trinite 57–91

February 21, 1956

My Dear Friend,

A small note to be close to you on March 2, to tell you my thoughts are with all that remains with us and enriches our days.

I was so happy for your news from Jacques Dupont and to know that you enjoyed New York, and had some fun.[75]

Forgive me for boring you, but Halffter is very anxious to know if you will agree to participate in the hommage to Manuel de Falla. He considers *you* of capital importance.[76]

Could you ask Vera or Bob to tell me if you *are able* to write something for Falla before September. I had told Halffter of the amount of work tying you down, but he thinks primarily of Falla and this memorial concert, and cannot conceive of the event without you.

I have completed my chore, doubtless upsetting you, but you love me enough to forgive me, no?

Fond wishes,
Nadia

ɞ   ɞ   ɞ

Stravinsky to Boulanger

Beverly Hills, California

Miss Nadia Boulanger
36 rue Ballu
Paris, IXth
France
February 27, 1956

---

75. Jacques Dupont was a set designer and the partner of French composer Henri Sauguet. Both were friends with Nabokov. See Giroud, *Nicolas Nabokov,* 101.

76. Ernesto Halffter (1905–89) was a Spanish composer and conductor. Halffter learned much from his mentor and friend Manuel de Falla, and after de Falla's death in 1946, Halffter aided in completing the unfinished opera, *Atlántida.* For more on the many homages to de Falla, see Nommick, "Des *Hommages* de Falla," 515–41.

My very dear Nadia,

I have just read your kind letter of Feb. 21 and thank you with all my heart for having thought of March 2.

What Halffter solicits is at the same time both touching and impossible for me. If you only knew everything I have to do before embarking in mid-June for Europe (Greece and Constantinople for our vacation, then concerts: Venice, Switzerland, Germany, Vienna and London, then returning to New York for Christmas, triple concert with the Philharmonic—*Rite* and *Persephone*—and recording *Persephone* with Columbia.)*

I finished my *Canticum Sacrum* (short, 16 minutes, and quite difficult) and now . . . proofs, which means—corrections!

Having finished the *Canticum,* I have put myself to work on an instrumental version (with choir) of J. S. Bach's Canonic Variations on *Vom Himmel hoch da komm' ich her,* which I have decided to do with my *Canticum* in Venice along with other compositions of a religious nature: Andrea Gabrieli, Schütz, Monteverdi, Gesualdo. The Bach Variations are taking more time than I thought. I am going to have Bob perform them here in the Ojai Festival in May where I am conducting my *Noces.*[77] This work is interrupted by all sorts of things and right at this moment, for at least a week, by an "abbreviated version of *Petroushka*" for TV cartoons, length—12 minutes.[78] They are making episodes of the start, of Petroushka's cell, of the Moor, one part of the Disguises and of Petroushka's death. In brief—a potpourri; and I am doing it for money!!! Yes, sir, it is certainly blameworthy but also excusable when one thinks of the taxes that gouge us without pity.

*All this at the beginning of January 1957 to which a showing of Vera's paintings has just been added. Tomorrow the showing of her work at the Santa Barbara Museum will take place . . .

Love,
I Str.

• • •

---

77. The Ojai Festival, see also chapter 3, n. 54.
78. See Walsh, *Second Exile,* 337; and Craft, *Selected Correspondence,* 396–97.

Boulanger to Stravinsky

36 rue Ballu
Telephone: Trinité 57–91

March 25, 1956

    May all of my thoughts go to you this Easter, Dear Igor, Dear Vera. Is there a way I might familiarize myself soon with the Venetian work for San Marco? At my peril, I dare confess a faint glimmer of hope.

    Marie Blanche is very sick, complications with the brain.[79] But one must not despair. It is a great sadness.

I send my love to you on the Day of Light and am your
Nadia

[P.S.] Many kind regards to Bob Craft

❧ ❧ ❧

Stravinsky to Boulanger

Good Friday, [March 30] 1956–

My very dear Nadia,

    Happy Easter to you as well!

    My cantata for Venice is called *Canticum Sacrum*—for tenor, baritone, choir, and a large instrumental ensemble. Not long (17 minutes), somewhat difficult (particularly for the singers' pitches). Latin text from the Vulgate. Vocal score will probably already appear in May, the full score—after Venice. Ask Dr. E. Roth (B&H in London) to send you the second set of proofs that I have just corrected—it will be easier, because here I have only manuscripts.

    I just finished (and sent back to London) an important arrangement of J. S. Bach's Chorale and five canonic variations—*Vom Himmel hoch da komm' ich her*—for instrumental ensemble and choir. I will conduct it with my *Canticum* in Venice and Bob [will conduct it] here, at Ojai, in the month of May.

    Poor Marie Blanche! Was it a stroke?

Love
I Str.

---

79. Marie-Blanche de Polignac (1897–1958) was dying of a brain tumor. The process was very painful. For more on Boulanger and Marie-Blanche de Polignac, see Kahan, "'Quelque chose de très raffiné," in *Témoignages et études*, 85–98.

❧ ❧ ❧

Boulanger to Théodore Strawinsky

The Palace, Principality of Monaco
April 5, 1956

Dear Théodore,

Would you please tell His Majesty[80] how much I am touched by His thoughts and am sorry that I am unable to accept His gracious invitation, but I am here to prepare the nuptial mass for the Prince of Monaco whom I knew as a child, and I am kept here for this ceremony with all my heart.

I regret missing the concert in every respect—how I would like to see all three of you again in Venice, in any case! Your Father seems to be involved in the most enriching activities—How delightful.

I send you all my most tender affection.
Nadia B.

❧ ❧ ❧

Boulanger to Stravinsky

May 6, 1956

1. Exact date of performance or rehearsal *Canticum* Venice
2. Which hotel will you be staying at? Bauer?
3. Would you prefer that Annette and I stay at a different hotel?
4. How long will you be in Venice?

[P.S.] Forgive me for bothering you with this . . . Plans must be made, rooms reserved. I've received *Canticum.* What marvelous and powerful music! Thank you,

Your
Nadia B.

❧ ❧ ❧

---

80. Despite not being able to attend, Boulanger noted the concert in her diary. Boulanger, "Agendas," F-Pn, Rés VmB Ms. 88 (1956).

Stravinsky to Boulanger

Hollywood

May 16, 1956

My very dear Nadia,

Excuse my silence—it's the fault of the Biennale! No one knows the date of my concert; all we know is that it will be no later than September 20. I cannot even obtain from them the smallest details about the choruses, orchestra, soloists; correspondence has been dragging on for months! It's horrendous.

I just changed the entire program, because they didn't want to make my job easier in letting Bob Craft conduct the old Venetian masters that he certainly knows better than I. I sent a cable to tell them that I will conduct at the Fenice, and not at St Mark's,* the following program:

Canticum

Mass

Canticum

Choral und Variationen (*Vom Himmel hoch*) of J. S. Bach in my arrangement for choir and orchestra. B. &. H. is in the process of printing it.

As usual we are staying at the Bauer Gruenwald Hotel. In a month we are taking the train to New York where we will set off (Vulcania) for Athens.

I am conducting *Les Noces* and Bob my Bach arrangement on May 27 at Ojai.

Fond and affectionate wishes,
I Str

*Because one does not give a concert performance of a mass intended to accompany a religious service in a church.

ॐ   ॐ   ॐ

Boulanger to Stravinsky

36 rue Ballu, 9th
Telephone: Trinité 90–17

Igor Strawinsky
1260 N. Wetherly Drive
Hollywood 46
California
U.S.A.
June 4, 1956

My very dear Friend,

"We leave the 27th"—May or June 27th? And I wonder *where* my wishes are going to find you. You are unbelievably lucky: I can't write—and besides, what letter [could I write] after meeting, after getting to know the *Canticum*!!

But, modestly, wisely, I send you my love, I thank you, and I profess myself yours,
N

[P.S.] I'll be in Venice at the Bauer from September 11 until . . . ! Everything depends on you.
[P.P.S.] All tenderness to Vera and kind regards to Bob.

❧   ❧   ❧

Boulanger to Théodore Strawinsky

August 13, 1956

Dear Théodore,

Although death may have been a deliverance for your dear Madubo, I understand your pain and I'm saddened not to have said so when I heard news of her death.[81] So now your dear old friend is in Peace—which she deserved so well. Like always, I am thinking of you—of our memories—of your mother. I send you my love and send to all three of you my deep affection.

---

81. She had died of "long-undiagnosed cancer" in Switzerland. Though she relocated to the United States shortly after the war, she had a falling-out with Stravinsky and his family and moved back to Europe. Walsh, *Second Exile*, 340; and Craft, *Dearest Bubushkin*, 179–80.

Nadia B.

[P.S.] Will you be in Venice? I do hope so.

[P.P.S.] And the work is so grandly austere, strong—its sonority must be extraordinary. And I am so happy at the thought of seeing your Father again.

❧ ❧ ❧

Boulanger to Stravinsky

Ecoles d'art américaines
Fondation reconnue d'utilité publique
Palais de Fontainebleau (S.-&-M.)
Conservatoire de musique
Le Directeur du Conservatoire

September 2, 1956

My Dearest Ones,

Will be at the Bauer on the 8th. It's terrible to wait, my impatience to see you again is so great, to hear the *Canticum* and *Choral.* I had better keep quiet, because I'm incapable of expressing what these works call for.

My love and deepest affection to you both,
NB

[P.S.] Impossible to obtain a room before the 8th, will therefore be at the Jolly Ravenna Hotel from the 5th to the 8th; am also looking forward to seeing the mosaics.[82] Annette Dieudonné, Winifred Johnstone, and one of my Indian students will all be there on the 8th.

[P.P.S.] What an *incredible* story concerning seats—Oh well, we'll fight them if we have to![83]

❧ ❧ ❧

---

82. Ravenna, Italy, is home to a number of remarkable early Christian mosaics, monuments that are now recognized as UNESCO world heritage sites. See Deborah M. Deliyannis, *Ravenna in Late Antiquity.* This visit to Venice is further discussed in Spycket, *Nadia Boulanger,* 134; Rosenstiel, *Nadia Boulanger,* 356; and Walsh, *Second Exile,* 342–44.

83. I suspect Boulanger had caught word that tickets would be difficult to acquire. There is not further explanation for this story elsewhere in the archives.

Boulanger to Stravinsky

[Undated]

My dear Friend,

I believed I knew the *Canticum* by heart, and the Variations. All that was left for me was to hear everything. I know that we bore you, we love you too much and without purpose. But our worth is so small beside yours. That night in San Marco warmed my heart. I felt you so alone, and never so alone, and our sorry tenderness was only bothersome. But I believe I truly understand this music.

God bless you, you who gives so much, and forgive me for not being able to stop myself from sending you these lines.

Fond wishes

❧   ❧   ❧

Théodore Strawinsky to Boulanger

Genève

October 16, 1956

Dear Nadia,

I imagine your concern if you've heard (as I am assuming) what public rumors are saying about my father. I am writing you these lines so you can find them upon arriving home from Poland.[84] Alas! The news is not good, and how can I hide this worry from you? The stroke my father suffered right after his Berlin concert is a truly serious shock. But what is and will be from now on a point of constant anxiety for us, is that he, at all costs, will henceforth have to take extra precautions in looking after himself, *to the utmost*, and you know how difficult that is for him. Thursday, I am going to join him in Munich where he is being taken care of in a clinic. I did not go there earlier, so as to avoid alarming him with an impromptu visit. Of course continuing the tour is out of the question (this is completely between us). I will write you a note from Munich. I know, dear Nadia, that we are united in our thoughts, and how deeply you share our despair. Your friendship is a comfort.

---

84. Boulanger's travels to Poland involved concertizing and providing lectures. She especially made note of concerts that contained the works of Karol Szymanowski and Witold Lutosławski; see Boulanger, "Agendas," September–October 1956, F-Pn, Rés. Vmf. Ms. 60 (3–4). Especially following the Second World War, Boulanger promoted the works of Polish composers; see, for example, her "Premières auditions" column on Szymanowski in *Le Spectateur*: Boulanger, December 24, 1946, "*Harnasie* de Carol Szymanowski," p. 2.

Denise and I send our love and our deepest commitment,
Théodore

❧   ❧   ❧

Théodore Strawinsky to Boulanger

Genève

November 7, 1956

Dear Nadia,
    Upon returning home from Warsaw you will have found my letter at rue
Ballu. I know that we see things in the exact same way. Thus, you will have
completely understood the fundamental motives of the three-week-long stay
that Denise and I just had in Munich; neither we nor others can do anything
for the situation,[but] we can save what can be saved for the good of my father.
This is because there is nobody around him to think reasonably both about his
health and his mental comfort. What is perhaps the saddest aspect of all of this
is the mental solitude in which he finds himself confined, to which he almost
surrenders at times, but he can't break out of. It is hard to understand from
the outside. We ourselves can only suspect the extent of it and now that we are
certain of it . . .
    With regard to the course of the disease, speaking of convalescence, it is
going satisfactorily at the present moment. The immediate moment is not
alarming. It is the future that worries us terribly, as nothing will be done to
look after him, despite what is said. And, alas, the problem is much more
complicated by the fact that Prof. Diehl (the doctor treating him), whom I
believe to be a good practitioner, but who committed, as soon as the treatment began, the incommensurable psychological error of leaving my father
with the hope of an *early resumption* of his activity! It's truly crazy, but that's
how it is. It is clear that it wasn't necessary to brutally tell him "Never again!"
but it would have been at least necessary to set aside the future and to expect
only a partial return to his activity in a future that is as vague and as far away
as possible. This is what should have been clearly established from the start.
The next scheduled concert (the 29th of this month in Rome) must then
take place, at least in principle, in three weeks! It's incredible! It is true that
he'll only conduct the *Canticum Sacrum* with the same choir as in Venice, but
still! The only thing we find reassuring about the situation is that our friend
Dr. Gilbert from Geneva—who came twice to see my father in Munich at our
request, and explained to him rather abruptly the very serious danger he is
now exposed to—will go to Geneva and Rome, specifically to be on site. He
will check everything just before the rehearsals, and if necessary, keep him

from picking up the baton. And above all, [he is going] especially to intervene in whatever way his status as friend and professional expert allows him,
in order to attempt [to convince] my father [not to do] the London concert
that should take place a few days later and that he doesn't want to give up for
anything in the world—only because of Professor Diehl's attitude. But at least
he accepted to submit, *in extremis*, to the verdict of Dr. Gilbert at the time of
the Rome concert. London, then, will ultimately be cancelled, but you see how
complicated all of this is. Good, but what next? Because it's upon returning to
America, first to New York, where they have quite a number of projects, then to
Hollywood, which will be the terrible danger. This is what terrifies us, because
there's nobody over there, I fear, to oppose him with the necessary authority,
in his most unreasonable undertakings . . . and we can do absolutely nothing
about it! There's nothing left for us but the consolation, which is very slight, of
telling you that without our time in Munich, *nothing* would have changed in his
life, either now or in the next few weeks. I am telling you this without modesty:
if Denise and I had not gone to Munich, I believe that we would already be in
the midst of running full speed directly toward catastrophe . . .

You come to mind, very dear Friend, among the very rare people who can
understand all of this and share in our worries, and to whom we can speak with
so freely. We are infinitely grateful to you for this . . .

Allow me to send you all of our friendly and affectionate devotion,
Théodore

P.S. Is it necessary to add all that we are feeling in regard to what is currently
going on in the world?! More than ever, our only comfort must be in the
Catholic faith.[85]

❧   ❧   ❧

---

85. October 23–November 10, 1956, marked the days of the Hungarian Uprising
    (also called the Hungarian Revolution.) This conflict was the first effective
    protest to Soviet rule since the installation of a communist government in the
    country after the Second World War. The uprising was ultimately crushed, and
    the Soviet government installed in January 1957 began a brutally repressive
    rule. See Rainer, Bekes, and Byrne, *The 1956 Hungarian Revolution.*

Boulanger to Théodore Strawinsky

November 11, 1956

Dear Théodore,

Your letter overwhelms and touches me—Your confidence consoles me—seeing as how my anxiety is so close to your own. Allow me to reassure you, however, that I was told a concert is no longer envisioned, but—it's not the same thing. And we suffer all the more when we listen again to the *Canticum*, however poorly performed. What spiritual significance and technique in a work so beautiful, so important and inevitably still misunderstood.

While my thoughts never leave your Father, I don't dare write there [to Munich]—I don't know what to say to him—I'm scared of words. You know that I love him as much as I admire and respect him. In the middle of the horror, of the disgrace into which we have plunged, your Father's illness is a terrible catastrophe.

Lovingly, and with a heart that belongs tenderly to you both,
Nadia

Chapter Six

Old Friends

1956–1972

Disruption and isolation marred the final years of Boulanger and Stravinsky's dialogue. Old age made it difficult for them either to write to others or to read letters they received, drawing into question the fidelity of texts they dictated. During this time, Boulanger remained an avid collector of Stravinsky's compositions, though for the most part his affectionate messages no longer adorned them. And Boulanger continued to attend performances of his works, but nothing comparing to the detailed parsing of the Parisian premiere of *The Rake's Progress* appears in these letters. Instead, Boulanger becomes rather taciturn regarding Stravinsky's music, remarking often that in each piece there resided "a great lesson" or that each work "spoke better for itself." Ultimately, her words reveal a dedication to her imagined concept of Stravinsky and an abiding devotion to their friendship that extended until Stravinsky's final years.

In his letters, Stravinsky becomes increasingly abrasive and at times defensive. Gone is the playful, kind man of the 1940s. In its place is an officious professional, occupied predominantly by tours and commissions. There are brief moments where one senses the Stravinsky of the past, such as in his telegram to Boulanger that Jean Cocteau had died (October 11, 1963). But otherwise Stravinsky's letters become a laundry list of places he has committed to visiting and concerts he has agreed to perform, even more so than before. Questions of who is behind the words found in these letters echo throughout this chapter.

Certain moments stand out as remarkable in this section. Among them is the discussion of Pierre Boulez from April to May 1967, as well as Stravinsky's palpable rage following the bungled Parisian premiere of *Threni* on November 14, 1958—and Boulanger's anticipation of his wrath. Similarly, Boulanger's despair at the passing of Prince Pierre of Monaco (November 14, 1964) and her disappointment at Stravinsky's refusal to accept a commission for the concert in celebration of Winaretta Singer, the Princesse de Polignac (November 7–24, 1964) are poignant moments in this last portion of the letters. Also present is the theme of coming together, and there are numerous references on both parts to in-person visits. Both Stravinsky and Boulanger continued to make a point of seeking out the other when Stravinsky was in Europe, retaining an underlying respect for their relationship that had at that point spanned nearly fifty years.

Finally, just as in the beginning portions of this edition, the final chapter of the correspondence is informed not by Stravinsky's words himself, but by those of his immediate family. In this section, the letters of Théodore Strawinsky provide a perspective both touching and vexing. He and Boulanger regularly corresponded as Stravinsky's health faltered, with Boulanger serving to calm and support Théodore. Once again, Boulanger acted as a surrogate family figure. It would be naïve to read Boulanger's veiled criticisms and condemnations of the acts of Robert Craft and Vera Stravinsky as complete truth; I wonder at times if Boulanger was telling Théodore what he wanted to hear. But considered in counterpoint with the words she sent Igor, these final letters flesh out the complicated situation in which Boulanger found herself during the last five years of Stravinsky's life. It is essential that Théodore Strawinsky's words also be viewed with some caution, given that he never seems to have forgiven his father for remarrying. And yet, Théodore's sorrow and frustration, especially as they are echoed in the letter from Stravinsky's daughter Milène Marion on October 27, 1969, cannot be rejected as outright petulance. And so the correspondence draws to a close with the words of family and faithful friends, with Boulanger's final letter in this collection sent to Théodore, containing words that celebrate his father's life and legacy as only Boulanger could describe it.

❧   ❧   ❧

Boulanger to Stravinsky

36 rue Ballu 9th
Telephone: Trinité 57–91

November 22, 1956

My dear Friend,
    I didn't want to bother you, but nevertheless I can't go on without telling you my thoughts. I have so much to tell you. *You* in Warsaw, which was one of the reasons for the Festival and the *Canticum* here. I haven't seen the reviews, [which I understand are] a bit harsh, but the musicians understood, at least the ones who *are* musicians.[1]

---

1.   Boulanger details the contents of the festival in her diary. There is no mention of Stravinsky's works in her description. Boulanger, "Agendas," October

With fond wishes, I am your
Nadia B.

❧ ❧ ❧

Boulanger to Stravinsky

36 rue Ballu, 9th
Telephone: Trinité 57–91

Mr. and Mrs. Igor Strawinsky
c/o Mrs. A. Sachs
The Ritz Hotel
Place Vendôme
December 1, 1956

You are going to spend a few hours in Paris, my dears, and I am stuck here in this clinic.[2] What can I say? The inevitability of the situation makes me so deeply sad.

I send my love and am with all my heart your
Nadia B.

Many prayers to God for you, you fight with such immense courage, but this does not surprise me. May He grant you His Saintly protection.

[P.S.] Just now, Théodore, whom I called, relayed to me what Dr. Gilbert said.[3] I am delighted the concert in Rome was so beautiful. I hope that you thought so and were satisfied in spite of everything.

❧ ❧ ❧

10–14, 1956, F-Pn, Rés Vmf. Ms. 60 (4). Stravinsky conducted the premiere of the *Canticum Sacrum* on September 13, 1956. Boulanger is concerned here about its reception. For one example of the American reception of the Warsaw Festival, see Paul Moor, "Warsaw Festival: Visiting Musicians Converge on Carnegie Hall this Week," *New York Times*, November 11, 1956.

2. This may have been because of her teeth, which Boulanger was losing at this time, or it may have been related to her cataracts. Rosenstiel, Boulanger's biographer who often mentions hospital visits or major surgeries, makes no mention of a hospital stay at this time.

3. Upon doctor's orders, Stravinsky agreed to cancel his January 1957 engagements in New York. After arriving in the United States, Stravinsky reversed his decision. Walsh, *Second Exile*, 354–56.

Stravinsky to Boulanger

LONDON

NADIA BOULANGER
36 RUE BALLU, PARIS
DECEMBER 5, 1956

THANK YOU FOR YOUR AFFECTIONATE LETTERS STOP INFINITELY
REGRET NOT HAVING SEEN YOU

TENDERLY,
STRAVINSKY

❧   ❧   ❧

Boulanger to Stravinsky

36 rue Ballu, 9th
Telephone: Trinité 57–91

December 9, 1956

Thank you for your telegram, Dear Vera, Dear Igor. I am so sad to have not
seen you Monday. Words seem so weak to me and become sentimental so
quickly. And I have difficulty saying what my tenderness would nonetheless
wish to express.

You are going to leave, but I cannot leave Europe this year, and much time
will pass without us seeing each other again. It is difficult for me [to accept it].

Every night here, I have heard your works all over, Dear Igor. I hope that
you take a little pleasure from all the joy we owe you and that you are happy to
do so much with all that you have been given. But forgive my nonsense.

Fond wishes. I love you with all my heart and am your
Nadia B.

❧   ❧   ❧

Théodore Strawinsky to Boulanger

Geneva

December 16, 1956

Dear Nadia,

I was so happy to hear your voice at the other end of the line the other day, but very upset to hear that you would be entering a clinic. Even when the operation is nothing serious, it's always bothersome to undergo anaesthesia [and] we hope you are now free of the effects . . . and we would be happy to have a little note to reassure us.

I don't need to tell you how sad I was to see my father leave, or more exactly to know he returned to America in less than perfect health (despite a . . . [illegibile] improvement) and the distance that will separate us can do nothing but add to our anxiety and our worry . . . And no one to watch over him.

I will have an exhibition at André Weil's, on Matignon Avenue during the last two weeks in February. Denise and I will be coming to Paris at the end of January, and we would be delighted to see you again.

In anticipation, dear Nadia, accept our heartfelt wishes. Wishes for you at the end of this year and on Christmas Eve.

Affectionately yours,
Théodore

P.S. Some very good news from Kitty, who is doing very well in her London life!

❧   ❧   ❧

Boulanger to Théodore Strawinsky

December 18, 1956

Dear Théodore,

Thank you for your letter—I think so much about you. I am slowly getting over this absurd adventure—but everything is returning to order.

I wasn't able to see your Father, but Mrs. Sachs, who was quite beside herself, was truly happy to find him back to his old self.

I understand your sorrow.

Know that I think of you both and please accept my wishes and deepest affection.
NB

ಶ್ಗ   ಶ್ಗ   ಶ್ಗ

Boulanger to Stravinsky

36 rue Ballu
Telephone: Trinité 57–91
[No Date]

My Dear Friend,

I've received numerous letters following *Perséphone*.[4] You must have been, I believe, content with this concert, with this program, with what you achieved for a performance. Father Fortier (the one who was at Santa Barbara) wrote to me that the broadcast in Canada was marvelous.[5]

What nostalgia at not being there!

You will receive a letter from Winifred Johnstone concerning the Lili Boulanger Foundation. I believe that you'll be able to sign the ballot sheet without reservation in support of Bhatia, a very gifted young Hindu who is very sick, [and] whom this bursary would help so much.[6] And for Per Nørgard, a young Dane, who is a real musician.[7] It seems to me that *these two* boys truly *deserve* this award.

I won't tell you again everything that keeps me close [to you]. My fond wishes to you both and a thousand to Bob,

Your
Nadia

ಶ್ಗ   ಶ್ಗ   ಶ್ಗ

---

4. Stravinsky conducted *Perséphone* in Manhattan on January 10, 1957. Walsh, *Second Exile*, 356.
5. See chapter 3, n. 29.
6. Vanraj Bhatia's letters to Boulanger can be found at: F-Pn, N.L.a. 55 (219–59). Little else about him is recorded in the archives.
7. For more on Per Nørgard (b. 1932), see Beyer, *The Music of Per Nørgård*; and Jensen, "At the Boundary between Music and Science," 55–61. For Nørgard's letters to Boulanger, see F-Pn, N.L.a. 91 (190–209).

Stravinsky to Boulanger

1260 N. Wetherly Drive
Hollywood 46, California

Miss Nadia Boulanger
36 rue [B]allu
Paris, 9th
France
January 18, 1957

Always happy to have a short note from you, if only to ask me to support your students' access to scholarships.

It is, of course, OK for the Hindu and the Dane
How are you doing?
Here everything is, for the moment, following its normal course.
Have you photographed the microfilms I sent with Bob in November for you [?]* If yes—be an angel and send them back to me with someone who's on their way to the United States. This film is very, very difficult to obtain, and I would like to make some reproductions here.

My most affectionate wishes, my dear Nadia,
I. Str

[P.S.] * That of Schütz—Webern.[8]

❧   ❧   ❧

Boulanger to Stravinsky

36 rue Ballu
Telephone: Trinité 57–91

February 19, 1957

My Dear Friend,
Once again, March 2 approaches. As always, I think of Catherine, of you.
[I hope you can] feel my faithful tenderness.

---

8. In his own letter, Robert Craft clarified that he was asking for the microfilm of the Schütz-Webern. Letter, February 18, 1957, CH-Bps In a later letter (May 12, 1957), Stravinsky calls this the "Isaak-Webern" microfilm. As early as during the composition of his Cantata, Stravinsky had grown interested in the music of Heinrich Isaac. Anton Webern had also been interested in Isaac and edited a portion of his *Choralis Constantinus*. Watkins, *The Gesualdo Hex*, 152.

At last, the *Canticum* takes its place. At first you speak alone, soon everyone follows, each at their own pace.

Théodore's exhibition was very striking. They make a beautiful ensemble [Théodore, Denise, and Kitty]. They dined here the other day with Dr. Gilbert's son, who is so refined and intelligent.

I love you more than I know how to say, you who have given us so much, and I am your faithful,
Nadia

❧ ❧ ❧

Boulanger to Stravinsky

36 rue Ballu, 9th
Telephone: Trinité 57–91

Mr. I. Strawinsky
1260 N. Wetherly Drive
Hollywood 46
California
U.S.A.
March 3, 1957

What joy your letter brought me, My Friend, it seems to me that you understand, and that does me good. It has been so long since I've seen you, [though] you are endlessly there. I know the music assures your presence—but, though it's a weakness on my part, that isn't enough for me. What emptiness you leave.

Did I tell you that *Perséphone* has been admirably heard everywhere? I hope creating this *folie* made you happy.

The power of life is stronger in you than reason, or rather your reason sees better. I am sending you the microfilm with George, or I'll send it by registered mail (What marvels in this volume!).

Sending all my love and tenderness,
Nadia

[P.S.] Give Vera and Miki my love, and my best to Bob

❧ ❧ ❧

Boulanger to Stravinsky[9]

36 rue Ballu
Telephone: Trinité 57–91

April 16, 1957

Sending all my thoughts to you for Easter, my Dears—what I wouldn't give to be close to you.

Boulez spoke to me with great seriousness about his trip to Hollywood.[10] I believe it will have a great influence on his development. Have you seen his music? What do you think of it? And your ballet with which I'm not yet familiar, is there a way to get me the proofs?

Excuse me—I know I'm being indiscreet, yet . . . how can it be avoided?

Fondly,
Nadia

❧ ❧ ❧

Stravinsky to Boulanger

Santa Monica, Calif.

Miss Nadia Boulanger
36 rue Ballu
Paris, IX
France
May 12, 1957

My dear Nadia,

This is to tell you I received your letter of April 16 and as always—no time for letters.

Boulez made an excellent impression on all of us: a musician of the first order, highly intelligent, he has good manners and is probably a generous man. His *Marteau sans maître*, which he conducted so well here, is an admirably well-ordered score, in spite of all the auditory and visual complications

---

9. This letter directly followed a personal invitation from Igor Markevitch to Stravinsky to attend Boulanger's seventieth birthday party, which Markevitch hosted at his home in Villars. On April 18, Stravinsky responded that he wished Markevitch well but could not attend the festivities in person.

10. Spycket discusses Boulanger's involvement with Boulez's trip to Hollywood in *Nadia Boulanger*, 130. Walsh discusses the visit as well as Stravinsky's response in *Second Exile*, 358–60.

(counterpoint, rhythm, tempo). Without being too familiar with Boulez's music, I find it, frankly, preferable to many other things from his generation.

I never received the microfilm (Isaak-Webern) that you had promised me from George Sachs, who was supposed to come to the United States this Easter. We haven't heard anything about it.

Just spoke with Nica Nabokov who will have returned to Paris when you read these lines. Telephone him to get the latest news.

Please respond.

Love,
I. Str

❧ ❧ ❧

Boulanger to Stravinsky

36 rue Ballu

May 16, 1957

Finally found someone, Dear Friend, to bring you your microfilm that I didn't dare trust to the mail service. The young Jean-Pierre Marty, a real *musician*, is leaving tomorrow for N.Y.[11] From there he'll deliver it to you by air to save time. When he arrives in Los Angeles he will ensure that everything is in order. If, by chance, you could see him for a moment, it would be such a great joy for him. He deserves it, but only if it doesn't bother you.

What you said about Boulez makes me happy—he is serious. He is a *good* musician, and there are no tricks or bluffs. He was so happy to have seen you.

I am overwhelmed by Marie-Blanche's slow agony. Operated on two months ago, she is in the most alarming state.[12] We expect her death at any time, yet something inside of her is so strong that she is still alive this morning. What sorrow.

Fond wishes and deep affection,

---

11. Jean-Pierre Marty (b. 1932) is a pianist and conductor. He eventually took over as director of the Ecole d'art américaines at Fontainebleau. He has published articles and books on the piano works of Wolfgang Amadeus Mozart and Frédéric Chopin. For his books, see *Vingt-quatre leçons avec*; and *The Tempo Indications of Mozart*.

12. Marie-Blanche (Comtesse Jean) de Polignac (née Margeurite di Pietro) (1897–1958) had cancer. On March 15, 1957, she was admitted to a clinic and stayed there until her death on February 14, 1958. For more on Boulanger's work and friendship with Marie-Blanche de Polignac, see Kahan, "'Quelque chose de très raffiné.'"

Yours,
Nadia

❧   ❧   ❧

Boulanger to Théodore Strawinsky

September 8, 1957
Hotel du Golf Chalet at Goblet

To be so close—and so far—I have arrived here, overcome by the tyranny of sleep—I am regaining my spirits—I'll see you upon my return from Villars, where I'm going to spend five days with the Markevitch family. But if you could send me the addresses of your Father before [he leaves Europe], you would make me very happy, as I must thank him. His writing seems to show he is doing well. To think that he passed by Ballu and I was in Fontainebleau—never suspecting that I was missing out on such a great joy!

To Denise and to you, dear Théodore, from my heart,
Nadia B

❧   ❧   ❧

Igor and Vera Stravinsky to Boulanger

VENICE

NADIA BOULANGER C/O MARKEVITCH
VILLARS SUR OLLON, SWITZERLAND
SEPTEMBER 16, 1957

OUR THOUGHTS OUR HEARTS WITH YOU DEAR NADIA ON THIS GREAT DAY OF YOUR BIRTHDAY[13] MANY HAPPY RETURNS

IGOR VERA STRAVINSKY

---

13. Boulanger celebrated her seventieth birthday on September 16, 1957. The occasion was marked with a lavish party in Switzerland held by Igor Markevitch. For more on the event, see Nadia Boulanger, "Hommages: 1939, 1957, 1977 et post mortem," F-Pn Rés Vm Dos 122. See also Rosenstiel, *Nadia Boulanger*, 371–72; and Spycket, *Nadia Boulanger*, 133.

🙠 🙠 🙠

Soulima and Françoise Stravinsky to Boulanger

URBANA, ILL

VIA RADIO SUISSE
NADIA BOULANGER C/O MARKEVITCH
VILLARS SUR OLLON, SWITZERLAND
SEPTEMBER 17, 1957

WITH YOU WHOLEHEARTEDLY A THOUSAND AFFECTIONATE THOUGHTS

SOULIMAS

🙠 🙠 🙠

Boulanger to Stravinsky

36 rue Ballu

December 20, 1957

Love, wishes, expectations, gratitude, finally a couple of words to say to you, Dear Igor—Happy Christmas.

Read your questions and responses (those which appeared).[14] What an ingenious and useful idea because even without good faith, one is obliged to think, to search, and the effort brings about better understanding. At least, let's hope.

I send you my wishes, I love you with all my heart and *thank you*. All best wishes to Bob,

Nadia B.

🙠 🙠 🙠

---

14. This letter references the first of Craft's published interviews with Stravinsky, first released as "35 Antworten auf 35 Fragen," *Melos* 24 (1957): 161–70; "Answers to 34 Questions: An Interview with Igor Stravinsky," *Encounter* 9, no. 7 (1957): 3–14; and "Entretiens d'Igor Stravinsky avec Robert Craft," in *Avec Stravinsky* (Monaco: Éditions de Rocher, 1958). Craft later expanded the format to ninety-two questions and published the exchange in book form as Craft and Stravinsky, *Conversations with Igor Stravinsky*. There is some question today regarding the veracity of Stravinsky's responses in these books.

Igor and Vera Stravinsky to Boulanger

> 1260 N. Wetherly Dr.
> Los Angeles 46 Calif

Miss Nadia Boulanger
36 rue Ballu
Paris, IX
France
January 1, 1958

Happy New Year, my very dear Nadia,
    Tomorrow we're going* with Vera to Houston (Texas) where I am conducting two concerts and Vera has her exhibitions.[15]
    Send us news. We should be back in a week.

All our love,
I Str.

*We're flying[16]

❧   ❧   ❧

Boulanger to Stravinsky

> The Palace of Monaco

January 9, 1958

How nice it is that you wrote to me. Sometimes we need a sign, and yours are [cause for] celebration. Dear Friend, My dear Igor, I've so many things to tell you to which you are central. Spoke at length with Rainier of Monaco. He is going to inquire about Villas that might suit you. However, he has no buildings that could be put at your disposal. Yet I believe, nevertheless, that you would have so many advantages in settling here. And [property values] are increasing at such a pace that what we acquire one year quickly *doubles* in value. One of my friends who bought a very nice apartment sold it two years later for *more* than double.

---

15. Stravinsky uses the singular "son" with the plural "expositions."
16. This letter concludes with a postscript from Vera Stravinsky specifying travel details.

If it's possible before I leave to visit the potential villas that would satisfy your *programme*, I will see them and keep you up to date as quickly as possible.

My love to you both, a thousand good wishes for Bob, and I am wholeheartedly yours,

Nadia B.

❧   ❧   ❧

Boulanger to Stravinsky

36 rue Ballu!!, 9th

May 25, 1958

Dear Friend,

[Sending] these lines to be with you on the 2nd. I see all of the past as if it were the present—I think of Them, of you, and am always there.

Need I tell you of my grief over the death of Marie-Blanche? I know . . . it's deliverance for her, but for me, it's a great pain.

You will receive a note from Winifred for the Lili Boulanger M. F. I believe it will be necessary to give:

$200 to Edward Ben Michael[17]
$200 to Geoffrey Grey[18]
$200 to Bruno Gillet[19]

They are serious boys who have talent and a great need to be encouraged, helped. Do you know the date for Venice? Will you be at the Bauer? How long will you stay there?

---

17. Edward Ben (Salim) Michaël (1921–2006) was a British composer who grew up in the Middle East (Iraq, Syria, Egypt, and Palestine) before returning to England prior to the Second World War. He studied with Boulanger in the early 1950s, and it was his *Nocturne* for flute and orchestra that won him this prize. His correspondence with Boulanger can be consulted at F-Pn, N.L.a. (201–36). For more on Michaël, see Culot, "Edouard Michael."

18. Geoffrey Grey (b. 1934) is a British composer. For his correspondence with Boulanger, see F-Pn, N.L.a. 73 (411–9).

19. Bruno Gillet (b. 1936) is a French composer. For his correspondence with Boulanger, see N.L.a. 72 (233–310) and N.L.a. 294 (070–076). His memories of studying with Boulanger were recorded as part of a roundtable celebrating Boulanger on the twenty-fifth anniversary of her death; see "Souvenirs de disciples de Nadia Boulanger," *Témoignages et etudes*, 17–32.

What can I tell you about the *Canticum*, about *Agon*?[20] I don't dare tell you anything, but I *thank you* from the bottom of my heart. You extract everything through the method you choose and you make it your own. All the art is there.

My tenderness to you both, and many thoughts for Bob,

Your
NB

❧   ❧   ❧

Stravinsky to Boulanger

Hollywood
March 2, 1958

Thank you, thank you, dear Nadia, for your letter—I am very appreciative, believe me.

We are going to Venice (certainly to Bauer) on July 29, embarking for New York on board the *Cristoforo Colombo* (which hit a whale between Genoa and Naples very recently). *Threni* (or *Lamentations after the Vulgate*) upon which the composition touches near the end, will be performed at the Scuola San Rocco under my direction around September 20; then I conduct *Oedipus* and *Le Sacre* and on Sept 24 I leave with my whole ensemble for Switzerland, where I am conducting *Threni* from Sept 25 to 29 in Geneva, Berne, Bâle, and Zurich. As for the desired allocation for the Lili Boulanger Fund: OK.

Poor Marie-Blanche. I am thinking of her and I sympathize with your grief because I know you were great friends.

I have as well just learned of a death that has greatly affected me—that of Alexandre Piovesan of the Venice Biennale, he couldn't have been more than forty years old![21]

Affectionately yours,
I. Stravinsky

---

20. Igor Stravinsky, *Agon* (New York, 1957). Boulanger owned only the miniature score, F-LYc, UFNB MEp STR 400. For more on *Agon*, see Joseph. *Stravinsky and Balanchine*, 211–27.

21. Alessandro Piovesan (1908–58) was director of the Venice Bienniale for the *Canticum Sacrum* and *Von Himmel Hoch Variations* performances. He was also present for the beginning of the *Threni* commission, though he died from pneumonia at the age of fifty before the piece was performed. See Walsh, *Second Exile*, 319–20 and 376–77.

❧   ❧   ❧

Boulanger to Stravinsky

Ecoles d'art américaines
Fondation reconnue d'utilité publique
Conservatoire de musique
Palais de Fontainebleau
Le Directeur

Mr. Igor Strawinsky
Hotel Bauer Grunwald
Venise
Italie
[September] 2, 1958

Dear Igor, Dear Vera,

I'll arrive in Venice with such joy! Read the score to *Threni*—daren't speak of it—what words would I use to describe such extraordinary pages?[22] Understand everything that my silence contains.

Leave tonight for Bucharest. Hope to arrive in Venice at the Bauer Grunwald on the 19th. To tell you of my joy and my impatience is impossible. I love you so and want you to know everything I cannot express!

Until the 19th, God willing,

I am your,
NB

[P.S.] Best wishes to Bob.

❧   ❧   ❧

.

---

22. Boulanger requested the score of Stravinsky on March 27, 1958. Igor Stravinsky, *Threni id est Lamentationes Jeremiae Prophetae* (New York: Boosey & Hawkes, 1958). Stravinsky's longest serial work—and arguably the most complicated—calls for vocal soloists, chorus, and orchestra. The text comes from the Book of Lamentations from the Latin Vulgate. Boulanger owned the full score, which she analyzed using serial techniques: F-LYc, UFNB ME STR 530. She also owned a copy of Roman Vlad's *Stravinsky*, in which she annotated portions of the text that discussed the serial techniques in *Threni*. Possibly she used this to aid her own analysis.

262   CHAPTER SIX

Stravinsky to Boulanger

Berkley
7 avenue Matignon
Rond-Point des Champs-Elysées
Paris, VII
Tel: Balzac 02.24
Telegram Address: Berkleyeb Paris 45

Mademoiselle Nadia Boulanger
36 rue Ballu
Paris, IX
November 13, 1958

My very dear Nadia,

    I was at your house today, but nobody was there. Too bad, I send you all my heartfelt love.

    Attached is a note for Bruno Gillet that I ask you to give to him,

Love,
I Str

🙢   🙢   🙢

Boulanger to Stravinsky

36 rue Ballu, 9th

17 November 1958

Dear Friend,

    What offensive absurdity! But is Gavoty worth worrying about?[23] Accept the attached letter.[24] The boy who wrote it was *sick* about what happened on Friday. He is *good* and he has talent.[25]

---

23. Gavoty, for whom Stravinsky had composed a chorale theme in 1952 (see chapter 4, n. 10), wrote a column on the *Threni* premiere in *Le Figaro* in which he criticized Craft for not conducting the Berg and Webern pieces with enough clarity. "Stravinsky a présenté ses *Threni*." *Le Figaro*, November 17, 1958.

24. The attached letter does not survive.

25. On November 14, 1958, Stravinsky conducted a concert including his work, *Threni*, alongside other pieces by Webern and Berg. The rehearsal on November 9 went terribly, the result of poor, underprepared performers. Stravinsky and Walsh both blamed Pierre Boulez for the situation. Boulanger and others tried to convince Stravinsky to cancel the concert, but he decided against it. Craft, *An Improbable Life*, 208. The concert held on the fourteenth

1. Would you allow your name to be put forth to the Committee for Father Desobry?[26]

2. Would you allow Charles Leirens to come and take a photo of you?[27] He takes very beautiful pictures.

I'm of course sad not to have seen you, and now it's too late. But I love you even though I cannot see you.

To you both,
Nadia B

❧   ❧   ❧

Boulanger to Stravinsky

36 rue Ballu, 9th
February 22, 1959

My Friend, the days have gone by. I have refrained from writing to you due to a useless discretion, but the resulting regret is too heavy to bear. As I believe you know, my thoughts never leave you. We don't see each other anymore, or very little, and each of us stays enclosed in our solitude, because we don't have enough time to get to the bottom of things, and our affection is too deep to be contented by gossip which neither of us believes in. But a date that links us is once again approaching, almost without our knowing it. Words would all be bothersome, useless, almost embarrassing. But only you know that I remain attached to the past that fills the present with what was and remains.

And I see again a calm face, a look lit up by the purity of its soul, and I send my very tender wishes. I keep in my heart the simple, sublime words I heard a long time ago. And you are twice as dear, though you certainly do not need

---

was a complete disaster, with *Threni* itself breaking down entirely at several points. Walsh, *Second Exile*, 386. Just the day prior, Stravinsky had tried to visit Boulanger at her Paris apartment, but she was not home. Letter, Stravinsky to Boulanger, November 13, 1958, F-Pn, N.L.a. 108 (264–5).

26. Most likely a reference to Father Jean Desobry, a priest in the Amiens diocese of Northern France, who was ordained in 1951. He was the archivist for the diocese from 1962 to 1975. "Jean Desobry," *Bibliothèque Nationale De France*, last modified March 23, 2016, http://data.bnf.fr/atelier/12601664/jean_desobry/. I have been unable to locate the nature of the committee or Boulanger's connection to Desobry.

27. Charles Leirens (1888–1963) was the founder in 1938 of the *Revue internationale de musique*. He was a renowned photographer.

me, and nevertheless show me that you know that my attachment is to your work as much as to you, My Friend,
Nadia B

[P.S.] So much affection for your household, including Bob

❧   ❧   ❧

Stravinsky to Boulanger

Los Angeles California

Miss N. Boulanger
36 rue Ballu
Paris, IX
France
February 25, 1959

My dear Nadia,
  Your letter is infinitely precious to me.
  This wound that I have carried now for twenty years still and always needs kindness.
  Thank you, very dear Nadia
  With all my heart,

Yours,
I Str.

❧   ❧   ❧

Boulanger to Théodore Strawinsky

March 2, 1959

Dear Théodore,
  It was on the 2nd of March that I learned about the death of your Mother. [This year] I wrote your Father a little in advance to be sure to be close to him. His response was the most moving testament that could possibly bring us together around a dear memory.
  I revered, I revere your Mother—thanks to you, her image is before my eyes always.

Lovingly, I am yours,
NB

❧   ❧   ❧

Stravinsky to Boulanger

Gladstone
114–122 East 52nd Street at Park Avenue
New York City—22
Cable Address
"Gladsto"
Plaza 3-4300

Miss Nadia Boulanger
36 rue Ballu
Paris, IX
France
November 20, 1959

Dear Nadia,
    Very touched by your letter which I read at sea on route back to America ("Liberty").
    Here in New York I am giving three concerts: two at Town Hall and one at Carnegie Hall *Dec. 20th (*Noces*), 3 January (*Sacre*), and 10 January (*Movements for Piano and Orchestra*).[28] Do you intend to come to the United States? If yes, when? We are staying here until January 15th.

With heartfelt fondness,
I Str.

❧   ❧   ❧

---

28. Boulanger received numerous accounts of the premiere of *Movements for Piano* (New York: Boosey & Hawkes, 1960), one of Stravinsky's more complicated serial works that far exceeded the capabilities of its first soloist, Margrit Weber. See "Spies to Boulanger," January 29, 1960, F-Pn, N.L.a. 107 (263–4); and "Soloist does not *understand* this music," September 20, 1962, F-Pn, N.L.a. 107 (275). Dr. Roth also contacted Boulanger saying he worried that Stravinsky's health would be too poor for him to conduct the premiere. Roth (Boosey & Hawkes) to Boulanger, November 12, 1959, F-Pn, N.L.a. 57 (174). Boulanger owned a copy of the score on which she wrote, "London, May 1960." The score contains no further markings. F-LYc, UFNB ME STR 401.11.

Boulanger to Stravinsky

36 rue Ballu
Paris IX
Tel: Tri 57–91

April 11, 1960

Easter has nearly arrived now—it seems to me that I haven't written to you in a very long time, my dear Igor, and yet I miss you more than I know how to say. But, in truth, I am slightly afraid of inflicting on you a useless letter full of my effusions—and what's more, I know how to listen to you without daring to speak to you. Perhaps because I admire you so much, I am acting silly.

A lot of disappointing concerts this winter—with many of the attempts showing both powerlessness and self-confidence at the same time. Out of clumsy hands and weak minds came a bunch of derivative, inadequate tricks and stuff. But it would only take *one* work and *one* will to put everything back in order.

You cannot imagine how angry I was at myself for not writing to you at the start of March—that month which is marked by such real pain for you.

I know, I know that the years change the outward appearance of what we allow to be seen, but the wounds never close.

Her photograph is here, near to me—the light given off by her being will never be extinguished—and . . . I know that She always prays for us.

I send my love and miss, more than you can know, the times which are now so far away, and during which we were so close. Yet what seems to have changed has not changed the essential [the essence of our bond]. And then, *you* are— and that is enough. With all my heart,

Your
Nadia

[P.S.] Best wishes for the household.

❧   ❧   ❧

Stravinsky to Boulanger

April 14, 1960

Very dear Nadia, Happy Easter. Your note touched me greatly.

Very busy: composition, treatments for my blood and my arteries (protection against new surprises!?), concert here (Mass and *Noces* in June), conducting there (*Oedipus* in Santa Fe in July), then we fly to South America for a concert tour (sharing the program with Bob), Mexico, Bogota, Lima, Santiago, Buenos

[Aires], Rio, Caracas, from August 1 to September 17. Then to Venice where Bob and I will be conducting at the Biennale, half and half, on September 26.

We're publishing the second volume of our conversations with Bob under the title of *Memories and Commentaries*.[29] This volume is dedicated to you. With all my love,

Write always—I'll be here until the beginning of July.

⁊⁰   ⁊⁰   ⁊⁰

Boulanger to Stravinsky

36 rue Ballu, 9th

April 24, 1960

You can't imagine the joy your letter brought me, Dear Friend. That you have thought to dedicate this book to me causes me—yes, don't smile—deep emotion. Thanks to you, and to Bob.

You provide such a service in setting the record straight—in clarifying what so many "amateur" pseudo-composers have naïvely systematized, exploited, or more often, stolen. So many cheaters.

As for your busyness, yes, perhaps it's terrifying. But it is still much more terrifying to *be* I. S., and . . . perhaps we must let him choose his own pace. And it seems to be suiting you quite well.

Could you tell Bob that I never received the parts of the funeral Ode?[30] It wasn't so important, but . . . I hope that they weren't lost. He responded so kindly to my request.

My love to you and to Vera and warm wishes for Bob. What an opportunity has been presented to you—Certainly to him, but to you, as well—it's good to have someone so young and intelligent close to you. Someone . . . who would not be envious to live in your shadow. But "They" never understand anything.

---

29. This was the second of the conversation books, eventually published in 1960. See Stravinsky and Craft, *Memories and Commentaries* (New York: Doubleday, 1960). For more about its content in relation to Boulanger, see Francis, *Teaching Stravinsky*, 236–38.

30. Boulanger attempted to acquire the parts to the *Ode* in advance and began by contacting Robert Craft. She then failed to respond to his request for further specificity about the parts and instead wrote Stravinsky the letter of April 24, 1960. See Craft to Boulanger, January 26, 1960, F-Pn, N.L.a. (63), 390. Boulanger's Lyon archives hold a copy of the pocket score that is annotated as having come from Stravinsky in April 1947, F-LYc, UFNB MEp STR 400. She owned no other copies or parts for the work.

And yet, the wind carries them away. You have, as you say, your compass in your pocket.

Again, wholeheartedly your,
Nadia B

                            ᔐ   ᔐ   ᔐ

Boulanger to Théodore Strawinsky

September 15, 1960

Dear Théodore,

I am thinking a lot about you right now. Are you going? Are you in Venice—is the past still living in the present? All of this is preoccupying me as I know you are tormented by it. And it's sad, as each loses and nobody wins. And what we lose, especially in this manner, is never to be found again. I want to hope that my worries are in vain, that you were able to spend some time with your Father, to hear his new work, well-performed.

Alas, new works always seem difficult, audacious pieces, or more accurately, incomprehensible. And in all his glory, your Father knows the bitterness of being, ultimately, rather alone with the present—so cruelly and blindly misunderstood. All of that seems paradoxical and is veiled by a small number of enlightened musicians and some courtiers.

Certainly, it does not matter: *Le Sacre, Noces, Œdipe* and soon *Canticum Sacrum*, then *Threni* will take their legitimate places. I am very sad not to be in Venice, close to him—you know what is in my heart, in my mind, in my life every day. But whether I'm close or far away, he always seems present to me, and my reverence never ceases to accompany him.

Dear Théodore, all of this tells you, does it not, how much I love you all, Denise, Kitty—in the memory of your Mother.

And I am your,
Nadia B.

P.S. I'll be in Lans en Vercors until the end of the month without a doubt

                            ᔐ   ᔐ   ᔐ

Boulanger to Stravinsky

Ecoles d'art américaines
Fondation reconnue d'utilité publique
Conservatoire de musique
Palais de fontainebleau
Le Directeur

Hotel Val Fleuri
Lans en Vescours
Isère
September 15, 1960

Very dear Friend, I'm sorry for this official paper, don't have anything else at hand, hardly dare to write to you dears [*illegible*] I were to come or stay. But there it is, I am sad to not see you, and have started, therefore, to feel sorry for myself.

I wanted to hear *Mouvements* and *Gesualdo*.[31] Knowing I won't see you, how I miss you. Not only because of my affection [for you], though this is somewhat the case, but also because of a necessity to see you, to refresh my ideas in the shadow of your own, and to know if I am capable of truly understanding everything.

Writing to you always makes me seem both proud and naïve. But I also know that so many things, so much is between us. How the path forward is sometimes only veiled, but never forgotten. It's our conscience that wants it this way, even when it bothers us. It saves us, it is the guardian of values that nothing could replace.

Sorry—I will leave you to your work, to your letters. Beings like you are not made to look back, but what they seem to no longer see does not cease to accompany them. I am waiting for the book in which you wished to inscribe my name, you cannot know what that means to me.

All my love to you and Vera, and please tell Bob how often I think of him,

Your
Nadia B

❧ ❧ ❧

---

31. Stravinsky, *Monumentum pro Gesualdo di Venosa* (New York: Boosey & Hawkes, 1960). Boulanger owned a copy of the score on which she wrote: "NB from IS, Oct 1960." The remainder of the score is without annotation. F-LYc, UFNB MEp STR 402. For more about Gesualdo's influence on Stravinsky, see Watkins, *The Gesualdo Hex.*

Théodore Strawinsky to Boulanger

Geneva

October 3, 1960

Dear Nadia,

Denise and I have just come back from Venice and I found your letter. Thank you for these lines, thank you for your thoughts, and above all thank you for your faithful friendship: it is so precious to us.

A present where the past ceases to remain alive would seem suspicious to me, not to mention a lie. And I am certain that the past is not dead for my father, but he shrouds in self-imposed silence—in addition to a certain innate sense of "modesty"—the whole array of exterior circumstances we know of.

We found him quite disabled because of his leg, which he can no longer rehabilitate—which humiliates him a lot and distresses us. He conducted *Orpheus* and *Monumentum Gesualdo* without excessive fatigue. These are not exactly the types of works to be appreciated by the public of Venice . . . Your presence (which we had hoped for) and the reassurance of your friendship were very much missed!

When will you see us, dear Nadia? Kitty joins Denise and myself in sending you our love, and we want to tell you of our great devotion and our affection,

Théodore

ᵃᵛ ᵃᵛ ᵃᵛ

Boulanger to Stravinsky

New York Office: Fontainebleau Schools, 122 East 58 St. N.Y. 22
Conservatoire de musique—Ecole des beaux-arts
Palais de Fontainebleau

October 29, 1960

The book has arrived, I am reading it eagerly and thank you both, Bob and you, Dear Friend, with all my heart. I hear again the comments made at Gargenville, here, at Foch Avenue—and you rekindle them in such a way that the eyes and ears are revived by these distant voices.[32]

---

32. The addresses mentioned here (Gargenville, "here," avenue Foch) are absent from the actual text of *Memories and Commentaries*, though they are all places associated with Boulanger. Indeed, despite its dedication to her—and despite several points of discussion relating directly to Boulanger—her name is never mentioned in the book. See also Francis, *Teaching Stravinsky*, 237.

And how many things most people, fortunately, will not see! Concerning the *Monumentum*—each note is significant . . . alas, I cannot write [about] it. It seems to me that I see, and read, and understand. It's sad not being able to communicate it, and above all perfectly useless.

All my heartfelt love,

Your
Nadia B

P.S. My tenderness to Vera and best wishes to Bob—how intelligent he is! A constant joy. And the strength of all that you keep silent wells up—and drives everything.

❧ ❧ ❧

Stravinsky to Boulanger

Hollywood

Miss Nadia Boulanger
36 rue Ballu
Paris IX
France
March 6, 1961

My very dear Nadia,

I was deeply touched by your affectionate message and send you all my love.

I've finished (we are in the process of correcting the proofs in London) the composition for Sacher (Basel*)—a sort of cantata (alto, tenor, choral, orch., and a narrator): *A Sermon, a Narrative, and a Prayer* and have put myself to work on "Flood."[33] That one will be good to compose.

---

33. Stravinsky, *A Sermon, A Narrative, and A Prayer* (New York: Boosey & Hawkes, 1961), calls for tenor and alto soloists with choir and orchestra. The work was commissioned by Paul Sacher. The "Sermon" portion quotes text from St Paul, the "Narrative" a text from the book of "Acts of the Apostles"; the "Prayer" sets a poem by Thomas Dekker (1572–1632). Boulanger owned two copies of the score, the first being a gift in 1962 from David J Adams, the Vice President and Managing Director of Boosey & Hawkes New York, the second bearing no annotation whatsoever. F-LYc, UFNB MEp STR 530 and UFNB ME STR 530. *The Flood: A Musical Play* (New York: Boosey & Hawkes, 1962) is a play with ballet and singing, based upon the biblical story of Noah. It premiered on CBS in 1962 with choreography by Balanchine and conducted by Robert Craft. Boulanger owned a copy of the full score, F-LYc, UFNB ME STR 560.

Good health for the moment. Beginning March in Mexico (for ten days—Easter), where I am conducting *The Rite* and Vera will have an exhibition of her gorgeous paintings.

Heartfelt wishes,

Yours,
I Str.

[P.S.] In July in Santa Fe—conducting *Oedipus* and *Perséphone.* End of August–September we are planning to go to Australia with Bob. October in Berlin with Santa Fe Opera, with Radio Brussels and BBC in London.

❧   ❧   ❧

Boulanger to Stravinsky

36 rue Ballu
Paris IX, France
Tel: Tri. 57–91

Dear Igor,

Many thoughts sent your way for March 2—so many thoughts for your work. We've just worked on *Threni*, this marvel in which every note has been chosen and found.

I don't want to bother you after you've started *Noah* [*sic*]. You are a world of energy, of invention, and of courage—always taking up the struggle again.

I'm sad to have no news of you, but I *understand.*

I am fondly your,
Nadia B

[P.S.] For March 2, 1961

❧   ❧   ❧

Boulanger to Stravinsky

Ecoles d'art américaines
Fondation reconnue d'utilité publique
New York Office: Fontainebleau Schools, 122 East 58 St. N.Y. 22
Conservatoire de musique—Ecole des beaux-arts
Palais de Fontainebleau
Le Directeur

October 26, 1961

Dear Igor,

Up to the last minute I held on to the hope of coming and greeting you in London. What disappointment I feel about it all. I had such a great need, such a great desire to see you. It has been so long!

And the time is equally as long because you use it in such a way that you are far ahead of the rest even before they get started.

And I needed to breathe some of your air (as if it were possible!) and to try to follow you. But to be honest, each of your steps is so decisive that unless we are hopelessly stupid and obtuse, we walk with you, renewed and new.

I love you so much, honestly as much as I admire you, and I'm sorry I can't rush to you.

To Vera, to you, and with many thoughts for Bob,
Nadia B

❧ ❧ ❧

Stravinsky to Boulanger

London

Mlle Nadia Boulanger
36 rue Ballu
Paris IX
October 30, 1961

Just a word, dear Nadia, to tell you that I was touched by your letter and that I am flying to New Zealand in ninety-four hours via Cairo and Sidney [*sic*].

I should be in Hollywood beginning of Dec.

With heartfelt fondness,

Yours,
I Str.

❧   ❧   ❧

Boulanger to Denise Stravinsky

February 18, 1962

Dear Denise,

Without news for a long time, but I feel close [to you] and my thoughts are always with you. I do hope that you are suffering less. But it has been so long—it's a burden to be so patient.

I saw your father-in-law upon his return from Moscow, walking with a bit of difficulty, but with an extraordinary presence—so preoccupied by you, by you all.[34]

The recording of the *Flood* is impressive and allows for an understanding of the grandeur of the work.[35] Regarding *A Sermon, Narration, Prayer* [*sic*], which I heard on the radio, it is profoundly moving. And if mastering these ever-new means is stupefying, the emotion that emanates from this sublime work is inexpressible. What a supreme force of thought and feeling—which [others] want to ignore!

Hug one another [for me] and know I am your,
Nadia B.

P.S. Not yet been able to write to Kitty. Going to do it one of these days I hope!

❧   ❧   ❧

---

34. In September 1961, Stravinsky traveled for the first time to the Soviet Union. His trip was covered widely in the press. It was his first visit to the country of his birth since the Revolution. Walsh, *Second Exile*, 461–65; Levitz, *Stravinsky and His World*, 8, 71, 279, 297–300; and Craft, "Stravinsky's Return: A Russian Diary," 33–48.

35. The original recording of *The Flood* took place in Hollywood on March 28 and 31, 1962, featuring Laurence Harvey as the narrator; Sebastian Cabot, Elsa Lanchester, and Paul Tripp in spoken roles; Richard Robinson as the tenor and John Reardon and Robert Oliver as basses. Everything was recorded with the Columbia Symphony Chorus & Orchestra, Columbia Masterworks Records, released on CD by Sony Classical Records (SM2K 46300). Igor Stravinsky, *The Flood*, Columbia Symphony Chorus & Orchestra, Robert Craft, Sony Classical Records, SM2K 46300, 1962, CD.

Boulanger to Stravinsky

Ecoles d'art américaines
Fondation reconnue d'utilité publique
New York Office: Fontainebleau Schools, 122 East 58 St. N.Y. 22
Conservatoire de musique—Ecole des beaux-arts
Palais de Fontainebleau
Le Directeur du Conservatoire

June 18, 1962

Very dear Igor,

Soon will be the birthday the entire world celebrates yet does not know how to celebrate enough. But once again I find myself near you in Hollywood—but also in Paris—I believe I'm sharing some of your views toward the Past, some of your silence in the Present, and your view of the new possibilities the material offers you and your mind.

I don't dare tell you what leads me always to this struggle before you, one that has no beginning and no end. In it I see your pain, your wounds, your aspirations, and I repeat, from the bottom of my heart, "May Peace be with you."

Your burden is heavy if it brings with it light, and I believe I feel and understand. I love you so much.

I send you all my love, I say to you *thank you,* and I hear you wherever you may be, always there,

Your
Nadia B

🕊 🕊 🕊

Boulanger to Théodore Strawinsky

[No Date] [1962]

Dear Théodore,

Sorry I still haven't written you. I am so shaken up. I spent Sunday afternoon with your Father—surprising strength, enthusiasm and tenderness. The worry he creates for himself, for Denise, for you, for Kitty. Perhaps he seems to remain silent, but he lives with those who are his life and every detail remains engraved—all hidden in a seemingly contradictory appearance, but nevertheless rooted within.

His impressions, his trip, this return to his childhood, his sense of modesty, his way of saying nothing but what he wants to, and how the words must veil or divulge. It is true, he walks with difficulty, it's the only time where one can see the signs of the shocks he has undergone. His spirit is young, alive, innovative, mobile, and what clairvoyance, what conviction as well, which sometimes creates incontrollable, spontaneous reactions.

Unfortunately, I must hurry, I can spare anything but time, but I am with you, sharing in your hopes, your expectations, knowing the weight of your intense patience.

Give Denise my love and know, both of you, that my thoughts never leave you. *Thank you again.*

Yours,
NB

❧   ❧   ❧

Boulanger to Stravinsky

Ecoles d'art américaines
Fondation reconnue d'utilité publique
Bureau New-York: Fontainebleau Schools, 122 East 58 St. N.Y. 22
Conservatoire de musique—Ecole des beaux-arts
Palais de Fontainebleau

March 2, 1963

My Friend,

So many thoughts go toward you as March 2 approaches, and so tenderly unites me to you, in the tenderness I am going to carry to Her, the one who knew the words to illuminate the shadows.

I've read your very important notes in *New Perspectives* with great interest.[36] What order they bring to such troubling confusion. We will all thank you—Bob and you—for the clarification. Bergson puts it well: the first sign of strength is precision.[37] And also [thank you] for, as much as you are able, protecting us and putting us on the right path. It's always with the same feeling when I think about this March 2, about these painful years, about Mika!

---

36. *Perspectives of New Music* was a new journal at the time, launched in 1962 by Boulanger's pupil Arthur Berger and by Benjamin Boretz. The first volumes included such seminal articles as Edward T. Cone's "Stravinsky: The Progress of a Method" and Berger's "Problems of Pitch Organization in Stravinsky." Also included in the first volume was an interview between Stravinsky and Craft, "A Quintet of Dialogues."

37. Henri Bergson (1859–1941) was a favorite French philosopher of Boulanger's, quoted often in her teaching. See Brooks, *Performing Past and Future*, 60–62.

My most profound tenderness,
Nadia B

♥   ♥   ♥

Boulanger to Stravinsky

36 rue Ballu

March 19, 1963

Your letter, My Friend, arrived on March 19. Twenty-eight years since Mother entered the Peace [of Christ]. And to feel you there, amongst our dear shadows, is such *happiness*. I love you so much.

The Holy Father's gesture is very significant, and I am sure you accept the honor with humility and emotion.[38]

I am doing better, but this absurd flu has a hold on me, and I am still a wreck, it's ridiculous. But a good lesson in patience! Thank you for having written me, I am in awe of your activity. The mind that sets the tempo—My love to Vera, best wishes to Bob, and to you, my friend, with my whole heart, I send fondest wishes.

Nadia B.

♥   ♥   ♥

Boulanger to Stravinsky

36 rue Ballu

June 18, 1963

It's Tuesday—your birthday, My Friend. We will be at the Champs-Elysées, *Le Sacre, [Les] Symphonie[s] [d']instruments à vent,* Boulez is conducting—and we'll be thinking of 1913, of the present, of all you have given to the world during these fifty years, of the doors you open at every step.

The words you are reading are my best. I recall everything we read [together], and more particularly, the audience granted by the Patriarco in Venice after the *Canticum Sacrum*. A phrase returns: "Yes, Igor Stravinsky gave us a lesson that evening before the altar of San Marco. Yes . . . yes a lesson."

---

38. This letter was written two years before Stravinsky received a Papal decoration from Pope Paul VI. Boulanger's subsequent letter (June 18, 1963) clarifies that she was referencing Stravinsky's audience with the "Patriarco" of Venice, a meeting granted following the performance of the *Canticum Sacrum*.

And this honor took on at that time a special significance. The Holy Father did not forget. He chose you, He gave you his blessing, and this June 18, it is this thought that lives in me and guides me toward you.

With all my heart, I send fond wishes,

Thank you
Nadia B

❧ ❧ ❧

Stravinsky to Boulanger

1260 NORTH WETHERLY DRIVE
HOLLYWOOD, CALIFORNIA

OCTOBER 11, 1963
NADIA BOULANGER
36 RUE BALLU, PARIS

JEAN IS DEAD AND I CAN CONFIDE ONLY IN YOU THE PAIN THAT ENCOMPASSES ALL MY THOUGHTS[39]

IGOR

❧ ❧ ❧

Boulanger to Stravinsky

PARIS

OCTOBER 12, 1963

IGOR STRAVINSKY
1260 N WETHERLY DR
HOLLYWOOD, CALIF

THANK YOU FOR SHARING YOUR PAIN WITH ME. AM AWARE OF ITS EXTENT AND SHARE IT ALL MY LOVE

NADIA

---

39. A reference to the death of Jean Cocteau (1889–1963). Cocteau was especially connected to Stravinsky during his early neoclassical years, particularly the work *Oedipus Rex*, for which Cocteau wrote the French text that was then translated into Latin by Jean Daniélou (1905–74). For more on *Oedipus Rex*, see Carr, *Multiple Masks*; and Walsh, *Stravinsky: Oedipus Rex*.

❧ ❧ ❧

Boulanger to Stravinsky

Ecoles d'art américaines
Fondation reconnue d'utilité publique
Bureau New York: Fontainebleau Schools, 122 East 58 St. N.Y. 22
Conservatoire de musique—Ecole des beaux-arts
Palais de Fontainebleau
Le Directeur

November 25, 1963

Oh, how sad, My Friend. I know that Aldous Huxley's death robs you of a very loyal friendship. Jean's death is such a heartbreak, and the tragic end to John Kennedy deeply upset you. And now December 2 approaches. But you have chosen St. Paul's text, and the light shines in the darkness.

Once more you bring us [the light] with *A Sermon, a Narrative, and a Prayer.* All of these exceed any words that could be used for such a masterpiece. May God bless you.

With tenderness and love, I am your
Nadia B.

❧ ❧ ❧

Boulanger to Théodore Strawinsky

December 15, 1963

Dear Théodore,

What comfort your letter brought me. I was tormented about your silence, without—how inconceivable—taking the trouble to write to you myself. How strange we are! At last, Denise can begin to see the end of her ordeal, thank God.[40] You are so often in my thoughts. Yes, it is very difficult to see time take

40. Since September 10, 1962, Denise had been undergoing treatment for what Théodore Strawinsky wrote to Boulanger was a tubercular (*tuberculine*) infection in her hip. She was sent to convalesce in a hospital in Leysin. The treatment was terrifically hard on her, and it took two years before she could return home and regain her ability to walk. Letters from Théodore Strawinsky to Boulanger, September 10, 1962, and June 27, 1964, F-Pn, N.L.a. 109 (21–22 and 28).

its toll on someone you love, and I understand your feelings in seeing your Father once again. His presence is shocking for everyone. It exposes one of the greatest mysteries there is. For you . . . I nonetheless hope you were able to scale the wall that long separations create. He needs this intimacy even more than you do—he who keeps his emotions secret, emotions that are so strong he hides them!

All my affection, I send you my love and my thoughts and am your
Nadia

P.S. Your card was so beautiful! It made the invisible visible.

❧   ❧   ❧

Stravinsky to Boulanger

1260 North Wetherly Drive
Los Angeles 69, California

Miss N. Boulanger
36 rue Ballu
Paris IX
France
June 10, 1964

Very touched, dear Nadia, by your letter for me of June 18—thank you!

We leave tomorrow to conduct a concert on June 13 in Red-Rocks, close to Denver. The 14th we fly to New York and then on to London on the 15th where for two weeks I am recording my *R[ake's] Progress* with Columbia.[41] The 28th or the 29th I'll conduct my *Bach Variations* and my *Symph. of Psalms* at Oxford (Bach Society)—then back to U.S.A.[42] I just wanted you to be up to date on our plans as much as possible.

---

41. This was Stravinsky's second recording of the opera, the first to be done in stereo. The sessions were held in London. Performers included: Judith Raskin (Anne Truelove); Jean Manning (Mother Goose); Regina Sarfaty (Baba the Turk); Alexander Young (Tom Rakewell); Kevin Miller (Sellem); and John Reardon (Nick Shadow). The Royal Philharmonic Orchestra performed and Stravinsky conducted. (June 16–20, 22, 23, 1964) It has since been rereleased by Sony as part of The Complete Columbia Album Collection. *Igor Stravinsky: The Complete Columbia Album Collection*, Royal Philharmonic Orchestra, Igor Stravinsky, Sony Classical Record, 88875026162, 1964, 57 CDs.

42. Stravinsky, *J. S. Bach Choral-Variationen* (New York: Boosey & Hawkes, 1957). Boulanger's copy was a gift from Boosey & Hawkes. Someone wrote over the "v" in Stravinsky's name on the cover of Boulanger's copy so that it read:

Your
I Str.

[P.S.] We bought the Baroness of Erlanger's house.[43] Immense amount of work to repair *everything.* This year (with so many trips), composing, the house (we are not selling the one where we live. I like it too much—it's been twenty-four years!).

❧ ❧ ❧

Boulanger to Théodore Strawinsky

July 25, 1964

Dear Théodore,
  I was going to write to thank you for the news about Denise when the news from Hollywood deeply upset me. I want to hope that this forced rest is not too worrisome a sign, but we are all sad, naturally.[44]
  All my love to you and Denise. I am so happy to think she's finally nearly through such a long, terrible hardship.

And as always, I send love to you both and Kitty,
Nadia B.

P.S. Sorry for this typed letter, just a bit of rest!

❧ ❧ ❧

"Strawinsky." The score is without additional annotation. F-LYc, UFNB MEp 530. The five variations are an orchestral arrangement of Johann Sebastian Bach's Canonic Variations on "Von Himmel hoch da komm' ich her" for organ (BWV 769).

43. A neighboring house, belonging to the Baroness d'Erlanger. Walsh, *Second Exile*, 495; Craft, *An Improbable Life*, 117.

44. Stravinsky had once again been advised not to travel. He explains the situation from his own perspective in his letter of July 30, 1964.

Boulanger to Stravinsky

36 rue Ballu
Paris IX, France
Tel. Tri. 57–91

Monsieur Igor Strawinsky
1260 N. Wetherly Drive
Hollywood 46
California
U.S.A.

Wherever these lines find you, My Friend, it will soon be your birthday and I cannot [even] give you a kiss. What regret. But I nonetheless feel very close. I envision you engaged with new problems—each work bringing along its own unknowns and demands. And this constant renewal of your thought is a renewal of life. Never any repeats, always rebounding toward new combinations. All of this is very mysterious and so clear once the work is completed.

You are constantly in my thoughts—what I wouldn't give to see you. You'll be in Berlin in September if I could come. More and more I feel we have to seize at any price the moments that are offered to us.

I don't know how to write to you. You are too great for me, and I love you too much, but you will understand that everything that [I send] to you is from the bottom of my heart.

My fond wishes, Dear Igor,
Nadia

❧ ❧ ❧

Boulanger to Stravinsky

36 rue Ballu
Paris IX, France
Tel. Tri. 57–91

July 27, 1964

My friend,

Knowing you [have been] stopped is a deep sadness. Have the courage to remain calm—after all, you will find there a new source of energy.

You have been put to the test so many times, and always seem to benefit from what seemed to stop you.

But we are sad, shocked, and good for nothing. Our prayers are with you.

I send my fondest wishes,

May God keep you, My Friend,
Nadia B.

[P.S.] How Nicolas loves you, it's very touching.

❧   ❧   ❧

Stravinsky to Boulanger

1260 North Wetherly Drive
Hollywood 69, California

Miss N. Boulanger
36 rue Ballu, Paris 9th
July 30, 1964[45]

My very dear Nadia,
    Thank you for your affectionate letter—don't worry about me: I am doing very well and I think Nabokov misinformed you: a month ago in London I had an ear infection and the doctors advised me not to fly too often, which is why I was thinking of canceling my concerts in Israel and in Berlin (end of August-September). But having learned that Israel was basing its entire season on my appearances and that they were already sold out (charity [events for] clinics, hospitals) I decided to fly there, but not to Berlin. A desolate Nabokov telephoned me from Paris asking me to come to Berlin as well. With great regret, I refused, not wanting to risk this flight as well. That's all. Certainly hundreds of letters and telegrams have arrived from everywhere wishing me a swift recovery and it is certainly more than doubtful that the newspapers are correcting these false declarations since these latest ones don't constitute the sensation that they are looking for [so as] to sell [issues]. After Israel (a concert in Jerusalem and two in Caesarea) two days in Rome (end of August) two days in New York and then Hollywood where we have bought and are renovating, furnishing, and organizing the late Catherine d'Erlanger's house for us to live in. We will put Bob Craft in the old house (who is conducting *Lulu* in Santa Fe these days and will meet up with us in New York to fly to Israel).[46]
    Thank you again for having written to me—am very touched.

Your
I Str.

❧   ❧   ❧

---

45. All errors appear as they are in the original.
46. For more about the Santa Fe production of *Lulu*, see Walsh, *Second Exile*, 482.

Boulanger to Stravinsky

Ecoles d'art américaines
Fondation reconnue d'utilité publique
Palais de Fontainebleau (S.-&-M.)
Bureau de New York
122 East 58th Street, N.Y. 22
Conservatoire de musique

Mr. Igor Stravinsky
1260 North Wetherly Drive
Hollywood 46
California
U.S.A.
August 6, 1964

My friend, what joy in reading that you are so especially well, active, and especially interested, I believe, in this new house where I dream of being [one day]. I spent such happy hours in the one that will become . . . "the old one."

No one in the world, and this is inevitable, has your vitality: you are always twenty years old. You'll remember that Clémenceau met with a gentleman who, stunned by his vivacity, said to him, "You are so young, Mr. President!" Clémenceau was at that point 88 years old.[47] His instantaneous reply: "When one is young, it is forever." But now, to more serious things.

You're coming to Berlin, aren't you? Think of poor Nicky who at first thought only of you, and now sees this festival centered on you, put together for you; he is frustrated that the inspiration [for the event] might be missing.[48]

But what am I saying is, if it is better for you to turn down this trip, then it goes without saying it needn't be thought of anymore. All the same, I'll still wager that you'll be in Berlin at the end of September. I would only go there for you, truth be told.

---

47. Georges Clemenceau (1841–1949) was the Prime Minister of France 1906–9 and 1917–20. He was heavily involved in the creation of the Treaty of Versailles and a prominent figure in Third Republic politics in general. For more, see Dallas, *At the Heart of a Tiger*; Newhall, *Clemenceau*; and Duroselle, *Clemenceau*.

48. Nabokov had organized another concert for the Congress for Cultural Freedom, this one centered on Stravinsky. Boulanger was to attend with Nabokov covering all of her expenses. Nabokov to Boulanger, June 11, 1964, F-Pn, N.L.a. 90 (220). Stravinsky turned the entire affair into a logistical nightmare by first canceling and then deciding at the eleventh hour to attend. Boulanger found herself placed in the middle. Nabokov to Boulanger, August 28, 1964, F-Pn, N.L.a. 90 (233). See also, Francis, *Teaching Stravinsky*, 216.

Best wishes to Bob, to Vera, to you. All my tenderness as always. Fondly,
NB

❧ ❧ ❧

Boulanger to Stravinsky

Ecoles d'art américaines
Fondation reconnue d'utilité publique
Palais de Fontainebleau (S.-&-M.)
Bureau de New York
122 East 58th Street, N.Y. 22
Conservatoire de musique

I. Strawinsky
1260 N. Wetherly Drive
Hollywood 46
California
U.S.A.
November 7, 1964

My Friend,

A rather important letter today. The Polignac-Singer Committee is preparing a concert for the celebration of Princess Winnie's Centenary.[49] We've come to ask you to write a work for the concert, for a small orchestra of a maximum of fifteen instruments, perhaps with a narrator.

It goes without saying that the Committee asks you to state the terms under which you would accept this commission. The concert would take place in October 1965. I can tell you that, in principle, the committee will accept your conditions. The President, Mr. Heim, believes your work alone would justify

---

49. Boulanger had been formally associated with the salon of the Princesse de Polignac since March 1923, Spycket, *Nadia Boulanger*, 77; and Kahan, *Music's Modern Muse* (Rochester, NY: University of Rochester Press, 2003), 234. Ten years later, she began to run a concert series for the Princesse, see Spycket, *Nadia Boulanger*, 81; Kahan, *Music's Modern Muse*, 301; Brooks, "*Noble et grande servante de la musique*," 100; Brooks, "Nadia Boulanger and the Salon of the Princesse de Polignac," 428–9. Following the Princesse de Polignac's death (February 25, 1943), Boulanger was appointed the director of concerts for the Singer-Polignac Foundation, Spycket, *Nadia Boulanger*, 122; Rosenstiel, *Nadia Boulanger*, 347; and Kahan, *Music's Modern Muse*, 367–68. It was in this capacity that Boulanger wrote this letter to Stravinsky. For more on the significance of the event and Stravinsky's refusal to accept the commission, see Francis, *Teaching Stravinsky*, 219–20 and 239.

the entire program.[50] Would you please tell me what you think about this, because our plans depend on you. Must I tell you my hope.

(I felt such deep emotion seeing you and Vera again, and I admired Bob who put everything in its place with such intelligence, such order. As for the work, how can one dare to speak of it. It is essential and we are so happy to understand it. Each of your steps is so decisive.)

Fondly,
NB

ᵂ   ᵂ   ᵂ

Stravinsky to Boulanger

NADIA BOULANGER
36 RUE BALLU
PARIS
NOV 12, 1964

PROPOSITION ATTRACTIVE REGRET TIME SO SHORT IS THERE CHANCE OF POSTPONEMENT AND COULD YOU CONDITIONS URGENT BECAUSE ANOTHER CONDITION PENDING ALSO LEAVING FOR NEW YORK IN A WEEK

AFFECTION STRAVINSKY

ᵂ   ᵂ   ᵂ

---

50. Roger Heim (1900–79) was a French botanist. He succeeded Edmond Faral as president of the Fondation. Heim was a professor at the Muséum national d'histoire naturelle from 1945 to 1973 and served as Director of the Museum from 1951 to 1965. He was appointed to the Académie des sciences in 1946.

Boulanger to Stravinsky

36 rue Ballu
Paris IX, France
Tel. Tri. 57–91

Mr. Igor Stravinsky
1260 N. Wetherly Drive
Hollywood 46
California
U.S.A.
November 14, 1964

Dear Igor,

Thank you for your telegram. I cannot respond with precise details, the Committee President is absent. But I believe the amount would be $10,000, and perhaps the date changed, but I believe it will [still] be in *1965*.[51]

You can imagine how much I hope this project becomes a reality. I am very sad, Pierre of Monaco died Tuesday. I still can't believe everything is finished. But what can I say, I will always feel his presence.

The heart is tired, yet God's will be done.

My fondest wishes.

I love you so, Dear Igor,

Your
Nadia

[P.S.] Tell me *as soon as you can* what you think of this offer.
[P.P.S.] I leave for Monaco but will be here on the 18th. Will telegram as soon as I've been able to contact Mr. Heim.

❧ ❧ ❧

---

51. Adjusted for inflation, $10,000 in 1964 would be almost $78,000 today.

Stravinsky to Boulanger

NADIA BOULANGER
36 RUE BALLU
PARIS
NOVEMBER 17, 1964
INFINITELY SORRY BUT TODAY I ASK 10 000 TO CONDUCT IN A
CONCERT AND NO LESS THAN 25 000 TO TAKE ON A SMALL PIECE
THANK YOU VERY MUCH NONETHELESS STOP
WHAT SORROW THE DEATH OF PIERRE OF MONACO

AFFECTIONATELY IGOR

❧   ❧   ❧

Théodore Strawinsky to Boulanger

Geneva
November 17, 1964

Dear Nadia,

Denise and I know you are in deep sadness. Our thoughts, on the announcement of the passing of Prince Pierre of Monaco, went directly to you, knowing what the heart of such a great and faithful friend as you can give . . . and how it can weep at the heartbreak of such separation.[52] We are in Geneva now and once again under our own roof.

Allow me, dear Nadia, to tell you again of our deepest affection and kindest thoughts,

Théodore

❧   ❧   ❧

52. Prince Pierre of Monaco's death was greatly upsetting to Boulanger. We now know him to have been one of Boulanger's romantic interests and someone to whom she was deeply devoted. For more on his passing, see Jérôme Spycket, *Nadia Boulanger* (Stuyvesant, NY: Pendragon, 1992), 134–5. For the romantic connection between Boulanger and Pierre de Monaco, see Laederich and Stricker, "Les Trois vies de Nadia Boulanger."

Boulanger to Stravinsky

36 rue Ballu
Paris IX
Tel. Tri. 57–91

November 24, 1964

My Friend,

I will be with you on Saturday with such great loyalty and emotion. I see everything again, as if it were yesterday . . .

Words are pointless, we know what lives in our hearts, protected by silence.

I've returned—from Monaco—days of intense sadness, and yet so luminous. I knew Pierre of Monaco very well and loved him a great deal. Everything he left behind will help us live despite what he takes with him.

I don't know if you could have known that he was truly so secret, so alone, and yet so rich.

The Foundation held on so tightly to the hope that this project would be realized, the only one that appeared to me as the most beautiful, most appropriate [one], so everything is under consideration again. But I believe their budget will not permit them to plan for what hasn't been discussed yet surpasses their available funds.

I am, as always, with you, and I believe I understand you, see you, and always love you with all my heart,
Nadia B

& & &

Boulanger to Théodore Strawinsky

November 24, 1964

Dear Théodore,

Thank you for your thoughtfulness, it is kind [of you] at a very painful time. Prince Pierre was so close, so necessary, [he has left] a very deep emptiness.

But I am happy to know that you are finally at home. I hope so much that Denise truly feels better.

Saw your Father in Berlin. His new work is moving, was very beautiful—he himself is full of ideas, of conviction, but it's sad that his physical state weighs so heavily on him. I was so happy to have spent those few hours with him. His joy about the new house is extraordinary. [He has] the enthusiasm of someone whose future lies before him, yet . . . He knows, but he acts, lives, and feels with a heightened acuity, as if he has nothing more to lose. A very beautiful courage and inner strength. You have told me nothing about Kitty, are you also preoccupied? How I think of you both, of your Mother, of Mika, on the 28th!

All my love,
Nadia.

❧ ❧ ❧

Boulanger to Vera Stravinsky

*annotations Stravinsky's

36 rue Ballu
Paris IX
Tel. TRI. 57–91

For December 25, 1964

Dear Vera,

New York—Hollywood—the ends of the earth . . . I do not know [where], but my wishes are sent to you with profound tenderness. Do not be overwhelmed by my sentimental outpourings! I will tell you again only that I love you so much, and pray to God for you, for your Peace and for all to go as well as possible.

NY and Boston were turned upside down by the concerts. Here, <u>Dirk Olsen understood Abraham and Isaac, a very good impression. Le Roux and the orchestra are very good. How you were missed</u>.[53]

My wishes for you both, for Bob, and for a little Vera born on an already long-ago [Orthodox] Christmas. No memories of that for you, but a rich, beautiful, and daring life awaited.

With all my love,

Your
Nadia

❧ ❧ ❧

---

53. This reference is a mystery to me, and possibly to its recipients, too, given the underlining.

Boulanger to Stravinsky

Mr. Igor Stravinsky
1260 or 1250 N. Wetherly Drive
Hollywood 46
California
U.S.A.
March 14, 1965

My friend,

March 2 has passed, it is far and yet always near. I didn't write to you, yet thought of Her, of you, of all who live in the shadows, and in the light.

I feel you very near. I live alongside the memories that remain of our origins, of *Abraham*, with *l'Élégie pour JFK*, of this music of which every note has a real density.[54]

I'm attaching a letter from Stoutz's son—if you like, I can act as an intermediary.[55] I doubt you want to accept and that he can [afford your fee]. *He is nevertheless very serious*, and his desire to obtain this work is at its height.

I have something to tell you. But all that we do not tell each other is there, very powerful, set in stone.

Thank you for not ceasing to hear this world in your own way, and for the joy of the supreme security of performance. "He who manages to see every detail sees the whole of everything."

All my love to you and many thoughts for Vera and Bob,
Nadia B

[P.S.] I was in Rome, hence the delay.

❧   ❧   ❧

---

54. Stravinsky composed the *Elegy for J.F.K.* in 1964 after feeling that Americans were moving on too quickly from Kennedy's assassination. The work calls for baritone or mezzo-soprano soloist and three clarinets. Four haiku stanzas form the text, poetry commissioned by Stravinsky of W. H. Auden. Boulanger's copy of the score contains one of the most thorough and provocative examples of her serial analysis in her entire library. See Stravinsky, *Elegy for J.F.K.* (New York: Boosey & Hawkes, 1964), F-Pn, Vmg, 12520A.

55. Edmond de Stoutz (1920–97), founder of the Zurich Chamber Orchestra and the group's conductor until 1996. He wrote to Stravinsky via Boulanger to praise him for his music and request a commission for the Chamber Orchestra. He promised the work would be performed on 40–50 concerts under the title of "Our Strawinsky." Stoutz to Stravinsky, February 19, 1965, CH-Bps.

Boulanger to Vera Stravinsky

Ecoles d'art américaines
Fondation reconnue d'utilité publique
Bureau New York: Fontainebleau Schools, 122 East 58 St. N.Y. 22
Conservatoire de musique—Ecole des beaux-arts
Palais de Fontainebleau
Le Directeur

Mr. Igor Stravinsky
1260 N Wetherly Drive
Hollywood 46
California
U.S.A.
September 8, 1965 (for the 29th)

Dear Vera,

It's soon your Saint's Day. Certainly, there is something naïve about sending wishes. But, do we not remain naïve in the deepest of sentiments? From the bottom of my heart, I send you warmest wishes—hoping that few responsibilities, [moments of] glory, fatigue, travels, and obligations will deplete your marvelous energy. Certainly, you have a unique opportunity, but how heavy [it is], and the melancholy of seeing the years accumulate, and their weight imposed on him and on you.

Yet his genius renews itself by an almost unbelievable miracle. His *Requiem for T. S. Eliot* is a masterpiece.[56] It is as monumental as it is condensed. And everything remains clarified by him who has carried the torch all these years. Always the same, always new.

May God keep you in His Peace

I send you both my love and am your
Nadia B

[P.S.] Best wishes for Bob

❧   ❧   ❧

---

56. *Introitus: T. S. Eliot in memoriam* (1965), for chorus of tenors and basses, harp, piano, two tam tams, timpani, solo viola and solo contrabass. Boulanger owned nineteen copies of the choral parts and had them mounted on cardboard for performance purposes: F-LYc, UFNB 525, STR. Boulanger also owned a copy of the pocket score: F-LYc, UFNB, MEp STR 530.

Stravinsky to Boulanger

1218 North Wetherly Drive
Los Angeles, California
90069

Miss N. Boulanger
36 rue Ballu
Paris, IX
France
November 30, 1965

Thank you, my very dear Nadia, for your kind thoughts and letter, I am very touched by them because the day of November 30, 1938 is always with me, until the end of my days, like that of March 2, 1939.

Thank you for having put *Introitus* and *Elegy* on the program for Aunt Winnie's centenary.[57]

Fond wishes,
IS
[P.S.] We fly to NY December 10—as always are staying at the Hotel Pierre (61st St. and 5th Ave, NY)—we'll be there until January 17.

Love,
I Str

❧   ❧   ❧

---

57. "Aunt Winnie" is the Princesse de Polignac's nickname. This is the event for which Stravinsky refused to accept a commission. (See letters of November 7–24, 1964.)

Boulanger to Stravinsky

Ecoles d'art américaines
Fondation reconnue d'utilité publique
Bureau New-York: Fontainebleau Schools, 122 East 58 St. N.Y. 22
Conservatoire de musique—Ecole des beaux-arts
Palais de Fontainebleau
Le Directeur

Mr. Igor Stravinsky
1260 North Wetherly Drive
Hollywood 46
California
U.S.A.
December 4, 1966

Dear Friend,

Today I'm spending an unofficial Sunday close to you. For Baudelaire's centenary, the Minister, Mr. André Malraux, would like to organize an event to pay tribute to the musician who has dominated, to say the least, this century.[58] Therefore, would you agree to come to conduct the French premiere of the work dedicated to the memory of Aldous Huxley along with the *Symphonie de psaumes* and [other pieces] of yours that you would choose yourself?[59]

In the event that you would be interested in accepting, under what terms would you like the concert to be organized? What fee, how many rehearsals, and naturally, Bob?

Could you send me a night letter *collect* telling the *dates, fee, number of rehearsals*, Bob?

You would then receive an official letter confirming the invitation. Malraux attaches extreme importance to this project ~~as does Rufina Ampernova~~. He'll write to you later, I'm so anxious to read this work dedicated to the memory of Aldous Huxley.

Could you help me with this?

I send all my love.
Nadia B.

❧   ❧   ❧

---

58. André Malraux (1901–76) was the French Minister of Cultural Affairs.
59. Igor Stravinsky, *Variations: Aldous Huxley in memoriam* (New York, London: Boosey & Hawkes, 1963–64), F-LYc, UFNB MEp STR 400. Boulanger's copy of the score lacks any sort of annotation.

Stravinsky to Boulanger

HOTEL PIERRE, NEW YORK

NADIA BOULANGER
36 RUE BALLU PARIS
DECEMBER 1966

~~AM TERRIBLY UPSET, CAN'T COME TO PARIS. I AM WRITING YOU~~
~~WROTE TODAY WHY I~~
AIRMAILING YOU TODAY WHY I DECLINE ~~CANNOT ACCEPT~~
~~YOUR AND PROPOSITION TO~~ ANY MUSICAL ~~MANIFESTATIONS~~
PARTICIPATION IN PARIS.

AFFECTIONATELY
I STR[60]

❧   ❧   ❧

Stravinsky to Boulanger

1260 North Wetherly Drive
Hollywood 69 California

Miss Nadia Boulanger
36 rue Ballu, Paris
December 11, 1966

My Dear,

No time to write to you properly. Excuse me.

1) *Variations* dedicated to the memory of Aldous Huxley has nothing to do with his work. The months that this composition took me [to write] were the months when dear Aldous left us (throat cancer) and it was only natural that I dedicated this work to his memory. Of the rest, I am certain (and this does not discourage me) that this music would mean nothing to him (or would displease him) because what he liked was romantic and classical music, to which my composition is very much foreign.

2) I am no longer going to give concerts in Paris after the public's and the press's affront at the premiere of my *Threni*, conducted by myself in one of Boulez's concerts. This decision is final.

---

60. Three versions of this telegram appear in the archives, one draft and two copies of what was actually sent to Boulanger. Text found in the draft that does not appear in the sent version appears here crossed out.

3) Moreover, let's not forget that André Malraux—who (very naturally) is organizing an official event for the centenary of the great Baudelaire—had said not long ago that he considers music to be a secondary art. It would thus be ridiculous to impose on him (Minister of Public Instruction) pieces of a secondary art on such an important occasion.

Those are the three things I wanted to say to you in response to your kind letter of December 4.

Despite this "business" letter, I wish to underscore my friendship and best wishes, with which you are already familiar.

Yours,
I Str.

P.S. Very touched by your letter in memory of my dear little girl.

❧   ❧   ❧

Boulanger to Stravinsky

Ecoles d'art américaines
Fondation reconnue d'utilité publique
Bureau New-York: Fontainebleau Schools, 122 East 58 St. N.Y. 22
Conservatoire de musique—Ecole des beaux-arts
Palais de Fontainebleau
Le Directeur

February 13, 1967

Dear Friend,

I counted on sending a young Italian's sheet music to you. He has just lost his mother in tragic circumstances and wasn't able to copy the scores.[61] He has *a great need* for this award, is *very talented*, and a worker—he needs to develop, but he is truly a musician. Did you agree to vote for him? I hope so. He deserves it and has such a need. Tell Winifred if you accept my proposal *or not.*

I think of you constantly, am immersed in the music of the recent meaningful years which were so beautiful, but I don't abandon the works of the past, which remain so new, so alive. But . . . I will leave off with my superfluous comments. The music *is*, we are nothing, and words add nothing to it.

I would like to see you so much. But I hear you in the silence, and believe I understand you, understand what will never be said. My fond wishes to you and also to Vera, my thoughts to Bob and my affection to Milène.

---

61. The artist in question is Giampaolo Bracali.

Your
Nadia

❧ ❧ ❧

Boulanger to Théodore Strawinsky

[No Date] [For March 20, 1967]

Dear Théodore,

I've tried in vain to call you, but no answer. I wanted to thank you for your thoughts. I wanted to share my wishes and to ask you to remember me to your Father—certainly [I love him for] his music, always, but also [for] that within him which is humane, humble before God, great, and tender. Tell him I still love him much more than he can know.

And I send you my deepest affection,
Nadia B.

❧ ❧ ❧

Théodore Strawinsky to Boulanger

Musée de l'Athénée
[n.d.]

Very dear Friend,

These quick words on the eve of my exhibition. Thank you, thank you for your letter, received in Hollywood where I finally had the opportunity to see my father privately. He is marvelous, as always, but alas, much less alert.
Théodore Strawinsky
[P.S.] Denise and I send you our heartfelt fondness.

❧ ❧ ❧

Boulanger to Stravinsky

2 The Grove
Highgate Village
London, N6
June 5, 1967

My Friend,

Everyone pays you homage, only I will keep quiet. I who love you greatly, admire you and, I believe, know you.

This is perhaps one of the reasons for my silence—having penetrated your thoughts, your most secret being, could I *betray* what you never cease to hide. And then, I am incapable of saying the things that are so serious, so important.

You have opened the doors that give true sense to music, to religion, to love—to *courage?*

I send my love, I pray to God for you, and express my profound tenderness. My respect cannot be defined, it surpasses all measure.

Nadia B

ᴲ   ᴲ   ᴲ

Boulanger to Stravinsky

Ecoles d'art américaines
Fondation reconnue d'utilité publique
Bureau New York: Fontainebleau Schools, 122 East 58 St. N.Y. 22
Conservatoire de musique

Mr. Igor Strawinsky
1218 N. Wetherly Drive
Hollywood D46
California
U.S.A.
January 15, 1968

My Friend,

This morning there was an admirable performance of *Le Sacre* under the precise, alive, and true direction of . . . Igor Stravinsky. And to think they argue: "[Is he a] conductor, yes or no?" And while witnessing the [only] one who could give such a performance, with real connections, his rhythms so perfectly set out and conducted. Sober, modest, and effective commentaries from H. Barraud.[62]

---

62. Barraud, *Pour comprendre les musiques d'aujourd'hui.*

No literature sheds light on audible acts—honestly, intelligently. And he has rightly noted that there was not one Stravinsky of yesterday and another of today, but *one* Stravinsky, for always, who is always new. I suppose he will give [a performance of] recent works here, the *Requiem Canticles* is a revelation for young people, not to mention those who are capable of hearing and understanding.[63]

I could go on and on, you give so much with work after work. Always new and always the same. I do not cease dreaming of seeing you, alas, [and] I hope you know that I always am near to you and to Vera.

Nadia

[P.S.] May God keep you and give you patience in the face of suffering.
[P.P.S.] And many kind thoughts for Bob.

❧   ❧   ❧

Boulanger to Théodore Strawinsky

September 21, 1968

Dear Théodore,

I will be passing through Geneva on the 7th, maybe the 8th, [and] would like so much to see you. (Not free for lunch on the 7th!) I think so faithfully of you, of Denise, of over there. A friend who saw your Father in NY found him well. What joy, what joy that he is able to travel.

Fond and tender wishes,
Nadia B.

---

63. Igor Stravinsky, *Requiem Canticles* (New York, London: Boosey & Hawkes, 1965–66), a setting for orchestra and choir of excerpts from the Latin Requiem Mass. Boulanger owned four copies of this score in various formats, all of which are housed at the F-LYc. She owned two copies of the conductor's score, both of which are annotated, though likely not in her hand (UFNB ME STR 530). She also owned a copy of the pocket score (UFNB MEp STR 530) and twenty-nine copies of the choral parts (UFNB 525 STR). The parts are all rental copies that were never returned. These scores suggest the work was acquired from Boosey & Hawkes for performance. Boulanger wrote on January 24, 1970, to Stravinsky that she had indeed been to hear a performance of the *Requiem Canticles* in Brussels. Perhaps these scores were related to that event. Boulanger to Stravinsky, January 24, 1970, CH-Bps.

P.S. Paris the 27th [en route to] Winterthur, [then] I'll be at the Montreux Palace on the 5th.

❧ ❧ ❧

Théodore Strawinsky to Boulanger

Almelo

October 15, 1968

My very dear Nadia,

It was upon arriving at the hotel in Holland, where we have settled for a few months, that I found your letter addressed to Geneva . . . it followed us here *where we were not!* We were actually in Switzerland at that time!! We could've had the pleasure of seeing you then. We were brought back here by an emergency surrounding Denise's mother, who had had an attack, and I had to leave my work here (large frescoes in a church) abruptly to go back to Geneva, but our mail continued to be delivered here. What bad luck for us, dear Nadia. How happy we would have been to see you again, to discuss so many problems we keep in our hearts . . . And during our unplanned stay in Switzerland, I heard from my sister, Milène, that my Father and Vera and Robert Craft were in Zurich!! Oh! Dear Friend, there is so much distress in this, I cannot find the words to write to you, but I know you can read between the lines. At moments, my dear Father gives the impression that he is doing better, and finds with his intelligence some critical responses, but it's impossible to find any sort of happiness in his eyes. His legs don't carry him anymore, that you know, but not at all anymore . . . and here he is travelling: after Zurich it will be Paris! My great, dear Friend, it's a tragedy, but what can be done? Zurich was nonetheless necessary so that Denise and I could have the great, great happiness of spending a few hours with him, and he also found joy in it, so he told us. How comforting for a son's heart. I know you were told, dear Nadia, that it tired him to have visits—and I feel so sad for you. They are going to go to Paris . . .

To finish off these heartfelt lines, I'll tell you again, dear Nadia, how upset we were to have missed you in Geneva, but I hope [we will see each other] in Paris . . . when? I don't know exactly.

With all our faithful attachment, Denise and I express to you our deepest affection and send tender thoughts,
Théodore

P.S. We will be with you in thought, especially the day after tomorrow, the 17th, at the emotional moment of noon. With you and all of your friends.

❧ ❧ ❧

Boulanger to Théodore Strawinsky

October 19, 1968

Dear Théodore,

What sadness in your letter, how sad it is to think of such a glorious, very old man who is battling with death, even more with illness, the decline it brings, all seen by a mind still so lucid it is capable of measuring his suffering, weakness, weariness, and the body's rejection.

How much I think of you, of Denise who is suffering as well, of this helplessness where you both are, and what is there to do, what to say, what to hope? May God support those who travel such a difficult road.

The ceremony on Thursday was very moving and to feel that her name was there where she lived a whole part of her life was, for me, very sweet.[64] [Now people will] become aware of her work, and I can greet death with tranquility. Her memory will not be forsaken!

I send you all my most tender love. May God keep you,
Nadia B.

❧ ❧ ❧

Boulanger to Théodore Strawinsky

November 30, 1968

Dear Théodore,

I am with you with such deep emotion on this November 30.

Words can do nothing, I send my love. I saw your Father again, you can imagine with what happiness and what sorrow.

I am always with you both, wholeheartedly.
Nadia B.

❧ ❧ ❧

---

64. A reference to the dedication of a plaque for the rue Ballu apartment, citing it as the place where Lili Boulanger had lived. The rue Ballu was renamed Place Lili Boulanger on May 5, 1970.

Boulanger to Stravinsky

Mr. Igor Stravinsky
1218 Wetherly Drive
Hollywood 46, California
August 31, 1969

My Friend,

I believe you would have been touched to see how attentively and precisely our students prepared your Mass. This is a group of young people who really know your work by heart.

The performance they gave was so clean, so sober, and so comprehensive. Among others, we have worked on *Dumbarton Oaks*, the *Symphonie*, *Deux Psaumes* [*sic*], the *Canticum Sacrum*, *The Flood*; you know what these works represent for me.[65] It does one good to see young people understanding works of such importance.

I send all my love and am always your,
NB

❧   ❧   ❧

Boulanger to Théodore Strawinsky

[September 20, 1969]

Dear Théodore,

How I think of you! Your Father's tragedy is still here, yet already absent. And is he aware of this, does he suffer, what relief does he receive from the only relief possible? Such anguish in these questions. And the Almighty, is He believed in, recognized?[66] Our hearts are linked, my prayers joined to yours in the faith and mercy of God.
To Denise and you in deepest commitment,
Nadia B.

P.S. Hope you can read this, my eyes are dying, sorry.

❧   ❧   ❧

---

65. An example of a dictated letter where the person writing did not entirely understand Boulanger. This is a reference to the *Symphonie de psaumes*.
66. There are similar issues with syntax in this letter, possibly the result of poor handwriting on Boulanger's part.

Théodore Strawinsky to Boulanger

Geneva

September 23, 1969

My dear and great Friend,

A single line from your letter tells us what you think, but what you tell us about it overwhelms us . . . and you wrote to us by hand![67] Thank you from the bottom of my heart! You understand the tragedy of the situation. When I wanted to go see my dear Father on June 18 for his birthday after his operation (double operation) in New York, I received a response from Vera asking me not to come for the moment . . . I don't want to add any commentary, but you can imagine my pain. My dear Father can no longer react, but he is perfectly aware of it and suffers profoundly from it, *that I know*. I am close to him through prayer—*with you*, dear Nadia, *we* are close to him, but [only] through prayer—and I thank you from the bottom of my heart that I can write these lines to you.

Denise and I express to you our deepest commitment.

Your
Théodore

🐦   🐦   🐦

Boulanger to Théodore Strawinsky

September 29, 1969

Your letter is overwhelming, dear Théodore, is there nothing to be done? Because it raises critical issues.

I am so near to you,
N.
P.S. Can you send Milène's address to me at rue Ballu?

---

67. Boulanger's eyesight had greatly deteriorated by this point in her life, the result of overuse and cataracts that she did not allow to heal properly. Yet, to those she cared about deeply, Boulanger continued to write by hand, even though she could not make out the details of what she was writing. After a point, the technique she used involved holding a ruler against the paper to guide an oversized marker with which she would then write. This process typically resulted in difficult to read if not entirely illegible letters (as evidenced by the letter of September 20, 1969). Théodore Strawinsky is here remarking how surprised he is that Boulanger did not dictate the letter but instead chose to write to him herself.

❧ ❧ ❧

Igor and Vera Stravinsky to Boulanger

NADIA BOULANGER
36 RUE BALLU
VIA PARIS

SEPTEMBER 30, 1969

DEAR NADIA, WE THINK ABOUT YOU WITH LOVE AND HOPE TO SEE
YOU IN PARIS IN ONE MONTH

IGOR, VERA

❧ ❧ ❧

Théodore Strawinsky to Boulanger

Geneva

October 2, 1969

My very dear Nadia,

Thank you, thank you for your note and for your unfailing friendship toward my father and us.

Yes, the problems that are cropping up are so painful, and, as you say, critical in any plans, but what and how should I feel when all access toward my father has been virtually blocked?! What a tragedy, foremost for him, but also for us, his children . . . In such a situation we are powerless, because what can we do that won't provoke too much of a painful shock for him, even though I know his deepest thoughts.

I have just received a heartbreaking letter from Milène. The poor girl has front row seats to this tragedy. They are in New York (I mean my father) and plan to go to Paris around the 15th of this month. Here is Milène's address:

Mrs. André Marion

146 South La Peer Drive
Los Angeles Calif. 90048
U.S.A.

I send my heartfelt love, dear Nadia. Perhaps we'll see each other soon,
Théodore

❧ ❧ ❧

Milène Marion [née Stravinsky] to Boulanger

October 27, 1969

Dear Mademoiselle Boulanger,

Your letter touched me deeply. The feelings of kindness and understanding that it expressed are a great comfort for us in the very difficult and troubling situation we find ourselves, which is even more difficult as my brothers and I are totally powerless to set it right.

Thank you for your loyal friendship and be sure of my deep and sincere respect for you,
Milène

❧ ❧ ❧

Théodore Strawinsky to Boulanger

Geneva

December 7, 1969

Dear Nadia,

Got home the day before yesterday from New York where I spent two weeks—I don't wish to let the days pass without writing to you, my dear Friend, at least a few lines, to open my very heavy heart.

The state of my very old and dear Father distressed me: he is so fragile! They say he is doing better—yes, better than June, when it seemed his days were numbered. Let us join our prayers so he might at least be spared the pain and sadness not caused by his physical state, alas! . . . Physically, he is suffering a lot, mostly because of how terribly thin he is. Yet, he eats well enough and happily. With regard to his morale, he seems immersed in his own impenetrable world and [then], suddenly, will offer a reflection that denotes a certain mental lucidity, but these instances are rare and brief. He says himself, for example, that he is conscious of no longer being able to coordinate things in his head. He dozes or sleeps a large part of the day. The only pleasure that remains to him—and this is deeply moving—is to listen to music. So, we played him records. It's very poignant to see him listening while following the score. With regard to the atmosphere surrounding him, you know yourself, dear Nadia, how heavy, painful, and troubled it is. My only consolation was to see how admirably well he is taken care of, insofar as the nurses who surround him day and night (there are four) are perfect in kindness and attention. This Vera knew how to successfully arrange for him, and I'm grateful to her. We would so like to come to Paris and hear your news and talk about everything that is important to you, but I don't believe it will be possible before the end of January. I send my love.

Yours faithfully and wholeheartedly,
Théodore

❧   ❧   ❧

Boulanger to Théodore Strawinsky

December 21, 1969

Dear Théo,

Your heart-wrenching letter haunts me. I know, I understand and am so near to you. Perhaps the light of Christmas will brighten things up over there and support you. I send my love to you and Denise. Do not worry, I see almost nothing anymore but I am well and work with joy and gratitude.

Always yours,
Nadia B.

P.S. But what [illegible] trouble it is to know these sufferings and not [illegible] for you.

❧   ❧   ❧

Boulanger to Stravinsky

Hotel Astoria
103 rue Royale
Brussels, Belgium

Monsieur Igor Stravinsky
1260 North Wetherly Drive,
Hollywood 46
California
U.S.A.
January 24, 1970

My friend,
On Wednesday we have the *Requiem Canticles* here. You can imagine how I felt, hearing at last this work that has for so long been in my heart and in my

thoughts. It seems that it was prepared with [illegible] attention and love. My fond wishes to Vera and to you, and give my best to Bob.

Yours, always,
Nadia B.

ᴥ ᴥ ᴥ

Théodore Strawinsky to Boulanger

Geneva

January 27, 1970

Dear Nadia,

Coming from you, nothing could have touched us more than this marvelous record. We listened to it with deep emotion. I send my love to you with *immense, immense thanks!*

If I didn't write you sooner, it is because, after barely making it back at midnight, I caught an awful flu and have only gotten over it recently.

I live in constant anguish—you'll understand it—being now completely deprived of news of my father. Everything has been broken off between Vera and us following a letter that I could not stop myself from writing to her—in only the most correct and moderate terms—to tell her of my indignation at the announcement that not only all of the manuscripts but also all of the archives are up for sale. Letting others believe that it is Strawinsky himself selling all of them. Not to mention my indignation over the articles, or "interviews" fabricated by Craft to bolster the legend that the master is still mentally in full form. My letter earned me a vile response from Vera. And when I think, my dear and good friend, that my poor father's completely shrouded mental state prevents him from even recognizing his own music when we play a record of it for him? It is tragic. The only consolation is to think that he is no longer in a state that would allow him to understand all the treachery unfolding around him. Never did I think Vera would one day stoop to this level!

Denise and I send our faithful wishes,
Théodore

ᴥ ᴥ ᴥ

Boulanger to Stravinsky

Ecoles d'art américaines
Fondation reconnue d'utilité publique
Bureau New York: Fontainebleau Schools, 1083 Fifth Avenue, New-York, NY
10.028
Conservatoire de musique
Palais de Fontainebleau
Le Directeur
36, rue Ballu, Paris IX

Monsieur Igor Stravinsky
Essex House
New York
NY
U.S.A.
Ash Wednesday [February 11, 1970]

My thoughts and prayers are united with yours.
May God keep you

Your
Nadia B.

❧　❧　❧

Boulanger to Stravinsky

Ecoles d'Art Américaines
Fondation Reconnue d'Utilité Publique
Bureau New-York: Fontainebleau Schools, 1083 Fifth Avenue, New-York, NY
10.028
Conservatoire de musique
Palais de Fontainebleau
Director
36 rue Ballu, Paris, IX

Mr. Igor Stravinsky
Essex House
New-York City
NY
U.S.A.
March 2, 1970

My thoughts are with you in steadfast loyalty, My Friend.

In her memory, I send you all my love,
Nadia B

❧   ❧   ❧

Boulanger to Théodore Strawinsky

May 8, 1970

Dear Théodore,
How kind of you and Denise to have written me.
Death's great mystery is around your Father, and whatever his faith and our submission may be, it is certainly a painful time in its stress and severity.

I am with you constantly and send all my love,
NB.

❧   ❧   ❧

Boulanger to Théodore Strawinsky

November 18, 1970

Dear Théodore,
Without a doubt you have received this interview with your Father, a seemingly implausible interview in all respects.[68]
What can you do, what do you think? Need I tell you with what fondness I am constantly near to you and Denise. Such drama has played out in this long and terrible battle,

NB.

❧   ❧   ❧

---

68. Robert Craft, "Igor Stravinsky: On Illness and Death," *Harper's Magazine* (New York, NY), Nov. 1, 1969. Soulima Stravinsky also began collecting at this point references to interviews with his father that he suspected to be falsified. His archives also hold numerous newspaper clippings and court documents concerning the Lillian Libman trial and the posthumous debate over the Stravinsky estate. See US-NYp, Soulima Stravinsky Papers, Newspaper Clippings.

Théodore Strawinsky to Boulanger

Geneva
November 20, 1970

Very dear Friend,

Once again your note upset me. No, I did not know anything about this interview or, rather, pseudo-interview: When I think about this summer when we saw my father in Evian every day, he was totally incapable of associating two ideas or two sentences in a row, having never even understood that he was in Evian and no longer in New York! But the drama that surrounds him is so great nothing surprises me . . .

Would you be so kind as to give me—by return mail if possible—the reference of the journal that published the text and the date it came out, so that I might find it?

You understand us, I know, and you know how much all this tears us apart. Thank you wholeheartedly. How I would love to see you!

Denise and I send our love and all of our deepest affection,
Théodore

❧   ❧   ❧

Théodore Strawinsky to Boulanger

Cavalière
December 27, 1970

Very dear Friend,

The year which draws to a close has been a sad, hard, and heavy one—for us and for all our friends. Denise and I have twice mourned [the loss of loved ones]: in addition to her mother, three months ago we lost our dearest friend in Geneva, Madame Casaï, (Marie-José's lady-in-waiting) who was a real sister to us.[69] And what can we say about the real drama that is playing out around my

---

69. Berthe Casaï (née Berthe Marie Madeleine Brolliet) (1905–70) was lady-in-waiting for Queen Marie-José of Belgium (1906–2001), the last ruling Queen of Italy. Casaï lived in the Merlinge Castle along with her husband, Marcel. Between 1957 and 1984, Théodore and Denise Strawinsky summered with the Casaïs at their home in Bastide Saint-Yves, Cap Nègre, France. Queen Marie-José was also linked to Pope Paul VI, and she may have played a role in Théodore's appointment to the Order of St. Gregory the Great in 1977. I am thankful to the Fondation Théodore Strawinsky for sharing this information with me.

father who is already three-quarters in the hands of God? It's in such moments that the real values appear to our eyes from the heart, and one feels their unique importance: real friendships, real commitment, and profound faith. You know, dear Nadia, the place in our hearts your friendship occupies, resolutely linked to my father and to my mother. It's all that matters. We would like to be able to erase all of the rest. Alas! It's not so easy.

We are just here a few days to rest, and we'll be returning to Geneva as of January 5 or 6.

On the threshold of 1971, Denise and I remind you of everything that our hearts so affectionately desire for you,
Théodore

❧   ❧   ❧

Boulanger to Théodore Strawinsky

February 1, 1971

Dear Théodore,

Your distressing letter affected me so painfully. All that is happening at the moment is unbearably heartbreaking, and we would like to think it untrue. I am with you with all my heart, in prayer for him and for those capable of such an act. May God have pity on their misery. We cannot.

Lovingly yours,
Nadia

❧   ❧   ❧

Igor Stravinsky died in New York on April 6, 1971

❧   ❧   ❧

Denise Stravinsky to Boulanger

Geneva
April 21, 1971

Dear Nadia,

Théodore wants to think of nothing but the deliverance, thank God, of his beloved father. With marvelous courage, he offers to God his pain as a son, and he confronts the whole situation, certainly with pain, but with a spirit that will keep its serenity. As much in New York as in Venice, we have constantly felt your faithful friendship, love, and the admiration that you have had for our dear father. For Théodore and for me as well, I say to you, our great and dear Friend, thank you for your prayers, for your constant thoughts, and your comforting friendship. I am attaching to this letter a text that Théodore wrote just a month ago (and dedicated it to you), and I would ask you be so kind as to have it read to you. I find it admirably refreshing, pure, and, today, so upsetting. It is to accompany an album of records [that were] edited in Japanese in Japan. We have to send it back to Tokyo at the beginning of May, but Théodore, according to his contract, is free to have it published wherever he wants beforehand.

Given the tragic events, we wondered if it wouldn't be an opportune moment to publish this text in France, without delay, in an important newspaper and we thought about [Le] *Figaro*, in the weekly literary insert. But unfortunately, we no longer know anyone! Nobody. In Geneva they would take it right away, but the circulation would be too limited. If the text resonates with you, dear Nadia, could you suggest to whom we should possibly address it, and better yet, could you yourself speak to the Editor?

We have a series of contemplative photos of my dear father-in-law amid the members of his family that (as is the case with Théodore's text) shows a little-known side of Strawinsky that the children would be happy to see returned to its [rightful] place, since, for a long time, [people] have been working to erase the memory of a family life that was so deep, so true, so beautiful, and which is engraved in the hearts of Igor and Catherine's children, hearts which today have been so painfully hurt.

I am ashamed to take your precious time, but I know you will forgive me.

Allow us to send you all our love along with our deep and grateful affection.
Denise[70]

❧   ❧   ❧

---

70. Letter accompanied by Théodore Strawinsky's article: "Igor and Catherine Strawinsky: My Parents at The Heart of My Childhood Memories."

Boulanger to Théodore Strawinsky

May 11, 1971

Dear Théodore,
    A letter from *Figaro* deeply disappointed me, "The article is too long," they say. I asked them to send it back to me, and as soon as I return to Paris, I will take care of its publication. I believe the performance of the Mass will work itself out one of these days, it has to, but . . . I want to hope.
    I never leave you!

Your
NB.

🐦   🐦   🐦

Boulanger to Théodore Strawinsky

June 16, 1971

Dear Théodore,
    How my thoughts are particularly close to you in these days once celebrated with joy, but nothing has disappeared and Peace prolongs the past. I'm happy that you gave the article to Zygmunt, he is so moved by it.[71] As for H. Monnet's article, he is certainly right in his enthusiasm, but is it his place to dig up these stories and stir up controversy?[72] I do not know what to think, because to let it happen is so revolting.
    If you only knew of Mitell.[73]

Yours with tenderness and in deep thought,
Nadia B.

---

71. It is unclear to which Zygmunt Boulanger is referring here. Zygmunt Krauze (b. 1938) and Zygmunt Mycielski (1907–87) both corresponded with Boulanger at this time (Karuze: F-Pn, N.L.a. 78 [206–8] and Mycielski, F-Pn, N.L.a. 89 [43–440] and N.L.a. 90 [51–136]).
72. Henri Monnet (1896–1963), was a pianist, violinist, lawyer and politician. He was a friend of Stravinsky's and in later years became involved in a domestic dispute between Kitty Stravinsky and her parents, in particular Denise. Boulanger is referring to his article "Stravinsky et son siècle," *La Revue des deux Mondes* (July 1971), 85–95.
73. It is unclear who Mitell was. A generous reading of the word could render it a misspelled reference to Mitteleuropa, another term for the Second Viennese School. The term is used in Monnet's article.

P.S. I have nevertheless telegraphed Vera, telling her that I understand her immeasurable distress, because I still hope that she gives in and can at least sleep. What a terrible ending.

❧　❧　❧

Boulanger to Théodore Strawinsky

November 24, 1972

Dear Théodore,

There is nothing to say to your letter, and yet everything to say to you.

We are "revolted" by some facts, which will basically disappear very quickly; and we hold on to such memories here!

Today we are going to sing "Ave Maria," "Pater [Noster]" and "Pastorale," and we have no doubt that everything else holds no weight next to this music of such spiritual and musical importance.

I am thinking of you, of Denise, and am, with all my heart, your
NB.

Bibliography

Primary Sources

Archives

British Broadcasting Corporation Written Archives Centre, Caversham, England.
Centre International Nadia et Lili Boulanger (Nadia and Lili Boulanger International Foundation), Paris.
Fondation Théodore Strawinsky, Geneva.
Fonds Boulanger, Bibliothèque nationale de France, Paris.
Médiathèque Nadia Boulanger, Conservatoire de Musique et de Danse.
Mills College Archives, Oakland, California.
Soulima Stravinsky Papers, New York Public Library, New York.
Stravinsky Sammlung, Paul Sacher Stiftung, Basel, Switzerland.

Secondary Sources

Ansari, Emily Abrams. *The Sound of a Superpower: Musical Americanism and the Cold War*. New York: Oxford University Press, forthcoming.
Baeck, Erik. *André Cluytens: Itinéraire d'un chef d'orchestre*. Brussels: Mardaga, 2009.
Barraud, Henry. *Pour comprendre les musiques d'aujourd'hui*. Paris: Éditions de Seuil, 1968.
Berger, Arthur. "Problems of Pitch Organization in Stravinsky." *Perspectives of New Music* 2, no. 1 (1963): 11–42.
Beyer, Anders, ed. *The Music of Per Nørgård: Fourteen Interpretative Essays*. Aldershot, UK: Scholar Press, 1996.
Blyth, Alan. *Song on Record*. Vol. 2. Cambridge: Cambridge University Press, 1988.
Boulez, Pierre. "'J'ai horreur du souvenir!' A propos de Roger Désormière." *Points de repère II: Regards sur autrui*, 48–64. Paris: Bourgois, 2005.
———. "Strawinsky demeure." In *Musique russe*, vol. 1, edited by Pierre Souvtchinsky. Paris: Presses Universitaires de France, 1953.
Bourne, Vincent. *La divine contradiction: L'avenir catholique orthodoxe de la France*. Paris: Librarie des Cinq Continents, 1975.
Brelet, Gisèle. *Le temps musical: La forme musicale*. Paris: Presses Universitaire de France, 1949.

Brooks, Jeanice. "Collecting Past and Present: Music History and Musical Performance at Dumbarton Oaks." In *A Home of the Humanities: The Collecting and Patronage of Mildred and Robert Woods Bliss*, edited by James N. Carder, 75–91. Cambridge, MA: Harvard University Press, 2010.

———. "The Fonds Boulanger at the Bibliothèque Nationale." *Music Library Association Notes* 51, no. 4 (1995): 1227–37.

———. *The Musical Work of Nadia Boulanger: Performing Past and Future Between the Wars*. Cambridge: Cambridge University Press, 2013.

———. "Nadia Boulanger and the Salon of the Princesse de Polignac." *Journal of the American Musicological Society* 46, no. 3 (1993): 415–68.

———. "*Noble et grande servante de la musique*: Telling the Story of Nadia Boulanger's Conducting Career." *Journal of Musicology* 14, no. 1 (1996): 92–116.

Byzantine Institute of America. *The Mosaics of St. Sophia at Istanbul*. Paris: Byzantine Institute, 1933 and 1950.

Carr, Maureen. *Multiple Masks: Neoclassicism in Stravinsky's Work on Greek Subjects*. Lincoln: Nebraska University Press, 2002.

Chamfray, Claude. "Additions aux biographies de compositeurs parues dans le *Courrier musical de France*." *Le Courrier Musical de France* (1967): 20.

Cingria, Charles. *Stalactites: Dessins de René Auberjonois*. Lausanne: La Guilde de livre Lausanne, 1941.

Clair, Jean and Viginie Monnier. *Balthus: Catalogue Raisonné of the Complete Works*. New York: Harry N. Abrams, 2000.

Cohn, Jan. *Creating America: George Horace Lorimer and the* Saturday Evening Post. Pittsburgh, PA: University of Pittsburgh Press, 1989.

Combarieu, J. and R. Dumesnil. *Histoire illustrée de la musique*. Paris: Plon, 1952.

Cone, Edward T. "Stravinsky: The Progress of a Method." *Perspectives of New Music* 1, no. 1 (1962): 18–26

Cotter, Jim. "Alan Hovhaness (1911–2000)." In *Music of the Twentieth-Century Avant-Garde: A Biocritical Sourcebook*, edited by Larry Sitsky and Jonathan Kramer, 211–16. Westport, CT: Greenwood, 2002.

Craft, Robert. *Dearest Bubushkin: The Correspondence of Vera and Igor Stravinsky, 1921–1954, with Excerpts from Vera Stravinsky's Diaries, 1922–1971*. London: Thames & Hudson, 1985.

———. *An Improbable Life: Memoirs by Robert Craft*. Nashville, TN: Vanderbilt University Press, 2002.

———. *Stravinsky: Chronicle of a Friendship*. Nashville, TN: Vanderbilt University Press, 1994.

———. *Stravinsky: Discoveries and Memories* Surrey, UK: Naxos, 2013.

———. *Stravinsky in Pictures and Documents*. New York: Simon & Schuster, 1978.

———, ed. *Stravinsky: Selected Correspondence*, vol. 1. London: Faber & Faber, 1982.

Craft, Robert, and Stravinsky, Igor. *Conversations with Igor Stravinsky*. New York: Doubleday, 1959.

———. *Dialogues*. Berkeley: University of California Press, 1982.

———. *Dialogues and a Diary*. London: Faber & Faber, 1962.

Crawford, Dorothy Lamb. *Evenings On and Off the Roof*. Berkeley: University of California Press, 1995.

Culot, Hubert. "Edouard Michael." *British Music: The Journal of the British Music Society* 25 (2003): 45–52.

Curtis, Michael. *Verdict on Vichy: Power and Prejudice in the Vichy France Regime.* New York: Arcade, 2002.

Dallas, Gregor. *At the Heart of a Tiger: Clemenceau and His World, 1841–1929.* London: Macmillan, 1993.

Deliyannis, Deborah M. *Ravenna in Late Antiquity.* Cambridge: Cambridge University Press, 2010.

Duchêne-Thégarid, Marie and Diane Fanjul. "Apprendre à interpréter la musique pour piano de Debussy au Conservatoire de Paris entre 1920 et 1960." In *Regards sur Debussy,* 79–99. Paris, France: Fayard, 2013.

Dufour, Valérie. *Stravinski et ses exegetes (1910–1940).* Bruxelles: Université de Bruxelles, 2006.

Duroselle, Jean-Baptiste. *Clemenceau.* Paris: Fayard, 1988.

Dushkin, Samuel. "Working with Stravinsky." In *Igor Stravinsky,* edited by Edwin Corle, 179–86. New York: Duell, Sloan, & Pierce, 1949.

Evans, Joan. *Hans Rosbaud: Bio-Bibliography.* Westwood, CT: Greenwood, 1992.

———. "Hans Rosbaud and New Music: From 1933 to the Early Postwar Period." In *Deutsche Leitkultur Musik? Zur Musikgeschichte nach dem Holocaust,* edited by Albrecht Rietmüller, 117–29. Stuttgart: Steiner, 2006.

Francis, Kimberly A. "A Dialogue Begins: Nadia Boulanger, Igor Stravinsky, and the *Symphonie de psaumes,* 1930–1932." *Women and Music: A Journal of Gender and Culture* 14, no. 1 (2010): 22–44.

———. "A Most Unsuccessful Project: Nadia Boulanger, Igor Stravinsky, and the Symphony in C, 1939–1945." *Musical Quarterly* 94 (2011): 234–70.

———. *Teaching Stravinsky: Nadia Boulanger and the Consecration of a Modernist Icon.* New York: Oxford University Press, 2015.

Giroud, Victor. *Nicolas Nabokov: A Life in Freedom and Music.* New York: Oxford University Press, 2015.

Glotz, Michel. *La Note Bleue: Une vie pour la musique.* Paris: Jean-Claude Lattès, 2002.

Griffiths, Paul. *Igor Stravinsky: The Rake's Progress.* Cambridge: Cambridge University Press, 1982.

Guillot, Nicolas, ed. *Roger Désormière (1898–1963).* Paris: Comité Roger Désormière, 1999.

Häusler, Josef. *Im Zeichen von Ernest Bour 1964–1979.* Stuttgart, Germany: Metzler, 1996.

Horowitz, Joseph. *Artists in Exile: How Refugees from Twentieth Century War and Revolution Transformed the American Performing Arts.* New York: Harper, 2008.

———. *Classical Music in America: A History.* New York: W. W. Norton, 2005.

Hunt, John. *The Post-war German Tradition, Five Discographies: Rudolf Kempe, Joseph Keilberth, Wolfgang Sawallisch, Rafael Kubelík, Andre Cluytens.* Exeter, UK: Short Run Press, 1996.

Jensen, Jørgen I. "At the Boundary between Music and Science: From Per Nørgård to Carl Nielsen." *Fontes Artis Musicae* 42, no. 1 (1995): 55–61.

Joseph, Charles. *Stravinsky and Balanchine: A Journey of Invention.* New Haven, CT: Yale University Press, 2002.

Judt, Tony. *Postwar: A History of Europe Post-1945.* New York: Penguin, 2005.

Kahan, Sylvia. *Music's Modern Muse.* Rochester, NY: University of Rochester Press, 2003.

———. "'Quelque chose de très raffiné et de très musicale,' la collaboration entre Nadia Boulanger et Marie-Blanche de Polignac." In *Nadia Boulanger et Lili Boulanger: Témoignages et études,* edited by Alexandra Laederich, 85–98. Lyon: Symétrie, 2007.

Kriebel, Robert. *Blue Flame: Woody Herman's Life in Music.* West Lafayette, IN: Purdue University, 1995.

Laederich, Alexandra, and Rémy Stricker. "Les Trois vies de Nadia Boulanger: Extraits inédits de la valise protégée." *Revue de la BNF* 46, no.1 (2014): 77–83

Lakond, Wladimir, trans. *The Diaries of Tchaikovsky.* New York: W. W. Norton, 1945.

Landormy, Paul. *La musique française après Debussy.* Gallimard: Paris, 1943.

Leonard, Kendra Preston. *The Conservatoire Américain: A History.* Lanham, MD: Scarecrow Press, 2007.

Levitz, Tamara. "Igor the Angeleno: The Mexican Connection." In *Stravinsky and His World,* edited by Tamara Levitz, 141–76. Princeton, NJ: Princeton University Press, 2013.

———. *Modernist Mysteries: Perséphone.* New York: Oxford University Press, 2012.

———, ed. *Stravinsky and His World.* Princeton, NJ: Princeton University Press, 2013.

———. "Who Owns *Mavra?* A Transnational Dispute." In *Stravinsky and His World,* edited by Tamara Levitz, 21–59. Princeton, NJ: Princeton University Press, 2013.

Liese, Kirsten. *Elisabeth Schwarzkopf: From Flower Maiden to Marschallin.* New York: Amadeus, 2009.

Ligeti, György. "Hommage à Ernest Bour." In *Gesammelte Schriften* vol. 1, 511–2. Mainz: Schott Musik International, 2007.

Locke, Ralph and Cyrilla Barr, eds. *Cultivating Music in America: Women Patrons and Activists since 1860.* Berkeley: University of California Press, 1997.

Lowe, Keith. *Savage Continent: Europe in the Aftermath of World War II.* London: Viking, 2012.

Marty, Jean-Pierre. *The Tempo Indications of Mozart.* New Haven, CT: Yale University Press, 1988.

———. *Vingt-quatre leçons avec Chopin.* St-Paul-Trois-Châteaux, France: L'Atelier d'Onze, 1999.

Milot, Louise Bail. *Jean Papineau-Couture: La vie, la carrière, et l'œuvre.* La Salle, Québec: Editions Hurtubise, 1986.

Mouron, Henri. *A. M. Cassandre.* New York: Rizzoli, 1985.

Murray, Williamson and Allan Reed Millet. *A War to Be Won.* Cambridge, MA: Harvard University Press, 2000.

Neret, Gilles. *Balthus.* New York: Tashen, 2003.

Newhall, David. *Clemenceau: A Life at War.* Lewiston, NY: E. Mellen Press, 1991.

Nommick, Yvan. "Des *Hommages* de Falla aux 'hommages' à Falla." In *Manuel de Falla: Latinité et universalité,* 515–54. Paris: Presses de l'Université de Paris-Sorbonne, 1999.

Oleggini, Leon. *Connaissance de Stravinsky*. Lausanne: Éditions Maurice et Pierre Foetisch, 1952.

Pâris, Alain. *Dictionnaire des interprètes et de l'interprétation musicale au XX siècle* (2 vols). Edited by Robert Laffont. Paris: Bouquins, 1982.

Paul, Christian. "L'enfance mal connue de Roger Désormière." *Musicologies* 6 (2009): 35–40.

Pauli, Hansjörg. *Hermann Scherchen, 1891–1966.* Zürich: Hug, 1993.

Pincus, Andrew. *Scenes from Tanglewood.* Boston, MA: Northeastern University Press, 1989.

Poray, Denise. "Letter from Aix-en-Provence: Denise Wendel Poray Savors the Particular Flavors of a Summer Festival that Blends the Old and the New." *Opera Canada* 52, no. 1 (2011): 18–19.

Powell, Neil. *Benjamin Britten: A Life for Music.* New York: Henry Holt, 2013.

Rainer, Janos, Csaba Bekes, and Malcolm Byrne. *The 1956 Hungarian Revolution: A History in Documents.* Budapest and New York: Central European University Press, 2002.

Ramey, Philip. *Irving Fine: A Composer in His Time.* Hillsdale, NY: Pendragon Press, 2005.

Rosenstiel, Léonie. *Nadia Boulanger: A Life in Music.* New York: W.W. Norton, 1982.

Rosenthal, Harold, John Warrack, Roland Mancini, and Jean-Jacques Rouveroux, eds. *Guide de l'opéra.* Paris: Fayard, 1995.

Roussel, Eric. *Charles de Gaulle.* Paris: Gallimard, 2002.

Schuster-Craig, John. "Stravinsky's *Scènes de ballet* and Billy Rose's *The Seven Lively Arts.* The Abravanel Account." In *Music in the Theater, Church, and Villa: Essays in Honor of Robert Lamar Weaver and Norma Wright Weaver,* edited by S. Parisi, 285–89. Warren, Michigan: Harmonie Park Press, 2000.

Scott, Michael. "Raoul Gunsbourg and the Monte Carlo Opera." *Opera Quarterly* 3, no. 4 (1985): 70–78.

Simeone, Nigel. "Messiaen, Boulanger, and Josée Bruyr: Offandres Oubliées 2." *The Musical Times* 142, no. 1874 (2001): 17–22.

Souvtchinsky, Pierre "Igor Strawinsky." *Contrepoints* 2 (February 1946): 19–31.

Sprout, Leslie A. "The 1945 Stravinsky Debates: Nigg, Messiaen, and the Early Cold War in France." *Journal of Musicology* 26 (2009): 85–131.

———. *The Musical Legacy of Wartime France.* Berkeley: University of California Press, 2013.

Spycket, Jérôme. *A la recherche de Lili Boulanger.* Paris: Fayard, 2004.

———. *Nadia Boulanger,* trans., M. M. Striver. Stuyvesant, NY: Pendragon Press, 1987.

Steane, J. B. *The Grand Tradition: Seventy Years of Singing on Record, 1900–1970.* London: Duckworth, 1974.

Strauss, Joseph. *Stravinsky's Late Music.* Cambridge: Cambridge University Press, 2001.

Stravinsky, Igor. *Chroniques de ma vie.* Paris: D. Gonthier, 1935.

———. *Poétique musicale.* Cambridge, MA: Harvard University Press, 1942.

Stravinsky, Vera, Rita McCaffrey, and Robert Craft. *Igor and Vera Stravinsky: A Photograph Album, 1921 to 1971.* London: Thames & Hudson, 1982.

Strawinsky, Theodore, and Denise Strawinsky. *Au coeur du foyer: Catherine et Igor Strawinsky (1906–1940)*. Paris: Éditions Aug. Zurfluh, 1998.

———. *Catherine and Igor Stravinsky: A Family Chronicle*. New York: Boosey & Hawkes, 1973.

Stricker, Rémy. "La Critique de Nadia Boulanger: A la recherche d'une passion objective." In *Nadia et Lili Boulanger: Témoignage et études*, ed. Alexandra Laederich, 131–38. Lyon: Symétrie, 2007.

Tanase, Virgil. *Saint-Exupéry*. Paris: Gallimard, 2013.

Tanasecu, Dragos and Griore Bargaunau. *Lipatti*. Edited by Carola Grindea. Translated by Carola Grindea and Anne Goosens. London: Kahn & Averill, 1988.

Taruskin, Richard. *Stravinsky and the Russian Traditions: A Biography of the Works through* Mavra. Berkeley: University of California Press, 1996.

———, ed. "Stravinsky and Us." In *The Danger of Music and Other Anti-Utopian Essays*, 420–46. Berkeley: University of California Press, 2008.

Valéry, Paul. *Monsieur Teste*. Paris: Gallimard, Editions de la nouvelle revue française, 1927.

Varga, Bálint András. "Ernest Bour." In *From Boulanger to Stockhausen: Interviews and a Memoir*, 67–75. Rochester, NY: University of Rochester Press, 2013.

Vlad, Roman. *Stravinsky*. London: Oxford University Press, 1960.

Wallace, Helen. *Boosey & Hawkes, The Publishing Story*. London: Boosey & Hawkes, 2007.

Walsh, Stephen. *Stravinsky: A Creative Spring, Russia and France, 1882–1934*. New York: Alfred A. Knopf, 1999.

———. *Stravinsky: Oedipus Rex*. Cambridge: Cambridge University Press, 1993.

———. "Stravinsky Remains." *Stocktakings from an Apprenticeship*. Oxford: Oxford University Press, 1991.

———. *Stravinsky: The Second Exile: France and America, 1934–1971*. New York: Alfred A. Knopf, 2006.

Walton, Chris. *Othmar Schoeck: Life and Works*. Rochester, NY: University of Rochester Press, 2009.

Watkins, Glenn. *The Gesualdo Hex: Music, Myth, and Memory*. New York: W. W. Norton, 2010.

Wearing, J. P. *The London Stage: A Calendar of Productions, Performers, and Personnel: 1930–1939*. Metuchen, NJ: Scarecrow Press, 1990.

Weber, Nicholas Fox. *Balthus, A Biography*. New York: Alfred A. Knopf, 1999.

Weeda, E., ed. *Yuriy Mandel'shtam: Sobraniye stikhotvoreniy*. The Hague: Leuxenhoff, 1990.

Weinberg, Gerhard. *A World at Arms*. Cambridge: Cambridge University Press, 1994.

Wellens, Ian. *Music on the Frontline: Nicolas Nabokov's Struggle against Communism and Middlebrow Culture*. Aldershot, UK: Ashgate, 2002.

White, Eric Walter. *Stravinsky, The Composer and His Works*. Berkeley: University of California Press, 1966.

Williams, Charles. *Pétain: How the Hero of France Became a Convicted Traitor and Changed the Course of History*. New York: Palgrave MacMillan, 2005.

Wolff, Stéphane. *Un Demi-siècle d'opéra-comique (1900–1950: Les Oeuvres, les intérprètes)*. Paris: André Bonne, 1953.

Index